Claude Etienne Savary

Letters on Greece : Being a Sequel to Letters on Egypt, and

containing

Travels through Rhodes, Crete, and other Islands of the Archipelago...

Claude Etienne Savary

Letters on Greece : Being a Sequel to Letters on Egypt, and containing
Travels through Rhodes, Crete, and other Islands of the Archipelago...

ISBN/EAN: 9783744756617

Printed in Europe, USA, Canada, Australia, Japan

Cover: Foto ©Andreas Hilbeck / pixelio.de

More available books at **www.hansebooks.com**

LETTERS

ON

GREECE.

GREECE:

BEING A SEQUEL TO

LETTERS on EGYPT,

AND CONTAINING

TRAVELS THROUGH RHODES, CRETE, AND OTHER ISLANDS OF THE ARCHIPELAGO;

WITH

COMPARATIVE REMARKS

ON THEIR

ANCIENT AND PRESENT STATE,

AND

OBSERVATIONS

ON THE

GOVERNMENT, CHARACTER, AND MANNERS OF THE TURKS, AND MODERN GREEKS.

———————

Translated from the FRENCH of M. SAVARY.

———————

DUBLIN:

PRINTED FOR MESSRS. L. WHITE, P. BYRNE, J. MOORE, AND B. DORNIN.

M,DCC,LXXXVIII.

LETTERS

ON

GREECE.

LETTER I.

Alexandria, 1779.

I ADDRESS to you, Madam, the following Letters, forming a sequel to thofe on Egypt. Deign to receive them with indulgence, and accept them as the offering of gratitude. They contain my obfervations on thofe parts of Greece which I vifited in the courfe of two years. Acquainted as you are with hif-

B   tory,

tory, guided by a natural good tafte, and enlightened by the ftudy of the fine arts, you
prefer to all other countries that which had
the glory of bringing thofe arts to perfection.
I am perfectly of your opinion: the country
of Homer, of Socrates, and fo many other
great men whom their virtues or talents
have immortalized, has a claim to the love
and veneration of all ages. The traveller of
fenfibility, led by the enthufiafm infpired by
thofe places, once the theatre of fo many memorable events, will long continue to vifit
them. But, alas! inftead of a free, learned,
and warlike people, he will find pufillanimous
and ignorant flaves; inftead of flourifhing
cities, he will meet with nothing but heaps of
ruins, and fcattered and mutilated marbles,
inftead of the famous monuments of ancient
genius. Yet if his refearches be conducted by
found fenfe, if he be exempt from prejudices,
and correct in his defcriptions, even this contraft will fupply interefting objects and ufeful truths. You already have a glimpfe, Madam, of one part of the fcenes about to open
to your view. The obfcurity, indeed, in
which they are enveloped, does not permit
you to difcern their effects. Let us approach
them

them fomewhat nearer, the darknefs will difappear; we fhall fee them as they have been
fketched by nature, for in her colours I fhall
endeavour to pourtray them.

I have the honour to be,
    with the utmoft refpect,
        Madam,
            Your moft humble and moft
                obedient fervant,

                        SAVARY,

L E T T E R II.

To M. L. M.

Alexandria, Sept. 1779.

I AM preparing, Madam, to leave the city of
Alexandria, where I have paffed four months,
fince my return from Cairo. My ftay here
has been exceedingly agreeable, thanks to the
kindnefs of M. Taitbout de Marigni, the
French conful, who invited me to his table,
and fhewed me every poffible politenefs. I
have employed my leifure hours in examining
this city, its harbours and environs, and in
defcribing them, as you have feen in my former work.

In confequence of the war between Eng-
land and France, the Mediterranean fwarms
with Englifh privateers, and our regular
trading veffels no longer make their ufual
voyages. I have therefore been obliged to
wait for a neutral fhip, and have agreed
with a captain of Zante, an ifland belonging
to the Venetians, to convey me to Candia.

He

He is at this moment ready to fail, and I muſt haſten on board : Adieu, ye burning ſhores of Egypt! I lay aſide with pleaſure the turban, the long robe, and the muſtachio, thoſe neceſſary habiliments for every European who is inclined to viſit theſe countries. Adieu, ye ſuperb monuments, on which I have ſo often gazed with admiration and aſtoniſhment! I rejoice that I have ſeen you; but wiſh not to behold you a ſecond time, till the country in which you rear your lofty heads ſhall be no longer under the dominion of a barbarous people. Adieu! ye ever verdant gardens of Roſetta and Damietta, and ye groves, the ſoft retreats of voluptuous enjoyment! How do your perfumes embalm the air! How delightful were the coolneſs of your charming ſhades, impenetrable to the ardour of a burning ſun, did not death await the raſh mortal who ſhall too thoughtleſsly dare to enter them. Such, Madam, were my reflexions, whilſt I caſt a parting glance on objects by which I had been ſo deeply affected, as I followed the Zanthiot captain to the ſhip. The boat glided gently over the ſurface of an unruffled ſea, and my reverie continued till ſuddenly it ſtruck againſt the veſſel,

when

when the fhock diflipated the illufion, and I
mounted the deck.

We have weighed anchor. A favourable
breeze fwells our fails, and wafts us from the
fhore. We have already pafled the Diamond,
a rock fo called, fituated at the extremity of
the Ifle of Pharos, which, when the fea is calm,
rears its threatening head above the waters;
but in ftormy weather is entirely covered by
the waves. Mariners muft pafs round it to
enter the harbour; but its fituation is well
known, and it is eafily avoided.

At the diftance we now are from Alexandria, that city appears, in perfpective, forming
a femicircle on the fhore. Part of the houfes,
illuminated by the fun, reflect a vivid light,
and advance forward in the picture, while the
reft, enveloped in the fhade, appear in the
back-ground. About them rife the flender
Minarets, which feem to lofe themfelves in the
air. The principal object in this landfcape is
the pillar of Alexander Severus *, which
commands the whole city. This is the
firft thing difcovered when we make the

* Commonly called Pompey's Pillar. See the author's
Letters on Egypt.

land;

land; and the laſt we loſe ſight of when we
leave it. Hail to the greateſt column human
power has ever erected! Still does this teſtify
to travellers, that the arts have once flouriſhed
in this country, now the ſeat of ignorance and
barbariſm. Adieu! magnificent monument,
which wert ſo often the object of my
walks! Never could I be weary of contemplating the majeſty of thy ſhaft, and thy
enormous capital. But while I ſpeak it
leſſens inſenſibly, and now appears only a
black ſpeck amid the vapours of the atmo-
ſphere. Has Egypt then ſo ſoon vaniſhed from
my ſight!

It is not without regret, Madam, that we
quit a country in which we have paſſed ſeveral years of our youth, in which we have
beheld the wonders of antiquity, and purchaſed a few tranſient moments of happineſs
by an infinity of fatigues and perils. A
kind of melancholy takes poſſeſſion of the
ſoul. The more lively our ſenſations have
been, the more difficulty do we find in de-
taching ourſelves from the ſcenes which gave
them birth. We are perpetually recalling the
images of objects, by which we have been
deeply affected, and, recollecting them, feel

anew

anew every paffion they have infpired. Not unfrequently do they excite tears, and we feel an irrefiftible charm, which we endeavour to prolong, till, fatigued with fenfibility, it becomes neceffary to give reft to the mind by transferring our attention to other objects.

I fhall continue, Madam, in the courfe of this work, to defcribe, with all the exactnefs I am capable of, the places I may vifit; nor fhall I omit the reflections they may fuggeft, or my own feelings, in every fituation. What can be more interefting than the hiftory of the human heart? And how can this be better written than by faithfully relating the impreffions made on us by each new object, and in every various fituation?

I have the honour to be, &c..

LETTER III.

To M. L. M.

On board.

WE enjoy, Madam, the finest weather imaginable : not a cloud obfcures the fky, and a fouth-eaft wind wafts us directly toward the port to which our wifhes tend. We have now entirely loft fight of land, and, as far as the eye can reach, only view the immenfe abyfs of the waters, and the vaft expanfe of the heavens. How awful is this fight! How does it infpire the mind with great ideas! How adventurous is man, who trufts his fortune and his life to this frail veffel he has built, which a worm may pierce, or a fingle blaft dafh to pieces againft a rock! Yet in this he braves the fury of the ocean. But how admirable is his ingenuity! He commands the winds, enchains them in the canvas, and forces them to conduct him where he pleafes. He fails from one end of the world to the other, and traverfes the immenfe

liquid

liquid plains, without any fignals to direct him. He reads his courfe in the heavens. A needle, which wonderfully points perpetually to the Pole, and the obfervation of the ftars, inform him where he is. A few lines and points mark out to him the iflands, coafts, and fhoals, which his fkill enables him to approach or avoid at pleafure. Yet has he caufe to tremble, notwithftanding all his fcience and all his genius! The fire of the clouds is kindling over his head, and may confume his dwelling. Unfathomable gulphs are yawning beneath his feet, and he is feparated from them only by a fingle plank. His confidence might make us imagine he knew himfelf immortal; yet he muft die— die never to revive again!

I have the honour to be, &c.

LETTER IV.

To M. L. M.

On board.

I HAVE risen before the twilight, Madam, to contemplate at my leifure the rising of the fun. This fight, in the wide and fhorelefs ocean, is the moft wonderful and glorious fcene that nature offers to the eye of man. I fhall endeavour to defcribe it, if not with all the eloquence and grandeur of imagery it deferves, at leaft, with as much fidelity as poffible.

The weather is ferene, the air calm, the frefhnefs of the morning delicious. A light, but favourable, breath of wind wafts us gently along, and nothing difturbs the profound filence that reigns upon the waters.

The few ftars which ftill fparkle in the firmament are about to difappear. Already the firft rays of day pierce through the blueifh vapour of the horizon; while retreating night collects her fleeting fhades in the weft.

The

The eaſt gradually colours, and ſtreaks the
azure vault with purple. The ſcene varies
every inſtant. Each object becomes more
enlightened, and its colours more lively. What
a ſcene at length opens! a thouſand golden
rays, iſſuing from one common centre, divide themſelves in the air. The whole eaſt
ſeems on fire. The ſun is about to appear;
already I perceive his radiant diſk upon the
horizon. He appears to riſe from the centre of
the waves, and ſeems to repoſe an inſtant on
the liquid ſurface, as on a throne. How is
the eye dazzled with his ſplendor, while he
riſes majeſtically above the waters, which re-
flects his image a thouſand and a thouſand
times! Hail, glorious luminary, great ſource
of light to the univerſe, all hail! Thy pre-
ſence reanimates every living being, and dif-
fuſes joy through every heart. Glory be to
the hand that traced out thy path through
the heavens!

I have the honour to be, &c.

LETTER V.

To M. L. M.

On board.

FIVE days have elapsed, Madam, since our departure from Alexandria, and our vessel has always gone before the wind. Had it blown a little stronger we should not have been far from Candia; but it has continued so weak that we are hardly half way thither. I never saw the sea more calm; we proceed as gently as if we were floating with the stream of a river. Nothing can be more agreeable than our voyage. Seated under a canopy which shelters us from the heat of the sun, and cooled by the refreshing zephyrs, which play among the sails, we continue to advance insensibly. Notwithstanding our progress is so slow, if the same wind continues all night, we shall to-morrow be within sight of Rhodes, which is but a small distance from Crete.

Till

Till five in the morning we have enjoyed
the moſt delightful weather; but the horizon
in the weſt appears now gradually to overcaſt;
vapours, at firſt light and ſcarcely perceptible,
begin to extend, heap up, and thicken. Already they form a circle of dark clouds, which
like mountains, hide from us the laſt rays of
the ſetting ſun. Is this the fore-runner of a
ſtorm? Our mariners are of that opinion.
We ſhall ſoon ſee how far their preſages are
right.

I have the honour to be, &c.

L E T T E R   VI.

To M. L. M.

On board.

THE fears of the sailors, Madam, were not without foundation, the wind has changed. The eastern gale no longer wafts us gently on our way. A torrent of air, bursting from the west, has driven us towards the burning countries of Asia, and opposes itself as a barrier to our passage. In vain do we struggle against its violence; we lose on every tack, and recede instead of advancing. Thick clouds obscure the face of the sun, and the darkened ocean is covered with foam. Roaring waves continually lash the sides of the vessel, and the winds howl horribly among the rigging. The over-stretched sails break with violence from the yards, and the masts bend and crack with the rolling of the vessel, which, every moment, seems ready to shiver into a thousand pieces.

All the sailors are in motion; the captain

is

is obliged to ftrain his voice to give his orders.
The helm is confided to the moft experienced
failor. Some attend the ropes, while others,
clinging to the end of a yard, are taking in a
fail, and, balancing themfelves as the fhip
rolls, grapple a rope with their feet, and labour with their hands, at the rifk of being precipitated every moment into the fea.

For feven days, fucceffively, we have never
ceafed tacking; but in vain. We are continually lofing way; and, fhould this weather
laft, we fhall make Cyprus, or the coaft of
Syria. I am now convinced our veffel is but
an indifferent failer, and the crew extremely
ignorant. Our failors are Greeks, who know
little of the working of a fhip, and are flow
in performing the little they do know. Never
have they once been able to put the fhip about
with the head to the wind, fo that as often as they
change the tack we lofe more way than we have
gained. Nor has the captain more knowledge;
he has not taken one obfervation of the latitude; nor has he on board either fector or
quadrant, with the ufe of which he is totally
unacquainted. He is equally a ftranger to the
ufe of fea-charts, or the method of meafuring
a fhip's way by the log. In fine, he is a

genuine

genuine boat-mafter, who finds his way
in the day, by following the courfe of the
fun, and at night, by obfervation of the
ftars. In cloudy weather, he fteers as well
as he can, by the compafs, of which he
knows not even the declination. I am almoft
tempted to fancy him one of the pilots of the
ancient Greeks, and to fuppofe that he was
at the fiege of Troy, and that one of the fabulous deities has reftored him to life, to prove
to us the truth of the everlafting voyages
of Homer's heroes. However that may
be, I do not think we fhall very foon reach
Candia.

Our doubts are ended. We give up, at
leaft for the prefent, all hope of reaching Crete.
Wearied with fruitlefs ftruggles againft oppofing
fortune, our captain has juft turned his prow
toward Afia Minor. We are going, he tells
us, to feek for fhelter in fome port, and when
the weather is more favourable, we fhall renew our voyage. He does not know where
we fhall touch; but if he once makes land,
he will do every thing in his power not to
lofe fight of it again. Thus do the Greeks
manage a fhip. As for myfelf, I begin to re-

C   pent

pent embarking with fuch a pilot. But the dye is thrown, and I muſt ſtand the chance.

I have the honour to be, &c.

LETTER VII.

To M. I. M.

OUR deftiny, Madam, has fuffered no change. The wind keeps conftantly in the weft, and has driven the clouds toward the frozen fummits of Lebanon. The fky, at length, clears up, and we are bearing down upon the land, which has been announced by the failors from the maft head. On deck, we could only difcern fomething refembling a cloud, which enlarged and extended itfelf as we advanced. We now know it to be the continent of Afia, and the certainty of this has diffufed a general joy; but ftill we are not free from anxiety. The captain having never taken any obfervation, knows nothing of our latitude, and cannot tell what land we are about to make. In the mean time, however, we keep advancing toward it.

Objects infenfibly become more diftinct, we perceive mountains, hills, and a promontory,

which.

which running out into the fea, prefents a
barren fhore and enormous rocks.   Our failors
affure us, the high land, that appears in the
back ground, is the Ifland of Caftel Roffo; they
affert we fhall be at anchor there before night,
and we are bearing down on it with a favourable wind.

　　We approach the fhore, which feems deftitute of verdure; but in fact, the fun is fetting behind the mountains, and fhines only
upon their fummits.   The fhade defcends
rapidly into the vallies, and the eye no
longer diftinguifhes any thing but as through
a veil.   We are now, thank Heaven, entering
the harbour of Caftel Roffo, and about to
anchor, at the foot of the rock on which
that fmall town is built.

　　　　　I have the honour to be, &c.

LETTER VIII.

To M. L. M.

Caftel Roffo.

WE have now, Madam, been three days at anchor in the port of Caftel Roffo, which time I have employed in vifiting the country, of which I can now lay before you an accurate account. But remember, that the truth here is hideous. The more faithful I am in my defcriptions, the more will you be fhocked.

This ifland is fituated in the weftern part of a femi-circular bay, on the coaft of Caramania, or the ancient Lycia. It is but half a league in circumference, and is only feparated from the continent by a narrow ftreight. The coaft is inacceffible, except on the fide of the harbour, where there is a fmall town, confifting of about one hundred houfes. It is built upon a rock, on the point of which is a fmall Turkifh fort, which ferves to frighten away the Corfairs. The fpace it occupies is ex-

tremely

tremely confined, both by fea, and a very
fteep mountain, above three hundred feet
high, which has the appearance of a wall,
from which huge maffes of rock feem ready
to fall upon the houfes, and precipitate them
into the waves. I climbed it with difficulty,
and found on its fummit a plain, about a
quarter of a league in circuit, uncultivated, and
nearly covered with grafs, half burnt up. In
the middle is a fmall chapel, very wretched,
and very folitary.

From this eminence we difcover the Mediterranean to the north and fouth, while
the reft of the horizon is bounded by the
lofty fummits of Mount Taurus. When we
defcend into the town, we find ourfelves in
a bottom environed by fteep cliffs, which lofe
themfelves in the clouds. Thefe are a circle
of bare and hanging rocks, which, heated by
the fun, reflect a vivid light, injurious to the
eyes. Never did verdure embellifh thefe melancholy fhores; we only meet with a few
bulbous plants, and thorny fhrubs, which delight in fuch fituations. Such is the profpect the inhabitants of Caftel Roffo have inceffantly before their eyes. It prefents the
image of eternal fterility; nor do I believe

the

the whole world affords a more defolate and horrid habitation.

You may imagine, Madam, how wretched the Greeks, who inhabit fuch a place, muft be. They can neither fow nor reap. The ifland produces neither vegetables, fruit, nor grain. Their plantations are confined to about fifty feet of olive trees, and they have no cattle but goats, which climb among the rocks to find fubfiftence. To complete their mifery, there is only one fpring in the ifland, and that is almoft at the top of the hill; from whence the women are obliged to fetch water. I have often feen them labouring up a fteep path, carrying large pitchers on their fhoulders, and returning heavily laden, at the rifk of being dafhed to pieces with their burthen. Such a place of abode is not to be envied. Accordingly, the handfomeft houfe lets only at twelve livres (or half a guinea) a year; and the bride who receives for her portion a foot of olive ground and a fhe-goat, is efteemed wealthy.

Fortune feems to have intended to recompenfe the inhabitants of Caftel Roffo, by giving them indolent neighbours. In the time of harveft, they pafs over into Caramania, and get in the corn for the Turks. They bring
back

back with them grain, wine, and various kinds of provifions. Their fituation has rendered them feamen, and they make voyages during three months of the year, and return in winter, to enjoy, with their families, the gains they have made. Moft of them carry on a trade in wood, which they purchafe at a low rate, and fell high at Alexandria. For carrying this, they make ufe of decked boats, which do not ftow much, but fail very quick, and require little care. They likewife fupply their wants by fifhing; and by thefe various means obtain a fubfiftence.

Could you imagine it, Madam; on this defolate fpot I found a native of Provence, who is fettled here, and connected in bufinefs with a Greek; they live in the fame houfe, and are partners in a veffel. The former trades with the Turks, and purchafes fire-wood, and timber for fhip-building, in Cara-mania, which the other fells in Egypt, from whence, in return, he brings various articles which are ufeful here. They appear to fubfift comfortably, and live in harmony together. The Frenchman confiders himfelf as the agent of his nation, and renders his countrymen all the fervices in his power; in return for which,

he

he receives from them fome little prefents.   I
have every reafon to be fatisfied with his politenefs.   To do us honour he killed a fheep,
perhaps the only one in the ifland, and regaled
us in the beft manner he could, with Mufca-
dine grapes, gathered on the Afiatic fhore.
The oriental cuftoms were obferved in every
thing.   We eat upon the ground, feated
round the difhes, on the carpet, and, afterward, all drank out of one large cup, the only
one, doubtlefs, in the poffeffion of thefe
partners.   Next came coffee, and then pipes,
of which we were obliged heartily to partake.
I afked our hoft many queftions, and among
the novelties I learnt from him, the following
appeared worthy to be preferved :

    " In my excurfions through the mountains
" of Caramania," faid he, " I found at the
" foot of a tree, fomewhat different from the
" mulberry, large balls or cones, of a white and
" fine filk, much bigger than thofe of the com-
" mon filk-worm.   On examining the leaves, I
" difcovered the infects that produced them,
" fome of which were ftill fpinning.   They
" were caterpillars of a blackifh colour,
" larger than filk-worms.   I brought away
" four of them, and fent them to the conful

                                " at

" at Rhodes; but they cannot have been re-
" ceived, as I have never heard of them
" more."

I repeatedly requested my host to conduct
me to the place where he had seen this species
of silk-worm; but he answered, that, war having broke out between the Turks of that province, it was impossible to go so far. He
promised me, however, as soon as peace
should be restored, to send me some of them
to Candia, with the leaves of the trees on
which they feed. I relate these particulars,
to induce travellers, who may hereafter visit
these countries, to endeavour to procure some
of these valuable insects. The trees which
grow on the high grounds of Caramania would
thrive well in France, and it would be an
advantage to mankind in general, and a source
of riches to our own nation in particular,
could we discover and multiply a new species
of worm which produces silk.

L E T T E R IX.

To M. L. M.

Caftel Roffo.

WHILE we remain at Caftel Roffo, Madam, I muft not omit to mention fome beautiful remains of antiquity fituated at a fmall diftance. I cannot fay whether they are known; but I have never read a defcription of them in any author.

About half an hour's fail to the eaft of the harbour of Caftel Roffo, is a creek on the Afiatic coaft, fituated in the wideft part of the bay, and near a league in length. It affords a commodious harbour, where veffels are fecure from ftorms. The firft object that ftrikes the eye on approaching the land, is a vaft amphitheatre built with beautiful ftones, and of a circular form. It is about feventy feet high, and has eighty rows of feats, raifed one above the other. At the fifth row from the top, you remark at each of the extremities of the femi-circle, a part furrounded by a baluftrade, in which,

doubtlefs,

doubtlefs, were the places affigned for the
principal perfonages of the country. This
immenfe amphitheatre might contain the inhabitants of a large city, and ferve for public
exhibitions given on land, or, poffibly, on the
fea.   It is built with fuch folidity as to be proof
againft the ravages of time; at leaft it has
hitherto fuffered but little from its injuries.
The arena alone has been wafted by the fea,
which feems to have gained upon the land.
Beyond this amphitheatre are a great variety
of ruins.   The moft remarkable are difpofed
around a vaft vacant fpace, and we efpecially
diftinguifh the fuperb remains of a fpacious
building.   Huge columns overthrown, others
ftill erect, thick walls half demolifhed, highly
finifhed capitals, and broken cornices, announce
the ruins of a temple; for the ancients difplayed
all their magnificence in the edifices confecrated to the gods.   At the foot of the rocks
which furround the town, our admiration is
attracted by tombs in perfect prefervation,
fome of which are furrounded with columns
fupporting a dome of great folidity.   Others
are merely Sarcophagi hewn out of the ftone.
Several of them confifting of a fepulchral
chamber, cut in the rock, have fteps in front

by

by which we afcend to a periftile fupported by columns. Avarice, which tramples under foot the moft facred laws, has violated thefe refpectable manfions of the dead, by forcing away the ftones which defended the entrance.

Such, Madam, is the deplorable condition of this ancient and once flourifhing city. The harbour deftitute of fhips, that magnificent amphitheatre without fpectators, thofe piles of ruins, thofe tombs, defpoiled even of the bodies they contained, infpire the traveller with melancholy reflections. Has the fury of a conqueror deftroyed this city? Has it funk under the ravages of time? or have man and the elements both confpired its ruin?

I am inclined to believe the dreadful earthquakes, which happened under the monarchs of the lower empire, have fwallowed up the lower part of this town. The ruins we find on the edge of the fhore, and even in the water, certainly favour this opinion. Another proof is, that, in the maritime towns, as we may obferve Telmiffus on the fame coaft; the amphitheatres were at fome diftance from the fea, and fituated on fuch high ground as

to

to fecure them from its waters. At prefent, when the fea is agitated, the waves enter that I have been defcribing, beat againft the walls, and ruin the arena. The tradition of the country, too, is, that half of this city was fwallowed up by an earthquake. I have not been able to learn the date of this cataftrophe, but the fact appears indubitable.

The fight of the ruins of a city, while it afflicts us with melancholy fenfations, only ftimulates our curiofity the more to difcover its ancient name, and what it was in former times. Let us endeavour to invefligate thefe, and take Strabo, one of the moft accurate of ancient geographers, for our guide. After defcribing the weftern part of Lycia, he adds,

" Afcending the river Xanthus for the
" fpace of ten furlongs, we arrive at the
" temple of Latona, and, fixty furlongs above,
" the city of Xanthus, one of the largeft of
" all Lycia. Beyond this is Patara, a con-
" fiderable city, which has a harbour and
" feveral temples. It was founded by Patarus,
" and enlarged by Ptolemy Philadelphus, who
" called it Arfinoë of Lycia, in honour of his
" queen. Farther on ftands the city of Myra,
" on a high hill, twenty furlongs from the
" fea;

" fea ; and proceeding onward, we arrive at
" the mouths of the river Limyrus, and the
" city of Limyra, a league diftant from the
" fea-fhore *(a)*."

Let us now examine the account of the
fame places in Pomponius Mela. This author proceeds in his defcription from eaft to
weft.

" Beyond the promontory formed by Mount
" Taurus, we find the river Limyra, with
" a city of the fame name. This diftrict con-
" tains feveral towns, of which none are of
" any importance except Patara. The latter
" is famous for its temple of Apollo, which
" formerly was as much celebrated for its
" riches and the refpect paid to its oracles, as
" that of Delphos. Beyond is the river Xan-
" thus, with a city of the fame name *(b)*."

Both thefe geographers, you perceive, Madam, place Patara between the mouths of
the Xanthus and Limyra, and in all that
fpace, mention no other city with a harbour;
it feems highly probable, therefore, that the
ruins in queftion are thofe of Patara, fince they
are fituated between thefe two rivers, and on a
harbour.

(a) Strabo, lib. xiv.
(b) Pomponius Mela, lib. i.

This may be further corroborated from hiftory. Livy gives the following account of an
expedition undertaken by the Romans againft
Patara: " Caius Livius, arriving at Rhodes,
" declared to the citizens the fubject of his
" miffion. Having obtained their unanimous
" fuffrages in his favour, he added three gallies
" with four benches of rowers to his fleet, and
" made fail for Patara. At firft a favourable
" wind bore them thither with rapidity, and
" the Romans hoped the terror infpired by
" their fudden appearance would favour
" their defign. The wind, however, foon
" changed, and the fea became tempeftu-
" ous, yet, by dint of rowing, they at length
" gained the land ; but as they could find no
" fhelter near the city, and the violence of
" the ftorm hindered them from keeping their
" ftation before an enemy's port, efpecially
" as night approached, they paffed it and
" took refuge in the harbour of Phœnicus,
" not quite two thoufand paces *(c)* diftant
" from Patara *(d)*."

(c) Two thoufand Roman paces make about three quarters of a league.

(d) Liv. lib. xxxvii. cap. 16.

The

. The harbour of Phœnicus can be no other
than Caftel Roffo. The diftance from that
ifland, to the ruins I have been defcribing, correfponds exactly with the two thoufand paces
affigned by the Roman hiftorian as the diftance from Patara to Phœnicus. Befides,
there are pofitively no other harbours but thefe
two in this whole bay. To which we may
add, that Stephen of Byzantium places, on
the coaft of Lycia, an ifland called Phœnice,
which is, no doubt, the fame with the Phœnicus of Livy (e).

Thefe authorities united, I imagine, are fufficient to remove all doubt. D'Anville, in
his map of ancient Afia, does not feem to have
been perfectly acquainted with the fituation of
Patara, which he places a little too far to the
weft. He has alfo omitted entirely the ifland
of Caftel Roffo, but this was, probably, becaufe
it is fo little, as he has laid down this whole
coaft on a very fmall fcale.

This city was founded by Patarus, fon of

___

(e) Phœnice is a town of Crete; we find alfo an ifland
of that name on the coaft of Lycia. Stephanus Byzantinus de Urbibus.

D   Apollo;

Apollo *(f)*; it is not extraordinary, therefore, that the inhabitants fhould have erected to that god the famous temple, mentioned by Pomponius Mela, of which we ftill difcover the ruins. Apollo there delivered oracles for fix months in the year, and the other fix at Delos *(g)*.

Permit me, Madam, before I conclude this letter, to lay before you a flight fketch of ancient Lycia and its inhabitants, copied from Strabo *(h)*. Lycia was formerly a flourifhing republic, confifting of thirty-three cities, that had all a right to vote in the national affemblies. The largeft, among which was Patara, had three fuffrages; thofe of the fecond order two, and the fmalleft one. In thefe affemblies, the people elected their magiftrates, and the *Lyciarch*, or chief of Lycia. Taxes were here equitably impofed, and the public employments conferred on thofe who would difcharge them honourably.

(f) Patara is a city of Lycia. It received its name from Patarus, fon of Apollo; Lycia was the name of the daughter of Xanthus. Stephan. Byzant. Hence the epithet Patareus is given to Apollo by Horace, lib. iii. Od. 4.

(g) Servius, in Æneid.

(h) Strabo, lib. xiv.

The wife government of the Lycians maintained a rigid morality; and, notwithſtanding
the bad example of their neighbours, they
never abandoned themſelves to piracy, nor
permitted any diſhonourable traffic. Victory
could not corrupt them. After repeated ſuc-
ceſſes, which rendered them maſters of the ſea
from Aſia Minor to Italy, they ſtill retained
their moderation, and the ſimplicity of their
ancient manners. When the Romans, whoſe
arms nothing could reſiſt, conquered theſe
countries, they were ſo ſtruck with the wiſ-
dom of this republic, that they left them in the
enjoyment of their liberty and laws. The
only privilege of which they deprived them
was, the right of determining on peace or
war, in their national aſſemblies, without the
conſent of Rome.

What cannot liberty, morals, and a wife
government effect for the happineſs of mankind! Lycia, which formerly poſſeſſed theſe
invaluable advantages, became happy and
powerful. Her navy gave laws to the greater
part of the Mediterranean. The ruins of Patara are a proof of the flouriſhing ſtate of the
arts in that city. Three and thirty cities in a
ſmall province ſufficiently demonſtrate its
great population. What a difference do we

find

find at prefent! Defpotifm, like a devouring fire, has paffed over this rich country, and its cities are changed into wretched villages; its inhabitants have difappeared, and the earth denies her fruits. The Greeks, who might increafe and multiply, and infure plenty, by applying themfelves to agriculture, prefer thefe fcarcely habitable rocks to fubjection under the rapacious tyrants delegated by the Porte to be their governors. Were the rulers of nations but to attend to thefe great examples which hiftory prefents; would they but deign to reflect on the effects of a juft and wife government, and labour to eftablifh it in their ftates, how powerfully, how glorioufly might they reign, and how might they blefs their fubjects with fecurity and felicity!

I have the honour to be, &c.

L E T T E R   X.

To M. L. M.

From on board.

OUR anchor has been weighed, Madam, since day-break. The wind fettled in the north promifes us a good paffage, at leaft as far as Rhodes. I muft own I quit Caftel Roffo without regret. The ftate of humiliation in which the Greeks live in the Ottoman em-pire, and the oppreffions they fuffer, can alone reconcile them to inhabit fuch a barren rock, where not one of the neceffaries of life is to be found; where the horizon is bounded on every fide by tremendous cliffs, and where they can only view that part of the glorious face of heaven which is directly over their heads. Yet do thefe unfortunate beings, at-tached to their prifon, drag on a miferable life, without ever thinking to fearch elfewhere for a more agreeable habitation; fo deeply is the love of his country engraven on the heart of man!

We

We have opened out the narrow ſtraight that ſeparates the iſland from the continent, and are coaſting along the ſhore at the diſtance of two leagues. Our captain is determined not to riſk himſelf a ſecond time in the open ſea: he likes to ſee the land. This voyage would be more amuſing, did the coaſt preſent us with habitations, foreſts, and pleaſing landſcapes. But it is entirely deſert; not a ſingle village is to be diſcovered; the ſun has burnt up the little verdure to be ſeen in the ſpring, and the eye can diſcern nothing but piles of rocks, againſt which the waves perpetually daſh with a horrid noiſe. The diſtant horizon is terminated by the ſummits of lofty mountains, which, ſtripped of their antient pines, appear wholly without ornament. The ſhades, the Lycian groves, formerly the delight of the Patarean Apollo (*i*), have vaniſhed. Be not ſurpriſed at this, Madam; the Turks are continually felling the woods of theſe countries, either for their own

<hr />

(*i*) ——— Qui Lyciæ tenet
Dumeta, natalemque ſylvam
Delius, & Patareus Apollo.
　　　　　　Hor. lib. iii. Od. 4.

uſe,

ufe, or the profit they can make of them, and never plant a fingle tree.

All our canvas is fpread, and the veffel rapidly cleaves the bofem of the waves, which whiten under its prow. We ardently wifh to reach Rhodes to procure fome refrefhments, for our captain, accuftomed to live, like his crew, on cheefe, falt fifh, dried figs, and a fort of bifcuit made in Egypt, which is extremely hard, had only laid in frefh provifions for ten or twelve days, and we have now been feventeen at fea. The ancient Phœnice could furnifh us with nothing, and we begin to fuffer from famine, as if we were returning from a voyage round the world. We have nothing left but a little water, and black bread as hard as ftone; but the fight of Rhodes, the mountains of which we difcover, confoles us. If the wind holds, we fhall anchor there to-morrow morning, and find relief from all our preffing neceffities.

A new fcene now prefents itfelf to view! an innumerable multitude of fwans and cranes are failing on the waters, ranged in files, like fol-diers in order of battle. Each of thefe files is upwards of a quarter of a league in length, and we have counted thirty of them, all fwim-ming

ming in a similar direction. The head of
this army terminates in a point, and resembles
the prow of a ship. They all keep their posts,
notwithstanding the motion of the waves,
with which they alternately rise and fall;
their plumage, which is of a dazzling white,
forms an admirable contrast with the transf-
parent greenness of the waters. Farther on,
we discern another troop, disposed in the
same manner: and all have their heads turned
towards Africa, to which they steer in con-
cert.

These birds, at the approach of winter, fly
the snows and ice of the north, to seek
a milder climate. They first arrive at the
Black Sea, where they remain for a time, and
when the cold begins to increase too much
there, again take their departure with a
northerly wind, traverse Asia Minor, and rest
a while on the shores of the Mediterranean.
They afterward pass this sea, partly by swim-
ming, and partly by flying. In this manner
they reach the coasts of Africa, and especially
Egypt, where the great lakes of Menzala
and Burlos furnish them abundant food. There
they remain all the winter; but the storks,
which appear to be fond of a still warmer cli-

mate.

mate, quit thefe lakes in November, proceed
towards the Said, and end their journey at the
lake Mœris, and the canal of Jofeph. They
free the country from innumerable frogs,
infects, and reptiles, which abound in the
marfhes. Such is the regular progrefs of thefe
birds. But hark! they are in full cry, their
leaders have given the fignal, and the winged
navigators, rife in the air, and fly altogether,
directing their courfe toward the fouth. To
cleave this element alfo, with more facility,
they range themfelves in the form of a triangle.
the vertex of which is a very acute angle.
What wifdom is difplayed in the actions of
creatures which to us feem deftitute of reafon!
Fortunate, perhaps, in not poffeffing that liberty fo frequently abufed by man; they do
not counteract the views of nature, and enjoy, without alloy, that portion of happinefs
affigned them by the Creator.

The ifle of Rhodes is now in full view, and
prefents a range of hills refembling an amphitheatre, and terminated by a lofty mountain.
We are going as near the wind as poffible, and
with a crowd of fail, to gain the harbour.
But we fhall not reach it before night. Already the fun is fetting behind the mountains,
which

which hide him from us, while his radiant
beams ftill ftreak the clouds with gold and
purple! How vivid are their colours! Some
of them concentering thoufands of his rays,
again reflect them, and refemble globes of
fire floating through the air. Others, the
lower parts of which are entirely dark, affume
the appearance of dufky mountains of various
forms, and emit, from their luminous points,
the flafh of the ruby, or the fire of the topaz;
fome opening in the centre, and edged with
the brighteft and livelieft colours, exhibit the
azure of the fky fet in gold. Others diverfified with fattiny ftripes, are flightly bounded
with a yellowifh border. How admirable,
how magnificent, is this fcene! What a fublime
idea does it give of Him who faid, *Let there
be light, and there was light!* Night has thrown
her dark veil over this glorious picture, yet
the eye remains ftill fixed on the heavens,
and the foul ftill feels deeply penetrated with
fentiments of admiration and gratitude. How
great are the works of the Creator! and how
feeble the conceptions of man!

I have the honour to be, &c.

LETTER XI.

To M. L. M.

WE flattered ourfelves too foon, Madam, that we fhould have been able yefterday to enter Rhodes; but this was to rely too much on the conftancy of the wind, which changed fuddenly in the night, and obliged us to continue tacking before the ifland. We have been very near it, and its groves, delicioufly verdant, feemed to invite us to take fhelter in their fhades. The town, whofe lofty towers we could diftinctly difcern, appeared to offer us the provifions of which we ftood fo much in need, and every thing contributed to heighten our defires; but, like Tantalus, we were only permitted to gratify our eyes. The wefterly wind, which has fo often proved contrary, has once more deceived our expectations, and after tacking for a whole day and night, our captain, who never ftruggles obftinately againft fortune, has a fecond time fteered for

the

the coaft of Afia, and taken refuge in the
gulph of Macri, in which we have this morning caft anchor.

The gulph of Macri, or, as it was formerly
called, Glaucus, runs about fix miles into the
land, between two very high fhores, which
bound it to the eaft and weft. It gradually becomes narrower, and terminates in a beautiful
valley, at the entrance of which ftands a fmall
village inhabited by Greeks. We loft no time
in getting afhore, in order to procure refrefhments; but, unfortunately, a Turkifh cara-
velle, which lay there at anchor, had carried off every thing. We have not found
fo much as a fingle morfel of bread. They
have promifed to bake us fome; and we hope
to *breakfaft* this *evening* with a very hearty
appetite.

In the mean time, I have been to examine
the valley, and the remains of antiquity it
contains. Whilft I was purfuing the winding
of a rivulet that waters it, known formerly
by the name of the river Glaucus, I difcovered, on its banks, a very large fig-tree,
loaded with fruit. Several wine fhoots, which
grew at its root, held it in clofe embrace, and
mingled their green branches with its foliage,
through

through which might be feen clufters of purple
grapes, and figs beginning to turn yellow.
With what delight my eye dwelt upon this
beautiful tree! and how did I blefs my good
fortune, which had conducted me to this
fpot! I inftantly flew to feize the prize. How
excellent a regale are figs and grapes, when
for four-and-twenty hours you have had no
other fuftenance than a morfel of black bread
as hard as a ftone, and only brandy to
quench your thirft! Never did I make fo delicious a repaft. The fruits were of an exquifite flavour; I thought I never could be
fatisfied. As foon as my hunger was appeafed,
I recollected the rill which bathed the foot of
my benefactor, and took a moft reviving
draught. The pure and limpid water appeared far preferable to the fineft flavoured
wines. This adventure naturally led me to
reflect on the many wretched beings who are
perifhing with want, whilft others are revelling
in abundance. Ah! let thofe who read this
feel compaffion when poverty, with downcaft eyes, and pallid countenance, fhall fay
to them in a faltering voice, *I am hungry :* —
for hunger is indeed a moft cruel torture.

Telmiffus was built at the foot of a hill,

which bounds the valley to the eaft *(k)*. The
ancients, who agree in the fituation of this
town, make it a dependency, according to
fome of Caria, and to others of Lycia; doubtlefs, from its being on the boundaries of both
thefe provinces. But this queftion may, perhaps, be beft determined by referring to the
accurate Strabo *(l)*.

" Beyond mount Dædalus, which is in
" Lycia, we find in the fame province the
" fmall town of Telmiffus, with a pro-
" montory of the fame name, near which is
" a harbour. We next arrive at mount Cra-
" gus, remarkable for its eight fummits, and
" which has given birth to the fable of the
" Chimera. At the foot of this mountain
" we perceive a fteep hill rifing from the fea,
" ftill known by the name of Chimera." This
hill, according to Pliny *(m)*, cafts forth flames
during

(k) Thelmeffus is a town of Caria. Cicero de Divinatione, lib. i. Stephen of Byzantium, de Urbibus, fays, Telmiffus is a town of Caria; but Philo and Strabo place it
in Lycia. In fact, it is near Mount Dedalus, and is on the
boundaries of each of thofe provinces. Thelmiffus terminates Lycia on the weft. Pomponius Mela.

(l) Strabo, lib. xiv.

(m) Mons Chimæra noctibus flagrans. Plin. lib. v. cap. 27.

during the night; and hence the origin of the fable.

Telmiſſus was not a very conſiderable town. Strabo does not reckon it among thoſe which had the right of giving three ſuffrages in the national aſſemblies. But it was renowned for is ſoothſayers. Here, ſays Cicero, the ſcience of augury eſpecially flouriſhed *(n)*. Its port is ſheltered from every wind, being defended to the weſt by mount Dædalus, to the eaſt by the promontory of Telmiſſus, to the north by high hills, which form the baſis of mount Cragus, and to the ſouth by ſmall iſlands, which, lying acroſs the gulph, break the violence of the waves. Even at preſent, veſſels which meet with ſtorms may anchor there with ſafety. This advantage, the moſt important of any for maritime towns, rendered commerce and the arts flouriſhing at Telmiſſus, as is ſufficiently proved by the beautiful theatre we ſtill admire. It is built fronting the harbour, within the hill, which overtops it on the eaſt; it is of a ſemi-circular form, and has

Mount Chimera, ſituated in Lycia, throws out flames during the night.

(n) Cicero de Divinatione, lib. i.

twenty-four rows of feats. You enter the arena by three gates, of very fimple archi- tecture. The right fide of it, which is built againft the hill, is thrown down, and the feats, difplaced, are piled up without order; but the reft is in tolerable prefervation. This theatre is much lefs than that of Patara, is neither fo large nor fo magnificent, nor has it been fo well able to refift the ravages of time. We cannot doubt but thefe edifices were pro- portioned to the extent and power of the cities by which they were built. I faw the name of Monfieur de Choifeul Gouffier in- fcribed on the ftones of the theatre of Tel- miffus, which he had caufed to be engraved with care.

At a little diftance, proceeding round the fame hill toward the north, we meet with a great number of tombs hewn out of the rock. They are in the fame ftyle with thofe of Patara, but not fo magnificent. The moft remarkable have a periftile, fupported by columns in front. But the thirft of gold has not fpared thefe any more than the others; they have almoft all been violated. The ftones which clofed them, and the bodies they contained, have been carried away, a great number

number of them are only fimple Sarcophagi
cut in the ftone.   Beyond, we find the ruins
of a caftle, which ferved perhaps as a citadel
to Telmiffus (o); nothing more is left of this
ancient town.   Mofs and briars almoft entirely cover its maufolea.   I remarked in the
environs young plane trees, and tufts of myrtle, which fomewhat confoled me for the fad
fcene I had before my eyes.

Fatigued by climbing up rocks during a
great part of the day, and fcorched by the
heat of the fun, I returned to the banks of the
charming rivulet, and the foot of my beloved fig-tree.   I there found a refrefhing
fhade, delicious fruits, and the comforts of
repofe.   Nothing difturbs the tranquillity of
this delightful fpot.   No noife of carriages,
no tumult, not even the found of a human
voice.   Every thing here is peaceful and filent.
Scarcely does the zephyr agitate the foliage,
or bend the fragile reed.   High mountains
feem to feparate this afylum of peace and filence
from the reft of the world.

(o) The reader may fee thefe ancient monuments deli-
neated, with great minutenefs and accuracy, in the *Voyage
Pittorefque de la Grèce* of Monfieur de Choifeul Gouffier.

E   The

The fun continues to enlighten this beautiful valley as in the ages or antiquity. Still is it warmed with the creative beams of that glorious luminary, and the prolific earth ftill produces in abundance vigorous plants, tufted thickets, and herbage maintained in conftant verdure by refrefhing ftreams. But the hand of man is wanting to aid the wild efforts of nature. Thorns fpring up inftead of ufeful trees, and rufhes now cover large tracts of land, which formerly were productive of golden harvefts; Were art to beftow ever fo little cultivation on thefe fields, they would foon be adorned with groves of myrtle, oranges and pomegranates, and all the treafures of Ceres and Pomona.

The Greeks, who inhabit this valley, leave it entirely wafte; not a cultivated acre is to be found. Difpirited and dejected as they are, what could they undertake? Should they fow, or plant, they would be deemed rich, and the Aga would come to feize on their property. The cultivator bedews the earth with his fweat only to reap the fruits of his labour. Deprive him of that hope, he labours no more; and this is the ftate of the Greeks under the Ottoman empire.

Such

Such were my reflexions while feated near
the ruins of Telmiffus, as my eye wandered
over the various objects which prefented themfelves to my view, when the coolnefs of the
evening, and the approaching darknefs apprifed me that it was time to quit this agreeable
retreat. I bade adieu to the ftream which
had quenched my thirft, to the fig-tree which
had refrefhed me, and haftened, once more,
on board, to join my companions, who feared
me loft.

I have the honour to be, &c.

L E T-

LETTER XII.

To M. L. M.

Rhodes.

FORTUNE, Madam, has perfecuted us
to the laft. We were on the point of entering the harbour of Rhodes, when a violent
gale of wind drove the veffel out to fea, and
it was with the utmoft difficulty we regained
the land. At length we have caft anchor in
a fmall bay, a league to the fouthward of the
town (p). Immediately after my landing I
went to vifit M. Potonier, the French conful, who received me very politely, and accommodated me with apartments in his houfe.
From thence, that is, from Neocorio (q) I

(p) This bay, which feems to have been taken from the
coaft, is probably the harbour which Demetrius dug during
the fiege of Rhodes, to fhelter his fhips from ftorms, and
the attacks of the enemy. It lies to the fouthward of the
town, precifely at the diftance affigned by Diodorus Siculus,

(q) A village near Rhodes, where the French conful
refides.

fhall

shall write to you, and give a defcription of ancient Rhodes, the moft eaftern and moft beautiful of the Cyclades. I fhall afterward lay before you a view of its prefent ftate, that you
may be able to compare what it is with what
it was, and form a juft idea of the ifland.
Permit me then, Madam, to go back into antiquity, and briefly prefent to you the principal outline of its hiftory. Thofe remote pe-
riods, in which imitative man engraved images
and fymbols, to preferve the memory of events,
are the reign of fable ; but remember that
truth is almoft always concealed under the veil
of allegory.

Several ancient authors affert that Rhodes
was formerly covered by the fea, and that it
raifed its humid head above the waters, and became an ifland ; but they do not fix the time of
this event, which is loft in the obfcurity of
ages ; tradition, however, has preferved the
memory of the fact, and the graveft writers of
antiquity have admitted it as certain. Delos
and Rhodes, fays Pliny *(r)*, thofe celebrated
iflands,

(*r*) Pliny, lib. ii. c. 87. This author mentions feveral
other iflands in the Mediterranean as having had the
fame origin. Such as Anaphe and Nea, between Lemnos
and

iflands, arofe out of the fea. So many other
authorities atteft the fame fact, that it cannot
reafonably be doubted. Philo *(s)* attributes this
event to the diminution of the waters of the
fea ; and were this opinion well founded, moft
of the iflands of the Archipelago, being
lower than Rhodes, muft have had the fame
origin. But we find nothing like this in hiftory. It is much more natural to imagine
that volcanic fires, fuch as, in the fourth year
of the hundred and thirty-fifth olympiad,
threw up from the abyffes of the ocean
Therafia and Thera, the modern Santorin,
and which, even in our time, have raifed

and the Hellefpont, and in the 4th year of the 135th olympiad, Therafia, and Thera, now called Santorin.

Pindar, Oly. Ode vii. Ancient Annals atteft, that at the
time when Jupiter and the immortals divided the earth,
Rhodes had not yet appeared in the midft of the fea, but
was ftill concealed in the profound abyffes of the ocean.
Ariftides *in Rhodiaca,* Ammianus, lib. xvii. fay likewife,
that Rhodes was formerly covered by the waters of the fea.

(s) Philo, de Mundo. The fea, fays this writer, has certainly diminifhed, as is proved by Rhodes and Delos, for
they were formerly covered with the waters of the fea.
After many ages, the waters having gradually funk, thefe
two celebrated iflands arofe above their furface.

above

above the waters feveral little iflands near them, gave birth, in the remote ages of anti- quity, to Rhodes and Delos (*t*).

The firft inhabitants of the ifland were the Telchines, called in fable Children of the Sea (*u*). Strabo (*x*) fays they came from Crete, and that they were believed to be magicians, on account of their extenfive knowledge. They were the firft who taught the ufe of iron and brafs, and made a fcythe for Sa- turn.

Helius, or the fun, enamoured with a nymph called Rhodes, gave the name of his miftrefs to this ifland (*y*). His children, named Heliades, fucceeded

(*t*) Strabo, lib. i. An ifland having fuddenly arifen be- tween Thera and Therafia, the Rhodians, who then pof- feffed the empire of the fea, had the courage to approach it with their fhips, and erected on it a temple to Jupiter Afphalius.

(*u*) Diodorus Siculus, lib. v.

(*x*) Strabo, lib. xiv,

(*y*) This allegory, fays Diodorus, fignifies, that the ifland being wet and marfhy, the heat of the fun evaporated the waters, and rendered the foil extremely fertile. This feems to corroborate alfo the opinion of the ancients on the origin of this ifland. For, fince Rhodes arofe out of the water, the

succeeded to the Telchines. Verfed in aftronomy, they divided the year into feafons,
and invented the fcience of navigation. One
of them, named Cercaphus, having married
Cydippe, had by her three fons, Lindus, Jalifus, and Camirus. At the death of their father, they divided the empire, and each of
them built a city bearing his own name (z).

(a) About this time, Danaus flying from
Egypt with his daughters, arrived at Lindus.
Being favourably received by the inhabitants,
he there built a temple to Minerva, in which
he confecrated the ftatue of that goddefs.
Three of his daughters died in the ifland, and
the reft followed him to Argos.

(b) After the departure of Danaus, Cadmus,
the fon of Agenor, feeking Europa, by order

---

the earth muft for a long time have been wet and marfhy.
The beneficent luminary, which dried and rendered it fertile, received the adoration of the inhabitants.

(z) Strabo, lib. xiv. Diodorus Siculus, lib. v. Others
fay thefe cities were built by Tlepolemus, fon of Hercules, who gave them the names of the three daughters
of Danaus, who died in the ifland. Others again, that
they were founded by Althemenus, the grandfon of Hercules.

(a) Diodorus Siculus, lib. v.

(b) Ibid.

of

of his father, met with a violent tempeft, during which he vowed, if he efcaped death, to
build a temple to Neptune. Having landed
at Lindus, he performed his vow, and left
priefts to officiate in the temple. He made an
offering to the Lindian Minerva of a golden
bafon with an infcription in Phœnician characters. Athenæus reprefents his landing here
as, a military expedition; he fays, that Cadmus took poffeffion of part of the ifland,
expelled the Heliades, and fettled the Phœnicians there in their ftead.

(c) At length the ifland was over-run with
ferpents, and thence received the name of
Ophiufa. Some of thefe were of a monftrous
fize, and devoured many of the inhabitants.
The oracle of Delos being confulted, declared
they muft fend for Phorbas, then in Theffaly
at the head of a body of troops. He accepted
the invitation of the Rhodians, deftroyed the
monfters that ravaged the ifland, and fettled
there. After his death, heroic honours
were decreed him for his important fervices.
Conon afferts that he drove the Phœnicians
from Rhodes.

(c) Diodorus Siculus, lib. **v.**

A fhort

(d) A short time before the Trojan war, Tlepolemus, son of Hercules, landed with his companions in the isle of Rhodes. Meeting with a favourable reception, he settled there, and, becoming king of the island, divided the lands among the inhabitants, and instituted equitable laws. On his departure for the Trojan war, he left the government to Butes, one of his companions; he greatly distinguished himself at that memorable siege, and died in Troas.

The Rhodians, even in those early ages, had a considerable navy. The island furnished them with timber for ship building, and their situation invited them to partake of the advantages of commerce (e). They made voyages into Spain, founded Parthenope, now called Naples, in Campania, and after the siege of Troy built Majorca and Minorca. The island was divided between the inhabitants of Lindus, Jalysus, and Camirus (f).

(d) Diodorus Siculus, lib. v.

(e) Strabo, lib. xiv.

(f) Homer names these towns in one line,

" Λίνδον Ἰηλυσόν τε ᾗ ἀργινοέντα Κάμειρον."—Il. ii.

" Lindus, Jalysus, and Camirus, white.—Pope.

This

This is what Homer gives us to underſtand, when he ſays, ſpeaking of the Rhodians, " They have three cities, three tribes; Ju- " piter, who governs the immortals, and " loves mankind, has heaped on them abun- " dant wealth."

I have paſſed rapidly over ſeveral ages, and omitting a number of mythological ſtories, haſten to the period when the Rhodians, united by a common intereſt, formed only one na- tional body, and founded the city of Rhodes, ſo called from the name of the iſland. This important event took place during the Pelo- ponneſian war (g). " It is known to almoſt " all of you," ſays Ariſtides, " that before " the naval expedition of Lyſander, the La- " cedemonian, the city you now inhabit was " not built. The iſland was called Rhodes, " but the city of that name did not exiſt. " The Rhodians dwelt in the three towns " mentioned by Homer."

(h) Rhodes had for its architect, Hippo- damus, of Miletus, who built the ſuperb walls

(g) Ariſtides, in Rhodiaca.

(h) The preſent city of Rhodes was built during the Peloponneſian war, by the architect who built the walls of the Piræus. Strabo, lib. xiv.

of

of the Piræus, deftroyed foon after by the Lacedemonians (i).

The people of Lindus, Jalyfus, and Camirus, united in one republic, were now all collected within this city, which was about three leagues in circumference (k); and capable of containing a prodigious number of inhabitants. It was fituated at the point of a promontory, that ftretches toward the eaft, on the fame fpot where the modern town ftands. The ground having a declivity, the architect adapted his plan to the fituation, and laid out the ftreets fo. artificially, as to convert this defect into a beauty. (l) " Rhodes," fays Diodorus, " refembled an amphitheatre ; " its numerous veffels, its towers, and fol- " diers, gave a high idea of its wealth and " power." Strabo, who had travelled through feveral countries, and had feen Rome, Alexandria, Memphis, and the moft celebrated

(i) Lindus, Jalyfus, and Camirus, were at firft feparate republics, but the inhabitants afterwards united under ene government in Rhodes. Ibid.

(k) According to Strabo, it was eighty ftadia, or about three leagues in circumference.

(l) Diodorus Siculus, lib. xx.

cities

cities of Afia, prefers Rhodes to any of them. (*m*) " The beauty," fays he, " of its harbours, " ftreets, and walls, and the magnificence of " its monuments, render it fo much fuperior " to all other cities, as to admit of no com- " parifon."

Ariftides (*n*) has defcribed it more circum- ftantially, and the account he has left us of it is calculated to excite our aftonifhment and admiration. " Within the walls of Rhodes, " we never faw a fmall houfe by the fide of a " large one. All were of the fame height, and " the fame order of architecture, fo that the " whole city feemed but one fingle edifice. " Wide ftreets croffed it from fide to fide, and " thefe were fo well difpofed, that from what- " ever part it was viewed the profpect was " truly magnificent. The walls and towers, of " a wonderful extent, height, and beauty, " above all excited our wonder. The lofty " fummits of the latter ferved as a Pharos to " mariners. Such, indeed, was the mag- " nificence of Rhodes, that, without having " feen it, the imagination cannot poffibly

(*m*) Strabo, lib. xiv.
(*n*) Ariftides, in Rhodiaca.

" form

" form any conception of its grandeur. All
" the parts of this immenfe town, mutually
" connected with each other, and moft beau-
" tifully proportioned, formed a perfect whole,
" of which the walls were the defence and
" ornament.   Rhodes was the only city of
" which it might be faid, it was fortified like
" a place of war, and decorated like a
" palace."

To this defcription we muft add, fuperb
temples, whofe porticos were enriched with
paintings of the firft mafters, a multitude of
Coloffufes, and ftatues of aftonifhing work-
manfhip, a magnificent theatre, extenfive arfenals, and fleets arriving from every part of
the world to pay the tribute due to the arts
from wealth : We muft likewife recollect, it
was inhabited by a free, brave, learned, and fortunate people, and we fhall be enabled to form
fome idea of this moft beautiful city of the world.
I cannot deny myfelf the pleafure, Madam, of
defcribing to you one or two of thofe wonders
of art which rendered it fo celebrated.   Pliny,
after enumerating the moft famous Coloffal
ftatues, adds: (o) " But none of thefe are to

(o) Pliny, lib. xxxiv. c. 7.

" be

" be compared to that which the Rhodians
" dedicated to the fun. This Coloſſus was
" the work of Chares, of Lindus (p), a pupil
" of Lyſippus (q). It was ſeventy cubits high
" (about one hundred and five feet), (r) and
" was thrown down by an earthquake fifty-ſix
" years after it was firſt erected (s). In this
" ſtate, its appearance is ſtill aſtoniſhing.
" Few men are able to embrace its thumb;
" and its fingers are larger than entire ſtatues
" uſually are; where it has been broken,
" we may diſcover, withinſide, deep cavities
" filled with enormous ſtones, which the
" artiſt had introduced to render it firm on
" its baſe. It is ſaid to have been the labour
" of twelve years, and that it coſt three

(p) One of the towns of the iſle of Rhodes.

(q) This Lyſippus, a celebrated ſtatuary, had caſt a
Coloſſus, forty cubits high, at Tarentum.

(r) Simonides, in the Anthologia, makes it eighty
cubits; but Strabo, lib. xiv. Iſidore Orig. lib. xiv.
cap. 6. and Feſtus, all agree with Pliny, and ſay its height
was only ſeventy cubits.

(s) Polybius, lib. v. Oroſius, lib. iv. Paulus Diaconus Hiſt. Miſc. all agree in ſaying, that at this time
the iſland of Rhodes, and the country of Caria, were agitated by a violent earthquake, that cauſed great devaſta-
tion, and threw down the famous Coloſſus.

" hundred

" hundred talents, a fum which the Rho-
" dians had gained by the fale of the warlike
" machines left by Demetrius before their
" walls, when he raifed the fiege. This city
" contains a hundred other Coloffal ftatues,
" lefs, indeed, than this, but each of them
" fuperb enough to render illuftrious any
" place where they might be erected. To
" thefe are to be added, five gigantic ftatues
" of the gods, the invaluable works of Bry-
" axis."

(t) Some modern hiftorians, wifhing to
add fomething of the marvellous to the account of the Coloffus, have pretended the
feet refted on two rocks, at the entrance of the
harbour, and that veffels paffed, with all their
fails fet, between its legs. This fable deferves
no regard, fince it is contradicted by the
filence of antiquity, which certainly would
not have neglected to record fo remarkable
a fact. On the contrary, the hiftorians who
mention the fall of the Coloffus, as well as
thofe who faw it, teftify, that it was lying on
the ground (u); but had it been placed at
the

(t) Rollin. Hiftoire Ancienne.

(u) Strabo, lib. xiv. The Coloffus of Rhodes, overthrown

the entrance of the harbour, it muſt have fallen into the fea, which circumſtance they certainly would not have omitted (x). It was ſtill in its fallen ſtate in the days of Pliny; as it likewiſe was as late as the twelfth year of the emperor Conſtans, when Moawiah, general of the Caliph Othman, taking Rhodes, deſtroyed this ſtatue, which had well deſerved to be enumerated among the ſeven wonders of the world (y). He ſold it to a Jew, who conveyed its fragments to Emeſa, on nine hundred camels (z), nine hundred and thirty-two years after it was firſt erected.

The arts ſeemed to vie with each other, to contribute to the embelliſhment of Rhodes. Painting there diſputed the palm with ſculp-

thrown by a violent earthquake, and at preſent lying on the ground, has its knees broken. The Rhodians are forbidden, by an oracle, from raiſing it up. This Coloſſal ſtatue, the moſt beautiful ever conſecrated to the Gods by man, is placed among the ſeven wonders of the world.

(x) Paulus Diaconus, Hiſt. Miſc.

(y) Conſtantine Porphyrogenetus ſays, it was ſold to a Jew of Edeſſa, and increaſes prodigiouſly the number of camels, which carried off its fragments, making them amount to thirty thouſand.

(z) Murtius, Diſſertation on the Iſle of Rhodes.

F

ture. The temples contained a multitude of admirable works, among which, fays Strabo (a), "two pictures of Protogenes were particularly admired, the one reprefenting "Ialyfus, and the other a Satyr, ftanding "upon a column, with a partridge at his "feet. The latter picture being expofed to ".public view, the bird attracted univerfal "admiration, fo that the Satyr, in the "finifhing of which the artift had employ-".ed his utmoft attention and abilities, was "almoft entirely difregarded. The wonder "and applaufe of the fpectators was ftill "more increafed, when, on bringing tame "partridges before the picture, they began "to call, as foon as they perceived the "painted bird, to the great delight of the "multitude (b). Protogenes was fo morti-"fied at the preference given to what was "intended merely as an ornament, that he "requefted permiffion from the prefect of the "temple to efface the partridge, and actually "did efface it."

(a) Strabo, lib. xiv.

(b) Protogenes was of Canna, a city of Caria, fubject to the Rhodians.

Pliny

Pliny (c) thus defcribes the picture of Ialyfus mentioned by Strabo: " The moft beau-
" tiful of the works of Protogenes, is the
" picture of Ialyfus, which is ftill to be feen
" in the temple of Peace at Rome. To fe-
" cure it, if poffible, againft the injuries of
" time, the painter placed four layers of colours
" one over the other, hoping that if the upper
" ones fhould decay, the lower would ftill
" remain. In this picture we fee a dog,
" exquifitely painted; chance having con-
" fpired with art to render it perfect. The
" painter, after finifhing every part of the ani-
" mal, and having furmounted every diffi-
" culty, was fo far fatisfied with his work;
" but one thing ftill remained, which he
" defpaired of being able perfectly to ex-
" prefs; this was the froth which whitens
" the mouth of a dog when panting; to
" reprefent this defied his utmoft art, and
" in every attempt he only feemed to de-
" part further from nature. The foam ap-
" peared always painted, and never natural.
" He was the more mortified, as he was ne-
" ver fatisfied with any thing lefs than what

(c) Pliny, lib. xxxv. c. 1c.

" might

" might be miftaken for nature itfelf. Of-
" ten did he efface his colours, and as often
" change his brufhes, without fuccefs.   Ir-
" ritated at the impotence of his art, he pee-
" vifhly threw his fpunge againft the picture,
" which by accident ftruck the mouth of
" the dog, and difpofed the colours more
" happily than his utmoft endeavours and
" fkill had been able to effect ; chance for
" once   moft   accurately   imitating   na-
-" ture (d)."

I have been fo particular in the defcription
of thefe two pieces, to prove how much the
ancients excelled in the art of painting. Protogenes, and Apelles his cotemporary, imitated nature fo perfectly, that their pictures feemed
living and animated beings. The refemblance
was fo exact, that animals, nay even men,
were not unfrequently deceived. Let it not
be imagined that the artift, born with the
happieft talents, can ever attain this de-

(d) Caius Caffius, who took Rhodes, and carried off
all the offerings, except the chariot of the fun, brought
away this fine picture. Dion Caffius. It was preferved
till the time of Commodus, under whofe reign the temple
of Peace was burnt, that is to fay, in the year 450.
Herodian. lib. i.

ᴛ   gree

gree of perfection, without prodigious efforts.
Genius muſt be ſeconded by the moſt per-
ſevering labour, and a profound knowledge
of every ſcience allied to his art. Without
this, the painter creates nothing for inmor-
tality. Protogenes (e) was ſeven years in
finiſhing the picture of Ialyſus; and, if Pliny
may be credited (f), during the whole time,
lived entirely on lupins, leſt, by too much
indulging his appetite, he ſhould obſtruct the
activity of his mind. Nothing can give a
ſtronger proof of the ſublime idea entertained
of perfection by the ancient artiſts, or more
clearly ſhew how much they were inflamed with
a noble thirſt of fame, than the readineſs with
which they made ſuch ſacrifices.

(e) Plutarch in Demetrio. Protogenes painted for
the Rhodians the picture of Ialyſus, which was carried off by Demetrius from a houſe in the ſuburbs,
while yet unfiniſhed. The Rhodians ſent a herald to
him, to conjure him to ſpare this piece. The prince
replied, that he would ſooner burn the images of his
father than ſuch a production of ſo wonderful an art.
It is ſaid that the painter was employed on it ſeven
years.

(f) Pliny lib. xxxv. c. 10.

Do

Do not imagine, Madam, that Rhodes contained only a fmall number of excellent
paintings.   The porticos of its temples
were decorated with pictures of infinite value. The poffeffion of one only of thefe immortal works, fays Ariftides (g), would have
fufficed to render a town illuftrious.   Lucian (h), who was no flatterer, has thefe words,
when fpeaking of his refiding at Rhodes :
" I lodged in the quarter of the temple of
" Bacchus, and, in my leifure hours, fre-
" quently rambled through the city to enter-
" tain myfelf with the admirable works of art
" with which it is enriched. Nothing can fur-
" pafs the exquifite pleafure I have experi-
" enced, from time to time, while walking
" under the porticos of the temple, and con-
" templating the admirable paintings which
" adorn that noble edifice.   My fatisfaction
" was the greater, as I was well acquainted
" with the fubjects, and recalled to memory
" the poetical ftories of the Gods and He-
" roes that are there fo admirably reprefent-
" ed."

(g) Ariftides, in Rhodiaca.
(h) Lucian, in Amoribus.

The fciences and literature ever go hand in hand with the fine arts, of which they are the inftructors and the guides. For the cultivation of thefe alfo were the Rhodians .diftinguifhed. Their fchools attained fo high a degree of celebrity, that they were reforted to by fome of the greateft men of Rome; among whom were Cato (*i*), Marcus Brutus (*k*), Cicero (*l*), Caffius (*m*), Cæfar (*n*), and Pompey (*o*).

Thefe men, born to command, did not confine themfelves to a few frivolous acquifitions; they all learnt Greek, then the univerfal language, and ftudied with attention the principles of legiflation, and the laws of various nations. Above all, they endeavoured to per-

(*i*) Aurelius Victor, Vit. Viror. Illuftr.

(*k*) Cicero, in Bruto.

(*l*) Appian, de Bello Civili, lib. iv.

(*m*) Caffius made a voyage to Rhodes, where he was inftructed in the fine arts, and the beauties and niceties of the Greek language.

(*n*) Plutarch, in Vita Cæfaris : He failed for Rhodes, there to ftudy eloquence under Apollonius Milo, whofe difciple Cicero had been.

(*o*) Plutarch, in Vita Pompeii : He repaired to Rhodes, and ftudied eloquence there, under the Sophifts, paying to each a talent.

fect themselves under the Greek rhetoricians
in the art of public speaking. Destined as
they were to discourse before an enlightened
people, concerning the most important in-
terests of the whole world, eloquence was
necessary to govern the minds of men, and
enforce persuasion by lively images, or co-
gent reasoning. Oratory was, at that time,
as indispensable to a Roman as courage or military abilities.

To what must we attribute this flourish-
ing state of the Rhodian republic? To the
fertility of the soil, the beauty of the climate,
or the excellent situation of the island?
These advantages, no doubt, contributed to,
but were not the efficient cause of, the wealth
of the Rhodians, which was owing to the
goodness of their laws, and the wisdom of
their government, the only solid foundations of the glory of empires. " We cannot
" too much admire," says Strabo (p), " the
" care with which the Rhodians preserve
" their excellent code of laws (q), and the
" wisdom

(p) Strabo, lib. xiv.

(q) The Roman Emperors adopted the naval code of
the Rhodians. Volutius Maximus, *de Lege Rhodiaca*
has

" wifdom confpicuous in the whole confti-
" tution of their republic, and efpecially, in
" the management of their navy. This has
" long preferved them the empire of the
" fea, which they have freed from pirates,
" and fecured to them the friendfhip of the
" Romans." In alliance with numerous
other powers, they artfully accommodated
themfelves to their various interefts, without
taking part in their private quarrels. This
fage policy procured them a long peace, and
rendered their commerce fo flourifhing, that
it extended over the whole Mediterranean.
Rhodes was the emporium of every trading
nation. " The mariner who touched there,"
fays Ariftides (r), " beheld, with aftonifh-
" ment, feveral harbours, formed by art,
" of piers of ftone, which advanced far

has preferved us the following declaration of the Emperor
Antoninus ; " I, the mafter of the world : Let every thing
" relative to naval affairs be determined by the maritime
" code of the Rhodians, as often as that fhall not directly
" contradict our laws."

M. Paftoret, in an excellent differtation, which obtained
the prize, of the academy of infcriptions, has demonftrated
the influence of thefe laws on the marine of the Romans.

(r) Ariftides, in Rhodiaca.

" into

" into the fea. One of thefe received the
" veffels from Ionia; another, thofe from
" Caria. Here a mole offered fhelter to the
" fleets of Egypt, Cyprus and Phœnicia, as if
" exprefsly formed for each refpective city.
" Near to thefe ports, arfenals reared their
" lofty heads, and aftonifhed the beholder
" with their magnificence."

The forefts of Mount Atabyris (s), which
were carefully preferved, furnifhed the Rhodians with excellent fhip timber. Their veffels were the beft failers in the world, and
their mariners the moft expert in navigation.
This gave occafion to the following apof-
trophe from Ariftides (t); " Oh, ye Rho-
" dians! if ever the tempeft warns you to
" think of your fafety; if ever you have to
" ftruggle againft the fury of the waves, re-
" collect the expreffion of one of your mari-
" ners, when his veffel was labouring in
" a ftorm: He faw the abyfs opening to
" receive him; when raifing his voice, he
" exclaimed, Oh, Neptune! know that I

(s) Atabyris, the higheft mountain in the ifle of Rhodes,
produces excellent pine trees.

(t) Ariftides, in Rhodiaca.

" will

" will not abandon the helm, and that if I
" muft be fwallowed up, I will fteer my fhip
" to the very depth of thy empire!" Such,
Madam, were the fources of the power and
glory of the Rhodians. Alexander (*u*), who
regarded their city as the firft in the univerfe,
chofe there to depofit his laft will.

The Rhodians were worthy to inhabit this
city. Their morals were mild and amiable,
and their manners polifhed, without affectation (*v*). When they appeared in public, they
were remarkable for the gravity of their de-
portment. They were not feen loitering in
the ftreets ; but ferioufly reproved foreigners
whom they faw ftrolling about in inconfide-
rate idlenefs. At the theatre, when a piece
deferved applaufe, all the fpectators kept a
profound filence. This they deemed the beft
homage they could pay to merit. At their
tables, civility and urbanity prefided ; and
all excefs was banifhed. They converfed
in a free and friendly manner with their
guefts, and never mortified them, by affuming
the fuperiority of a mafter. " Thefe are the

(*u*) Diodorus Siculus, lib. xx.
(*v*) Dion. Chryfoftom, Orat. 32.

" virtues,"

" virtues," fays Ariftides (*w*), " which render
" your city fo renowned.   Thefe raife you
" above every other nation, and attract the love
" and admiration of every people.   Your an-
" cient, and truly Grecian manners, render
" you far more illuftrious than your ports,
" your walls, or your arfenals!"

Such a people could not but be humane.
As for myfelf, I doubt whether men poffefs a
right to put other men to death, even when
guilty of great crimes.   The Rhodians, however, it is certain, fpared their fellow-citizens
the horror of thofe bloody tragedies, which
difhonour our cities.   Far from preparing
fcaffolds in public places; far from hiring
defpicable mercenaries to publifh in the ftreets
fentences which condemn unhappy wretches
to the flames, or the wheel; the law prohibited
any executioner from entering Rhodes (*x*).
Even the fentence of death was pronounced
without the gates of the city (*y*).   And they
would have confidered it as an impiety, to
ftain their ftreets with human blood.

(*w*) Ariftides, in Rhodiaca.
(*x*) Dion. Chryfoftom.
(*y*) Ariftides, in Rhodiaca.

The

The ancient writers, neverthelefs, reproach the Rhodians with the vices infeparable from great wealth : luxury, and voluptuoufnefs. " They build," fays Stratonicus, " as if they " were immortal, and ferve their tables with " as much profufion, as if they had but a " few days to live." The veffels they made ufe of in their repafts, were of an exquifite invention (z), and greatly renowned for the pleafure they gave in drinking. In their compofition they employed myrrh, the flower of an odoriferous reed, faffron, balm, amoma, and cinnamon, baked together. Anacreon, reciting the number of his miftreffes, fays, " For Rhodes, write down two thoufand." And we find, the ancients called it the city of gallantry (a).

The government of Rhodes was always republican. At firft, the fupreme authority was lodged with the people. The nobles, afterwards, got poffeffion of it ; and formed an ariftocracy (b). But they did not abufe their power. Humanity led them to fuccour their

(z) Athenæus, lib. vii.
(a) Athenæus, lib. viii.
(b) Ariftot. Politic. lib. v.

fellow-

fellow-citizens; and true policy taught them, that the lower claffes of fociety are of the moft real importance; becaufe, without them, a ftate cannot even fubfift. They took care, therefore, to prevent the wretchednefs which is fo deftruÉtive to population (c), and created magiftrates, whofe fole employment it was, to prevent or relieve, the neceffities of the poor; to provide them with wholefome food, and employ them in the public works. This ex-cellent regulation fecured tranquillity to the republic, which never experienced thofe vio-lent and repeated convulfions, that, at length, overthrew thofe of Athens and Rome. It, indeed, fuffered from fome tranfient ftorms. Alcibiades, at the head of a numerous fleet, rendered them fubject to the Athenians; but the republic, entering into an alliance with the inhabitants of Byzantium and Chio, fhook off that yoke (d). Maufoleus made himfelf mafter of Rhodes, by ftratagem, and eftablifhed a tyranny. Artemifia, his queen, making ufe of a like artifice, cut off fome of the principal

(c) Strabo, lib. xiv.
(d) Libonius, de Rhodiorum Libertate

in-

inhabitants.   But the Rhodians expelled their tyrants, and recovered their liberty.

The Rhodians were peaceably enjoying the fruits of the wifdom of their government, when Antigonus (*e*), irritated at not having been able to detach them from the alliance of Ptolemy, king of Egypt, declared war againft them.   He made immenfe preparations, and fent his fon, Demetrius, to fubdue the ifland. That prince, excellently fkilled in the art of taking towns, befieged Rhodes by fea and land.   To reduce it, he invented new ma-chines.   He advanced, to the foot of the walls, a moving citadel of wood plated with iron. This edifice, called the Helepolis, was of a prodigious fize; had nine ftories, and might be moved every way.   Catapultas were employed againft the walls, which threw prodigious ftones and beams of an immenfe fize, headed with iron, while battering-rams, two hundred feet in length, and worked by a thoufand men at once, were fhaking them with repeated ftrokes. A multitude of archers, placed on the top of the moving tower, fhowered down their ar-

(*e*) Diodorus Siculus, lib. xx. defcribes this fiege at length.

rows on the befieged. Thirty thoufand foldiers were employed to put the helepolis in
motion; and fight under its fhelter. The
ltrongeft tower of Rhodes, and great part of
the wall, were thrown down; but the courage
of a free people triumphed over the fleets of
Demetrius, the numerous army he had in
his pay, and all the military talents this great
captain difplayed, during a whole year, in his
various attacks. At the moment when the
befieged were moft brifkly preffed, fome
of the fenators propofed to throw down the
ftatues erected in honour of Antigonus and
Demetrius, in happier times : but the people
rejected this mean counfel, and treated it as
criminal. The generofity of the Rhodians,
toward their enemy, did them honour in the
eyes of all Greece; and hiftory has preferved,
and long will preferve, the memory of fo
glorious an action (f).

(f) Ptolemy rendered them great fervices during this war,
by fending them troops, and fhips, laden with corn. They,
in gratitude, fent to confult the oracle of Ammon; and, on
its anfwer, confecrated, within their walls, a magnificent
monument; to which they gave the name of Ptolemy : It was
a large fquare, with a portico on each fide, a ftadium (fix
hundred feet) in length. Diodorus Siculus. lib. xx.

Mithri-

Mithridates (g), who so long withstood the fortune of the Romans, and conquered Greece, and the islands of the Archipelago, failed in his attempts on Rhodes (h). Caius Cassius took it, during the civil war, and despoiled it of a part of its treasures. Nevertheless, the republic again gloriously reared her head, and the services rendered the Romans by the Rhodians, procured them both their liberty and new towns in Caria. In fine, ever observant of their laws, and careful to maintain the commerce to which they owed their power, they remained independent till the reign of Vespasian (i), who first reduced their island to a Roman province. Since that time, Rhodes has been only one of the finest isles of the Archipelago. The power and riches of the inhabitants have disappeared. It seems as if their genius became extinct with their liberty, that sacred fire, which had caused them to produce so many wonders. Literature, the sciences,

(g) Aurelius Victor, de Viris Illustribus.
(h) Diodorus Siculus, l. xx.
(i) Suetonius, in Vita Vespasian. cap. 8.

G   and

and arts, loft with their freedom, have never more revived.

Under Conftantine this ifland remained a part of the Eaftern empire, which was greatly weakened by its divifion. The pufillanimity and vices of the princes who fucceeded, fhook it to its very foundation. The Arabs, led on by the enthufiafm which Mahomet had infpired, invading and giving battle in the name of the Almighty, conquered the fineft provinces of the empire; and in the twelfth year of the reign of Conftans (*k*), Mowiah, Othman's lieutenant, made himfelf mafter of Rhodes. The Greek emperors, however, at length expelled the infidels, and kept poffeffion till the time of Baldwin; who, becoming fovereign of Conftantinople, fent a prefect to Rhodes (*l*). Some time after, John Ducas conquered it. The brave warriors, then known by the name of the Knights of St. John, led on by their grand mafter, Foulques de Villaret, attacked and took it, after a bloody battle, in which heroifm triumphed over numbers and va-

(*k*) Zonoras, Annal. 3.
(*l*) Nicephorus Gregorias, lib. ii.

lour.

lour (*m*). Mahomet the fecond, who made the Chriftian world tremble, and feemed to have enchained victory to his car, tarnifhed the luftre of his laurels, by befieging this place, defended by a handful of heroes. In 1552, Soliman faw a numerous army perifh under its walls; and if this redoubtable conqueror of Hungary and Perfia did at length fubdue Rhodes, attacked, as it was, on all fides by the forces of the Turks, the greater was the fhame for the Chriftian princes, who did not fend a fingle veffel to the aid of its intrepid defenders. Deftroyed, rather than vanquifhed, they were almoft all buried under the ruins of their forts. Soliman could not enter the town, but through torrents of the blood of his foldiers. He found it nothing but heaps of ruins, defended by a fmall number of knights, covered with wounds, at the head of whom appeared the famous Villiers de l'Ifle Adam, a brave old man, who united to the coolnefs of age, the intrepidity of a hero, and the greatnefs of foul of a philofopher.

I have, now, given you a fummary of the hiftory of Rhodes, from the earlieft anti-

(*m*) Paulus Langius, in Chronico Citizenfi.

quity,

quity, to the period in which it fell under the power of the Turks : it now remains for me to lay before you fome account of its prefent ftate.

I have the honour to be, &c.

LETTER XIII.

To M. L. M.

Rhodes.

I HAVE no longer, Madam, the pleasure of presenting you the description of a magnificent city, a wise government, or a free and glorious nation. The ambition of the Romans, the degeneracy of the monarchs of the Lower Empire, the fanaticism of the Arabs, and destructive earthquakes, have alternately laid waste the isle of Rhodes. The despotism of the Turks, succeeding to these calamities, has been the cause of no less fatal evils; and utterly destroyed monuments, sciences, and arts.

The modern town, built on the ruins of the ancient city, occupies only a quarter of its extent, and possesses no remarkable antiquities. Not even the smallest remains of the theatre, temples, and portico, are to be discovered. Statues, colossuses, paintings, all have been destroyed, or carried off. To wide and

and fkilfully difpofed ftreets; to thofe regularly ranged edifices, where each front prefented the fame order of architecture, have fucceeded narrow and winding lanes, and houfes
without tafte, regularity, or decoration. I may
venture to affert, Madam, that if a Rhodian
of the days of Alexander were to revifit his
native city, he would find himfelf abfolutely
a ftranger; he would not recollect the fmalleft
monument; but muft imagine himfelf tranfported into a country inhabited by barbarians.

The knights of Rhodes have left various
traces of their refidence in the ifland. Their
armorial enfigns, and fome bufts of the grand
mafters, fculptured in relief, on marble,
decorate the front of feveral buildings.
The walls and towers they erected ftill
fubfift, and bear the glorious marks of their
obftinate defence, The church of St. John
has been converted into a mofque. The vaft
hofpital, in which Chriftian charity received
the faithful from all parts of the world, and
furnifhed them with fuccours, at this day
ferves as a granary for the Turks. The barbarians fuffer it to go to ruin, as well as the

government

government houfe, in which we find antique
marbles, and columns.

Rhodes has only two harbours. The
fmalleft faces the eaft, and is called Darea.
Rocks, at a fmall diftance from each other, in
the front, block the entrance, and only leave
room for one veffel to pafs. Moles, raifed
on each fide, defend it from every wind.
The Turks, who, fince the conqueft of the
ifland, have not removed from it a fingle grain
of fand, fuffer it gradually to choak up. There
is only water enough for merchant fhips, and
even they are obliged to unload a part of their
cargo, before they can enter it. Ships go
thither to careen, and caravelles are built
there for the Grand Signior. This handfome
bafon might be made fit for the reception of
large veffels, if the fame means were employed to clear it, as at Marfeilles and other
ports.

The other harbour is large; it bears the name
of Rhodes; and in this, frigates of thirty
guns may anchor. Veffels are here defended
from the wefterly winds, which, in thefe lati-
tudes, prevail nine months in the year.
North and north-eafterly winds blow full
into the harbour; and, when violent, fhips
are

are in danger of driving on the rocks, or againſt the walls of the town. Though Rhodes has retained none of its ancient ſplendor, its advantageous ſituation, on the point of a promontory, its houſes diſpoſed in the form of an amphitheatre, the ſolid ſtructure of its walls, and its towers advanced upon the ſhoals, give it an air of ſtrength and importance to mariners, as they approach the city (*n*). But there are no ſoldiers on the iſland. Its forts are without defenders, and will become the conqueſt of the firſt nation, which ſhall think proper to attack them.

The Pacha is the governor general of the iſland. He poſſeſſes abſolute power; and pre-ſides at once over civil juſtice and military diſcipline. He nominates to employments that fall vacant; ſentences to death, and is to watch over the maintenance of good order,

***

(*n*) The Rhodians have no troops in their iſland. They are not warriors. Knowing themſelves incapable of refiſting the weakeſt enemy who may attack them, in time of war they hire ſoldiers from Caramania, to defend their city. Theſe are undiſciplined troops, who aban-don themſelves to all the exceſſes of a blind ferocity, and are more to be dreaded by the inhabitants, than by the enemy.

through

through the whole extent of his government.
This supreme officer, finding no one who
dare refist his will, may be guilty of the utmoft exceffes of tyranny, without fear of
punifhment or controul.

All private litigations are decided before
the tribunal of the judge, called the Cadi.
His decifions are without appeal. He partakes
alfo of the ecclefiaftical jurifdiction with the
Muphti. The latter is the interpreter of the
Koran, prefides over religious affairs, and
expounds the divine law ; nor can the Pacha
put a man to death, until he has given his
fanction to the juftice of the fentence.

The Greeks and Jews have a chief named
the Mouteveli, who is their intendant general ;
and has the regulation of the tax called Carach *(o)* (a capitation tax, impofed by the
Grand Signior on all his fubjects who are
not Mahometans, but which is paid only by
the men). He decides all differences that arife
among them, without its being neceffary to
have recourfe to any other jurifdiction. When
the Cadi has condemned a Greek or Jewifh
debtor to pay the money due to his creditor,

(o) This word is Arabic, and fignifies tribute, or tax.

he

he fends his fentence to the Mouteveli, who, if he thinks proper, carries it into execution. Thefe are the principal officers in the ifland, who all feem to confpire its ruin. As a proof of this, I fhall give you a flight fketch of their adminiftration; for the truth of which I can fafely vouch.

The foil of Rhodes is dry and fandy; but the numerous fprings which water it render it extremely fertile. Corn thrives there admirably. Its yellow and heavy grain affords a flour as white as fnow, which makes excellent bread. If half of the country, capable of growing it, were cultivated, the Rhodians would have far more than fufficient for their confumption, and might export to foreign countries. But the Turks are no cultivators; and the Greeks, weighed down by the fervices exacted from them by the Mouteveli, for his own profit; and difcouraged by the fear of not enjoying the fruits of their labours, let the fineft fields lie barren. It is certain, Madam, that a fingle word from the Pacha would enrich the country with the treafures of agriculture. He is abfolute, and has but to command, and affure the hufbandman of his protection: but he knows not

whether

whether he fhall himfelf be in place to-morrow, and would be fearful of labouring for
the advantage of his fucceffor. Befides, a ftill
more powerful reafon prevents him from
endeavouring any improvement : the mifery
of the country conftitutes his wealth. Rhodes
not furnifhing fufficient corn for the fupport of
its inhabitants, he fends to purchafe the grain of
Caramania, which is of an inferior quality,
at a low rate. He has this conveyed to
market in fmall quantities, to enhance the
price. But, what is ftill more oppreffive, is
that the rate fixed for the firft bufhel of the
new crop, ferves as the ftandard price for all
that is fold during the remainder of the year ;
which rule is not to be departed from, though
one half of the people fhould perifh. This
infamous monopoly, which rapidly enriches
thofe who are concerned in it, is productive
of the moft fatal confequences to commerce,
agriculture, and the induftry of the inhabitants. What, indeed, can be expected from
a nation, in want of the firft neceffaries of
life ? What exchanges can they make with
foreign countries, if their own be infufficient
for their fupport, and they have neither arts
nor manufactures ? and, indeed, the univer-

fal

fal poverty and frightful depopulation of the
ifland, are indelible proofs of the vices of this
wretched government. The following ſtate-
ment will be a ſufficient demonſtration of
what I have ſaid.

The ifland of Rhodes contains two cities;
the capital, of the fame name, of which I have
been ſpeaking, and the ancient Lindus. The
former is inhabited by Turks, and a ſmall
number of Jews,

Five villages inhabited by Mahometans, and

Five towns and forty one villages inhabited
by Greeks.

Number of families.

Turks	-	4700
Greeks	-	2500
Jews	-	100
Total		7300

Suppoſing five perſons to a family, we
ſhall have 36,500 inhabitants. But the ifland
is more than forty leagues in circumference.
Here then is a vaſt ſpace occupied by few-
er people than is contained in a moderate

town

town in France. Might we not fay that at
Rhodes the earth devours its inhabitants? By
no means; the foil is fruitful, and would produce abundantly, now, as well as formerly,
corn, oil, excellent wines, wax, and even
wood for fhip-building. Defpotifm, and the
monopolies of the great, alone prevent the
increafe of the inhabitants. The ftate of the
revenues of the ifland perfectly correfponds
with the fmall number and poverty of the
Rhodians. Permit me, Madam, to lay it
before you; without thefe particulars, what
I relate would appear incredible.

Table

Table of the revenues of the ifland of Rhodes.

Duties of carach or capitation	42500	
Tenths on all produce of the land	23050	
Cuftoms	3500	
Tax on houfes	6250	
On the farm of wax	10300	Piaftres, or crowns of 3 livres—half a crown Englifh.
On cattle	800	
At the gates	200	
On the farm of the baths	1200	
On falt	700	
On vineyards	600	
New poll tax on every Greek and Jew	900	

Total 90,000

Here then we have 90,000 Turkifh piaftres which the ifland produces the Grand Signior, from which we muft deduct   55,500 Piaftres

Employed in paying the guards of the town and villages, the infpectors of eftates in the country, the repairs of the mofques, and the bread and foap diftributed to the poor, by order of the Sultan. So that the Grand Signior really receives no more than   34,500 Piaftres

From

From this calculation, Madam, on the accuracy of which you may rely, it appears that this large ifland produces lefs to the Ottoman emperors, than many eftates, of only fome leagues extent, in France, are worth to their poffeffors. Do not afk me what has become of that powerful people, who, profiting by their advantageous fituation, their forefts, their harbours, and the fertility of their country, covered the Mediterranean with their victorious fleets : I have already faid they loft their liberty; and with it fcience and national genius. The Turkifh government has put the finifhing hand to their misfortunes ; Rhodes now only affords a few indigent wretches, without commerce, arts, or induftry, becaufe they can have no property, who wander over the defolated plains of this once flourifhing ifland.

Of the three cities founded, according to the fable, by the children of the fun, Lindus alone has left any remarkable veftiges. Camirus and Jalifus are totally deftroyed (p).
" Leaving Rhodes, fays Strabo, and failing
" on with the coaft on the right, the firft

(p) Strabo, lib. xiv.

" city

" city we arrive at is Lindus, fituated on a
" hill on the fouth fide of the ifland, and
" oppofite Alexandria. The traveller here
" admires the famous temple of the Lindian
" Minerva, built by the daughters of Da-
" naus *(q).*" Cadmus enriched it with magnificent offerings. The inhabitants here confecrated
the feventh ode of Pindar's Olympics, which
they infcribed in letters of gold *(r).* The
ruins of this noble edifice are ftill vifible
on an eminence near the fea. The remains
of its walls, which were built with enormous
ftones, difcover the Egyptian tafte; but
the columns and other ornaments have been
carried off. On the higheft part of the rock,
we perceive the ruins of a caftle that ferved
as a fortrefs to the town; it occupied a large
fpace which is now filled with rubbifh.

The modern Lindus is fituated at the
foot of this hill; a deep bay, which runs
up far into the land, ferves it as a harbour.
Veffels find here good anchorage, in eight
and twelve fathom water, and are fheltered

(q) Diodorus Siculus, lib. v. fays it was built by Danaus
himfelf.
(r) Demetrius Triclinius.

from

from the fouth-wefterly winds, which prevail during the rough feafon of the year.
At the beginning of winter, they fhould anchor clofe to a little village called Maffary.
Before the building of Rhodes, Lindus was
the port reforted to by the fleets of Egypt, and
of Tyre. It was enriched by commerce,
and a wife government, profiting by its
harbour and fituation, might ftill render it
a flourifhing city.

About the middle of Rhodes is a high
mountain, which commands the whole ifland.
It is called Artemira, and I imagine it to
be the Mount Atabyris of Strabo (s). On
it formerly was a temple of Jupiter, now
no longer in exiftence, but its place is fupplied by a fmall chapel, to which the Greeks
make pilgrimages. Mount Artemira is very
fteep, fo that it is impoffible to afcend it on
horfeback, and on foot it takes four hours
to reach the top. When there we enjoy a
moft magnificent profpect. On the edge of
the horizon, towards the north-eaft, we difcover the fummits of Mount Cragus; to the

(s) We next arrive at Atabyris, the higheft mountain
in the country, on the fummit of which is a temple of
Jupiter. Strabo, lib. xiv.

H   north,

north, the high coaſt of Caramania; to the
north-weſt, the ſmall iſlands of the Archipelago, which appear like luminous points;
to the ſouth-weſt, the ſummit of Mount
Ida, capped with clouds; and, to the ſouth,
and ſouth-caſt, the vaſt expanſe of waters
which bathe the coaſts of Africa. This extenſive proſpect varies every inſtant, as it
is more or leſs illuminated by the rays of
the ſun, and exhibits a moving ſcenery which
aſtoniſhes and delights the beholder. After
contemplating this grand picture, the eye
looks down with pleaſure on the iſland which
rounds itſelf beneath our feet; and here and
there we perceive, on the tops of the moſt
lofty hills, ancient pines, planted by nature,
that in ages paſt formed thick foreſts, which
the Rhodians carefully preſerved for their
navy. At preſent theſe trees are not very
numerous, as the Turks make uſe of them
to build the Grand Signior's caravelles, and
cut down without ever planting. Their
ſolitary ſhades are at preſent the retreats
of the wild aſſes, which are remarkable for
their ſurpriſing ſwiftneſs.

Beyond theſe firſt heights, we meet with
various amphitheatres of eminences, which

become

become gradually lower till we reach the fea. In the greater part of the ifland, the coaft is a gentle and almoft infenfible declivity; therefore, fhips may almoft every where anchor at a cable's length from the fhore. The hills in general are covered with thorns, or brambles; but on fome of them we find vineyards, which ftill produce the perfumed wine in fuch requeft among the ancients (t). This wine is very pleafant to the tafte, and leaves an exquifite flavour in the mouth. The Rhodians added the luxury of drinking it out of voluptuous cups. It would be eafy to multiply thefe vines, and cover with them hills of a great extent, which are now lying without cultivation.

On the fhady fummit of Mount Artemira a great number of fprings arife, which fertilize the plains and vallies. Around the villages, we find a few cultivated fpots, and orchards, where the fig, pomegranate, and orange trees, though planted without regu-

---

(t) Pliny. The wine of Rhodes refembles that of Cos. Theodorus adds, Some praife the wine of Rhodes, on account of its exquifite perfume, and agreeable flavour.

larity

larity or tafte, afford, neverthelefs, pleafing
fhades. The peach trees, which, in the time
of Pliny (*u*), produced no fruit at Rhodes,
are at prefent very fruitful; but the peaches
they bear have neither the flavour, nor the
delicious juice of ours; as in this country they
know nothing of the art of grafting. The
palm flourifhes here, as in the days of Theophraftus (*v*), but produces no fruit. There
feems to be a certain line drawn by nature
for each fpecies of tree, beyond which fome
will not grow at all, and others become barren.

In pafling over the ifland, we traverfe with
regret beautiful vallies, without finding fo
much as a village, a cottage, or even the
fmalleft traces of cultivation. The bottoms
of the rocks are covered with wild rofes.
Myrtles in flower perfume the air with

(*u*) The peach trees were tranfmitted to us late, and
with difficulty. They produce no fruit at Rhodes, which is
the firft place they were tranfplanted to from Egypt. Pliny.
l. xv. cap. 13.

(*v*) The nature of the foil contributes much to fecundity
or fterility. This is vifible in the peach and palm trees.
The latter bears fruit in Egypt, and the adjacent countries;
at Rhodes it only flowers.

their

their delicious emanations, and tufts of the laurel-rofe adorn the banks of rivulets with their beautiful flowers. The inhabitants fuffer the earth to nourifh an infinity of ufelefs plants, without endeavouring to direct or profit by its fecundity.

But let us not too heavily cenfure the Greeks for this torpid indolence. They are utterly unable to attempt any thing for private advantage, or public utility. The deftructive monopoly of the Pacha prevents all exertion, and the continual fervices impofed on them by the Nazir wear them down with labour. This officer, who is fuperintendant of naval affairs, employs them, the greateft part of the year, in cutting down wood to build the caravelles; which they are obliged to convey, with infinite difficulty, to Rhodes. What do you fuppofe he gives, Madam, for the conveyance of a large tree, which has employed feveral men a confiderable time? Fifteen fols (feven-pence halfpenny). But how much do you imagine each of thefe beams, delivered at the arfenal, cofts the Grand Signior? Sixty livres! (fifty fhillings.)

The prefent Nazir, not being able either to read or write, is obliged to employ Greeks

to

to manage his accounts, and thefe make no fecret of his knavery. The pay of the build-ers, who labour in the dockyards, is fixed by the Porte; but this too he diminifhes one half. If it happens to rain but an hour, that day's work is not reckoned; add to this, that in his accounts, he doubles the real number of the workmen.

The confequence is, that the caravelles built at Rhodes are very indifferent veffels; they remain fo long upon the ftocks, that their ribs fometimes become rotten before they are finifhed; but this does not hinder the builders from going on with the work. By this the Nazir foon amaffes great riches. The cries of the oppreffed are heard on every fide againft his injuftice; but they are not regarded. The oppreffor replies to every complaint with money; he purchafes with a number of purfes the protection of the Captain Pacha, and the profits he makes by his crimes enfure impunity.

It is diftreffing, Madam, to dwell on fuch acts of injuftice, and to reflect that all the officers of government in thefe countries are alike guilty of them. Thefe wretches, blinded by ambition, think only of amaffing wealth,

to

to procure higher employments at court. Can they be ignorant that they themfelves muft then become the victims of the rapacity of the Grand Signior, who never fails to find them guilty, to profit by their fpoils? But fuch is the manner in which the Ottoman provinces are governed ; all· the gold they poffefs is fwallowed up in Conftantinople ; and while the capital overflows with riches, they are languifhing in the extremeft poverty. The people, therefore, in defpair, are every where ripe for rebellion, and fhake the throne with violent concuffions. The empire, tottering to its foundations, is on the brink of ruin. Such are the effects of defpotifm. May fovereigns never lofe fight of the important truth, that in proportion as they render their authority more abfolute, they really lofe their power, and that they are never nearer deftruction than when a whole people tremble in their prefence !

I fhall finifh this long letter, Madam, by faying a word or two of the national character of the Rhodians. This, like that of every other people, is modified by climate,

mate, government, and religion. The ifland
enjoys the happieft temperature, and its air
is pure and falubrious. No epidemical diforders are known, but what are imported
from other countries. The wefterly winds,
which prevail for nine months in the year,
moderate the heats of fummer ; and, in the
winter, ice, fnow, and even hoar-frofts are
unknown. In the dulleft day, the fun difperfes
the clouds, and fhews himfelf at leaft for
fome hours ; through the whole year he
enlightens the ifland with his beneficent rays,
fertilizes the earth, and purifies the air, which
is naturally humid. " Tiberius," fays Suetonius (x), " made a ftay for fome time at
" Rhodes, enchanted with the beauty and
" falubrious climate of the ifland." So fine
a fky, fo delightful a temperature, have a
manifeft influence on the inhabitants. The
Turks born in the ifland are of a milder
difpofition, and poffefs more politenefs and
urbanity, than in the other provinces of the
empire. Lefs expofed than the Greeks to
the rapacity of the great, and peaceably enjoying their property, they here lead a hap-

(x) Suetonius in Tiberio, cap. xi.

py

py life in the bofom of their families, and among them we meet with cheerfulnefs, integrity, and focial manners. The Greeks live under the fame fky ; but, accuftomed perpetually to crouch beneath the iron fceptre that crufhes them, they become hypocritical, deceitful, and difhoneft. The proudeft of mankind in profperity, they are equally mean and cringing in misfortune. They are infected with all the vices which are the confequence of fervitude ; yet, compelled, as it were, by the force of climate, they fometimes indulge in merriment : their joy, however, is not the mild and tranquil joy of the Turks; but a clamorous and irrational mirth ; the feftivity, in fhort, of flaves, who, forgetting, for a moment, their wretched condition, dance amid their chains.

I did not myfelf continue long enough in Rhodes, to have made all the obfervations collected in this letter : I am indebted for them to M. Potonier, my hoft, who had refided five years in the country, and knows it perfectly.

I have the honour to be, &c.

L E T.

L E T T E R XIV.

To M. L. M.

Syme.

I QUITTED with regret, Madam, the ifle of Rhodes, where fo many memorable events were continually recurring to my mind. While the veffel was bearing us far from its fhore, my eye ftill continued fixed on this ancient country of the arts, and I could not but lament its deftiny. Will thofe happy days never return, when every po-lifhed nation did homage to this ifland ; when the talents of her artifts, and the eloquence of her orators, attracted a crowd of foreigners? When fcience has once ceafed to enlighten a country, muft it remain for ever obfcured by barbarous darknefs ? No : I would rather wifh to believe that the glorious days of Greece will again return, and that a people inimical to defpotifm, again eftablifhing a wife fyftem of government, will reftore its fciences and arts. Such were my reflections as we failed through the ftrait which feparates

Rhodes

Rhodes from the continent of Afia. If this
ifland had a navy, it might become miftrefs
of that paffage, and command the entrance
of the Archipelago to the Eaft ; which poft,
in the hands of any other nation but the
Turks, would be of the greateft importance.

We continued advancing flowly. The
wind, impeded by the high lands, fcarcely
fwelled our fails, and, at length, entirely
ceafed, and left us, for two days, becalmed.
The fea was perfectly unruffled, and reflected
the rays of the fun like a polifhed mirror,
while the motionlefs veffel feemed nailed to
its furface. The firft time we fail in thefe
feas we imagine ourfelves in the midft of a
great lake, as we are continually furrounded
either by iflands or the continent. The land
appears on every part of the horizon, and,
whichever way we direct our view, we perceive perpendicular rocks, or threatening fhoals.
The fight, however, has nothing terrible
in it to the mariner, who well knows he can
eafily find fhelter from the tempeft in innumerable harbours.

Proceeding onward, with a favourable
breeze, we had overfhot Syme, fo famous for
its fpunges ; and, leaving Telos, the high grounds

of

of which we perceived on the edge of the horizon to the fouth, we were about to enter
the bay of Cos, at prefent commonly called
Stanchio.

I was ardently wifhing to fee the country
of Hippocrates, and Apelles, when the wind
fuddenly died away, and left us in fight of
Nifyros ; which Neptune (z), as fables tell,
raifed out of the fea by a ftroke of his tri-
dent.

The calm we had enjoyed was deceitful ;
beneath it lurked the tempeft. The weft was
overcaft with dark clouds, and the wind foon
began to blow from that quarter in violent
fqualls. The captain inftantly put about his
fhip, and, far from endeavouring to gain the
port of Nifyros, fteered directly from it before the wind, and took refuge in a deep
bay of the ifle of Syme. Thus, in a few
hours, we loft all the way we had gained in
feveral days.

This ifland, which received its name from
Syme, a (y) daughter of Jalyfus, is a dependency of Rhodes. It is only a rock of fmall

(y) Stephanus Byzantinus.

(z) Ibid.

extent,

extent, the foil of which, extremely ftony,
and burnt up by the heat of the fun, produces neither grain nor fruit. A few vineyards among the rocks yield a good wine,
but the reft of the ifland is barren ; and nothing is to be found upon it but briars, wild
almond-trees, thorns, and tufts of myrtle in
the more moift places.   The fifhery for
fpunges, which grow in abundance round the
ifland, is the only fupport of its inhabitants.
Men, women, and children, all know how to
dive, and plunge into the waters in fearch of
the only patrimony beftowed on them by
nature. The men, efpecially, are inimitable
in this dangerous art ; they throw themfelves
into the fea, and dive to a very great depth ;
but they frequently ftrain themfelves by re-
taining their breath too long, and, on coming
out of the water, often vomit great quantities
of blood. Sometimes they are in danger
of deftruction from the monfters of the
deep.   The knife they carry in their hands
would be but an inadequate weapon for their
defence ; but, accuftomed perfectly to diftinguifh objects through that pellucid element, as foon as they difcover thefe voracious
fifh, they fhoot up with the greateft rapidity
from

from a prodigious depth, and in an inftant are in their boat. Thefe particulars I learned from a diver of the country ; he complained of violent pains in his loins, the hardfhips of his condition, and the little profit he derived from his occupation ; and I cannot doubt but he had fufficient reafon. He had a fon with him in his boat, ten years of age, whom he was teaching his trade, the only inheritance he had to leave him.

The bad weather detaining us fome days in the harbour of Syme, I made an excurfion into the ifland, and vifited the village inhabited by the divers. Every thing I faw was a proof of poverty and diftrefs : the ftreets are narrow and dirty, and the houfes only miferable huts, into which day-light can fcarcely penetrate. The people, who have a referved and melancholy air, appear abforbed in their own wretchednefs, and exhibit none of that lively curiofity ufually infpired by the fight of ftrangers. Both men and women are dreffed in the fame manner; they all wear the long robe, the fafh, and a fhawl round their heads, and are only to be diftinguifhed by the difference of features. Thefe miferable people are, befides, fubject to a cruel malady. Leprofy,

the

the moſt hideous of all the ſcourges that afflict
humanity, is very common at Syme. The
wretched victims, who ſuffer from it, are ſeen
ſtretching out their hands to paſſengers at a
diſtance, and begging alms with a voice
ſcarcely audible; they are ſeparated from all
ſociety, and drag on the remainder of a
dreadful life in torments. Shuddering at
what I ſaw, I was about to return to the
ſhip, when a Greek prieſt forced me, by
repeated ſolicitations, to go into his houſe.
He made me ſit down on a ſmall wooden ſeat,
the only one he had, while he himſelf
ſquatted down upon a wretched mat. He told
me that he had been at Rome, where he had
ſtudied in the ſeminary *de propaganda*; that
he had been made choice of for paſtor of
Syme, and that he preferred this country to
all the charming ſcenes of Italy. I congra-
tulated him on his taſte and his travels, but
could not help inquiring within myſelf how
it was poſſible to like ſuch a place of abode.
This good father was very old; a long white
beard deſcended on his breaſt; his appearance
was venerable; and whether he really thought
himſelf happy in the ſtation where Heaven
had placed him, or whether he felt a ſatis-
faction

faction in converfing with an European in the Italian language, which he had almoft forgotten during forty years abfence from Rome, I know not, but pleafure fparkled in his eyes, and he loaded me with compliments. He quitted me for an inftant, dived into a dark hole he called his cellar, and returned immediately with a large pitcher of wine; out of which he poured fome into a fmall wooden porringer, and, after moiftening his lips, defired me to drink. The appearance of the veffel gave me fome difguft, and I wifhed to decline the compliment, but the laws of hofpitality forbade me. It would have been improper to offend my hoft: I therefore took the cup, and drank his health; he drank alfo to mine, and again prefented it to me, but I politely refufed. I remembered that Baucis and Philemon dwelt in a little cottage, and that their table was only three feet long; but could not but recollect that their veffels, fimple as they were, were neat and fhining, and that cleanlinefs in every thing about them almoft concealed their indigence. My good old man was as poor as that virtuous couple; but his ragged mat, his fmoaky roof, and his cup as black as foot,

had

had nothing in them to gratify either the fenfe of fmelling, or of fight. I left him with thanks for his politenefs ; he wifhed me a profperous voyage, and we parted good friends.

I have the honour to be, &c.

LETTER VIII.

To M. L. M.

AFTER three days ftay in the harbour of Syme, we fet fail, intending to return to the bay of Cos, make the north part of the ifland, and then take our departure for Candia. The wefterly winds would then no longer have been unfavourable : but our evil genius again met us at the opening of the Straights. Twice were we prevented from entering, and twice driven back toward Nifyros. Our captain, confidering this difappointment as the confequence of a decree of fate, paffed the fouthern point of Stanchio, and bore away directly for the ifle of Crete. The wind continued to blow with violence from the north-weft : the waves beat furi-

I   oufly

oufly againft the fides of the veffel, and fometimes broke over the deck with a dreadful
noife. During the night we were greatly
alarmed; a large wave forced into the captain's cabin, where I lay, and my fervant's
bed, which was next the door, was laid under
water: he jumped out of his fleep, thought
himfelf drowning in the fea, and fet up a
hideous cry. I got up in a fright, and, feeing
the cabin full of water, thought the veffel had
opened her fides; but we were foon relieved
from our fears; the water had entered by the
hatches, which had been left open, and, on
fhutting them down, we were fufficiently
fecured from fuch accidents.

At day-break we difcovered the ifle of Dia,
now commonly called Standia, where veffels
touch in their way to Candia, being obliged to
unload here part of their merchandize, as the
harbour of the capital, almoft choaked up
fince it has been in the poffeffion of the Turks,
will not admit veffels of more than two hundred tons when fully laden. We were making great way, and entertained hopes of, at
length, reaching our defired haven. All on
board were in high fpirits, and congratulating
each other that we had only one hour's fail,
when

when the wind fuddenly fhifted to the weft, and blew very hard. The fhip began to drift, and folicitude and difappointment fucceeded to our flattering hopes. The captain in vain ufed every effort not to lofe way, by making repeated tacks, in which we approached the ifle of Crete near enough to difcover the verdant flopes of the hills near the fhore; but this delightful profpect only aggravated our misfortune. For two days and nights we have continued tacking before Standia, without being able to gain the harbour.

The wind continuing to increafe, the fea became furious, and the waves broke violently over the deck. The veffel, too deeply laden, would but ill obey the helm, and every moment feemed ready to be fwallowed up amid the liquid mountains that hung over us on every fide. The captain, yielding to neceffity, once more put before the wind, and fteered for the ifle of Cafos. We now went at a great rate, and, in a few hours, the rocks, which fhut in the road, opened to our view : the fea dafhed againft them with a dreadful noife, and the foaming breakers rofe to a prodigious height. As we drew nearer, our fituation appeared ftill more perilous.

None of the crew were acquainted with the road, or knew where to caſt anchor. They had intended at firſt to come within the ſhoal to the weſt, and were on the brink of certain deſtruction. In an inſtant we found ourſelves amid the breakers, which are there almoſt level with the ſurface of the water. The crew turned pale at their danger, inſtantly put about the helm, and we eſcaped ſhipwreck only by the length of the veſſel. Had the ſhip refuſed to obey the helm, ſhe muſt have driven on ſharp rocks, which would have daſhed her into a thouſand pieces. A large bark, which lay at anchor behind a ſmall iſland on the north ſide of the road, ſaved us, by pointing out the true anchoring ground.

We have now, Madam, been at ſea above ſix weeks, conſtantly buffeted by the winds, driven from iſland to iſland, from country to country, and ſeeking Candia, as Ulyſſes ſought Ithaca. His voyages every day appear to me more probable. Our ſailors, it is true, are unworthy of the days of Homer: on the ſmalleſt appearance of bad weather, they run to hide themſelves in the neareſt harbour. Since our departure from Alexandria, a French captain would have made ſix voyages to Crete.
The

The fuperftition of thefe Greeks is equal to their ignorance. They really believe their fhip enchanted, and look on me with an evil eye : I am pofitively afraid they confider me as the magician, whofe forceries occafion their mif-fortunes. Fanatic as they are to an excefs, they may take it into their heads, that their difappointments are occafioned by an heretic, and that, by throwing him into the fea, the perfecution of Heaven will ceafe. Be that as it may, fome of them have actually been in the boat, in fearch of a Greek prieft, to de-ftroy the enchantment. He, not long ago, came on board in his ceremonial habit, with a cenfer in one hand, and a *goupillon* (a veffel for fprinkling the holy water) in the other. He wore a long gown over his black robe ; and his long beard, contracted eyebrows, and point-ed bonnet, made him rather appear the magi-cian himfelf. A bafon of holy water was car-ried before him by a boy ; and the grave father began by fprinkling our chamber, without fparing any who were prefent. He gave his benediction to the crew, the decks, the mafts, and every rope ; repeating a great variety of forms of exorcifm, to free us from the power of Satan. He afterward went over the

whole

whole ſhip, with the cenſer in his hand, and burning perfumes, of which each of us had his ſhare. After the ceremony was over, the prieſt held out a little baſon, into which a few pieces of money were thrown, and he departed promiſing us a proſperous voyage, and much good fortune. The ſailors now believing themſelves unbewitched, appeared perfectly ſatisfied ; and cannot perceive that their ignorance and inexperience is the only charm that has obſtructed them in their voyage : to diſcover this would imply a degree of knowledge to which they are utter ſtrangers. Superſtition is the daughter of ignorance, which is born with the human race, and with that alone will be deſtroyed. The Greeks, endowed with a lively and active imagination, appear at all times to have been more ſubject to this weakneſs than other nations, as ſeems ſufficiently proved by the multitude of temples dedicated to Neptune in the iſlands of the Archipelago, and the tragical ſtory of the ſacrifice of Iphigenia, to obtain favourable winds.

I have the honour to be, &c.

L E T T E R XVI.

To M. L. M.

Cafos.

WE muft not always confider the obftacles
we meet with at fea, Madam, as a misfortune,
fince fometimes we may derive more advantage and improvement from adverfe winds
than from profperous gales. After having
been for two days within fight of the fmiling
fhores of Crete, without being able to land
there; and after contemplating, not without
repining at our fate, the verdant fields and
beauteous profpects of that country, I murmured againft the wind, which had compelled
us to abandon them, and our anchoring in
the road of Cafos feemed to me a misfortune.
Since I have become acquainted with the inhabitants of that ifland, however, I have feen
reafon to alter my opinion, and the wind
muft detain us here a long time before I wifh
it to change.

  " (a) Cafos is one of the Cyclades. . . . It
" received its name from Cafo, father of

(a) Steph. Byzant. The French captains, by a corrup-
tion of the name, call it *l'Ifle du Gaze.*

" Cleo-

" Cleomachus. This little ifland fent a co-
" lony to Mount Cafius, dependent on Syria."
" (b) Cafos," fays Strabo, " is diftant from Car-
" pathus (now called Scarpanto) feventy fta-
" dia, or two leagues and a half, and two
" hundred and fifty ftadia, or nine leagues,
" from Samonium (c), a promontory of Crete.
" It is eighty ftadia (three leagues) in circum-
" ference; on it is a town of the fame name,
" and round it feveral fmaller iflands." Pliny
(d) gives the diftances very differently; but
he was miftaken. I have vifited the places,
and muft pronounce in favour of the accuracy
of Strabo.

The ifle of Cafos has fuffered the common
fate of the Archipelago. It is now fubject to
the Turks, but they dare not inhabit it, becaufe it has no fort. They would be afraid
of being made prifoners by the privateers of
Malta, as has happened to them more than
once at Antiparos, and other places deftitute
of fortreffes. This fear is a moft fortunate
circumftance for the inhabitants, who owe to

(b) Strabo, lib. x.

(c) This promontory, fituated on the eaft fide of the ifland
of Crete, is now called Cape Solomon.

(d) Pliny, lib. iv. c. 12,

that

that alone the tranquility, happinefs, and liberty they enjoy.

The day after we caſt anchor, I was impatient to go on ſhore. The boat accordingly was launched, and we rowed towards the rocks which ſurrounded the iſland, but were at a loſs where to land. Every part of the ſhore was defended by dangerous ſhoals, over which the foaming waves broke with great noiſe and violence. On whichever ſide we caſt our eyes, Caſos appeared inacceſſible. At length one of the inhabitants perceiving our embarraſſment, came down from the village, and pointed out to us, by waving his handkerchief, the place to which we ſhould direct our courſe. We reached the place, after coaſting about a league along the iſland. The ground here becomes lower, and forms a valley, at the extremity of which a ſmall baſon has been dug for the reception of boats. The entrance is only twelve feet wide, and very difficult of acceſs, as it muſt be paſſed through exactly in the middle. If the boat ſhould touch the ſides, which are ſharp rocks, it would be in great danger of being daſhed to pieces. Add to this that, when we arrived before the entrance, a violent ſwell was ebbing out of it. The

Caſiot

Cafiot called one of his countrymen, and placing themfelves on each fide, they made a fign to us to pull ftrong. As foon as our boat had entered the dangerous pafs, they guided it with long poles, to prevent it from ftriking againft the rocks, and thus conducted it into port. Through this paffage alone is it poffible to get on fhore in the ifland. The inhabitants might widen it if they chofe, but they prefer leaving it thus dangerous, fince while it remains fo, they are under little ap- prehenfion from their enemies.

The Cafiot, who had fhewn us the harbour, politely invited us to go up to the village, and we followed him with pleafure. I was dreffed in the French ftyle, with a fword, hat, and every other appurtenance of the drefs of my nation. The news of the arrival of ftrangers foon fpread, and the women and children came out of their houfes, and waited for us at the top of the hill. They fhewed a great deal of curiofity, and examined us at- tentively. When we paffed them, they all modeftly caft down their eyes. Among the crowd, there were fome very handfome. Se- veral of them faluted us, wifhing us a good day, faying : " You are welcome !" and we

anfwered

anfwered them with the ufual eaftern expreffion :
" May the day be happy for you and for your
." guefts !"

The guide, who conducted us, was one of
the principal inhabitants of the ifland. He
preffed me to ftep into his houfe, and introduced me into a hall, which, though not
magnificently furnifhed, was fufficiently provided with every thing conducive to cleanlinefs and convenience. Around it was a fopha.
He feated me on a raifed bench, and placed
himfelf below, while breakfaft was preparing.
Soon after, his wife and daughter appeared,
with new-laid eggs, figs, and grapes. The
girl blufhed at fight of a ftranger, whofe
drefs muft, no doubt, appear to her very extraordinary. Whilft we were breakfafting with
a good appetite, and my hoft was pouring
me out fome excellent wine in a large glafs,
moft of the women of the village came to
pay him a vifit. They faluted us, and feated
themfelves, without ceremony, round the
apartment. They had been brought by curiofity, and foon began to whifper one another, and make their remarks on the French
drefs. Europeans rarely land in this folitary
ifland, and the inhabitants, accuftomed to fee
nothing

nothing but bald heads, wrapped round with fhawls, long robes faftened with fafhes, and venerable beards, could not but view with aftonifhment a foreigner with long plaited hair, without muftachios, and wearing a cocked hat, and fhort coat, that came no lower than his knees. They appeared greatly ftruck with the contraft, and a half fmile, which was fometimes vifible on their coun-tenances, was not improbably a fign-they were employed in making fatyrical obfervations on the peculiarities of my habit, while I, on my fide, was no lefs amufed with them. My at-tention was efpecially engaged by two young females, who would have been acknowledged to be handfome, even in Paris.

The leaft of the two had eyes full of fire, and fine black eyebrows, equally arched. Her complexion was rather brown, but her fea-tures extremely animated. Her cheeks, deli-cately rounded, were every inftant adorned with frefh rofes. Her delicate little mouth feemed formed to fay charming things. When fhe fmiled, teeth white as fnow agreeably contrafted the vermilion of her lips; and a moft enchanting vivacity animated her whole countenance, which feemed to fparkle with

with wit and repartee. Her ebon locks faftened, according to the manner of the country,
to the crown of her head, fell negligently on
a neck which feemed of polifhed ivory,
and terminated with a delightful fwell in the
moft charming bofom ever feen. A boddice
without fleeves, opening a little towards the
top, afforded a glimpfe of the exact proportion of her beautiful fhape. A robe of the
whiteft and fineft cotton, edged with a purple
border, four fingers wide, and elegantly embroidered, defcended to her feet, and her waift
was loofely girded by a fafh, which floated
round her.

The fecond difputed with her the palm of
beauty. Her fhape was more elegant, and her
carriage more noble. Her eyes' fhone with a
foft languor, and feemed formed to infpire ·
love and delight, while her long eye-lafhes,
modeftly lowered, concealed their fplendor,
as if fhe were afraid of betraying the fecrets
of her foul. Her complexion was fairer, and
her cheeks, lefs coloured, difplayed the lily
flightly tinctured with the rofe. Her features, though fcarcely fo expreffive as thofe
of her companion, had more regularity, and
were models of fymmetry and juft proportion.

At

At the firft glance, fhe but juft appeared what
may be called handfome, but on more mature
confideration, the perfection of the whole of
her beauties enforced the higheft admiration.
The charms of the former infpired a fudden
joy, and it was impoffible to look on her
without pleafure. Thofe of the latter made
lefs impreffion at the firft view, but, on examination, an irrefiftible attraction forced
every heart of fenfibility to pay her fincereft
homage.

All the women, who honoured us with
their prefence, were dreffed in the fame manner. They all wore the jacket, the fafh, and
the long robe of cotton. The only difference
confifted in the embroidery, which varied according to their different taftes, and in the
manner of wearing their hair, which fome of
them fuffered to flow upon their fhoulders in
one or more treffes, while others faftened it
to the crown of the head, letting it fall down
again upon the neck. The two I have juft
mentioned were not the only ones who were
handfome, but their beauty appeared to me
moft attractive.

You may poffibly imagine, Madam, that,
after the fad fcenes to which I had been for

fome time accuftomed, my imagination was
inflamed at the fight of thefe lovely females,
and that I have taken a pleafure in embellifhing
them. That may indeed be the cafe; but if
it be, the illufion was of fome duration. I
paffed eight days in the ifland, and would
not wifh to alter a fingle feature in the por-
traits I have drawn. I have defcribed what
I faw, and what I felt. I own to you, however, that my furprife was equal to my pleafure. I expected to find on this rock, only
miferable flaves, groaning under the oppreffions of the Turks; inftead of which I met
with a cheerful and happy people, who were
fortunate enough to be able to preferve their
liberty amid the defpotifm and tyranny with
which they are furrounded.

As foon as breakfaft was over, the ladies
retired. My hoft conducted me into another
apartment; and, to infpire me with confidence
in his countrymen, and efpecially in himfelf,
he drew out of a cheft two certificates, figned
by two captains, of Provence, which he defired
me to read. The firft of thefe contained the
following words:

    " Frenchmen, whom the tempeft may
" throw upon this ifland, confide in the in-
        " habitants.

" habitants. I was fhipwrecked on thefe
" rocks, and they afforded me every fuccour
" that men owe each other in fimilar mif-
" fortunes."

The other ran thus : " I warn fuch of my
" countrymen, as chance may bring into the
" *Ifle du Gaze*, to be upon their guard, and
" put no confidence in the inhabitants.
" They are a fet of thieves and knaves, and
" ftrangers have every thing to apprehend from
" their rapacity."

I returned this fingular writing to my hoft
with an air of fatisfaction, telling him, I had
no occafion for thefe teftimonies, to convince
me of his honefty. He locked it up carefully,
thinking he poffeffed a treafure, and this confidence gave me a favourable opinion of him.
It was true, that he was ignorant of the con-
tents, and that the fecond captain had deceived
him, but I could not wifh to rectify his miftake
in a thing on which he feemed to fet fo great a
value : efpecially as this paper, at the worft,
could only produce a falutary diffidence in fuch
as might read it. As for myfelf, I adhered to
the firft teftimonial, and continued to live in
familiarity with the Canots. The only precaution I took was, never to be feen without
being

being well armed and attended by a fervant; even this, however, was unneceffary,
for I never experienced any thing from thefe
people but the kindeft treatment.

Defirous of obtaining fome knowledge of
the ifland, I fet out from the village, and directed my courfe toward the higheft mountain, which I reached in an hour's walk.
From hence we may difcover Carpathus,
which appears to be at no great diftance,
and extends from eaft to weft. In front of
the village, three little iflands fituated to the
eaft, weft, and north, form the extenfive road
in which our veffel lay at anchor. They
are uncultivated, and produce nothing but
brambles. Below the hill from which I made
my obfervations, ftands a fmall chapel furrounded by fig-trees. Here begin a chain
of hills, that, bending into a femicircle,
leave in the middle a plain of a league in circumference, which has been cleared out by
the inhabitants, with infinite labour. They
have torn up large pieces of rock, and removed heaps of ftones, with which they have
formed the walls of the inclofure. All this
fpace is divided into compartments, and fhared among the Cafiots. They fow barley and

K   wheat

wheat here at the commencement of the rainy
feafon, which lafts from October to February.
The rain is not continual in thefe months,
but none falls in any other; the remainder
of the year the air is pure and ferene, and
both days and nights are continually fine and
clear. The heats are moderated by the
fea breezes, and beneath fo beautiful a fky
the inhabitants enjoy a delightful temperature,
and are almoft ftrangers to every kind of difeafe. The fides of the hills are covered with
vineyards, the grapes of which produce a
very agreeable wine. I could not help admiring the induftry with which thefe iflanders have been able to cultivate rocks, hardly
covered with a few inches of earth, and re-
joiced in the reflection that they were recom-
penfed for their labours, and that the ifland
fufficed for their fubfiftence.

When I had fatisfied my curiofity, I returned to the houfe of my hoft, where they were
waiting for me to dine. A hen, with rice, new-
laid eggs, excellent pigeons, fome cheefe, and
a glafs of good wine, made me amends for
the miferable repafts I had made on board.
The men dined together, feated in a circle
on the carpet, and the women in a feparate
apart-

apartment. This is the cuftom, and, though
not in the French tafte, I was obliged to con-
form to it. Towards the end of our meal the
cup was circulated from hand to hand. The
company drank to me, wifhing me a profperous voyage ; and I returned the compliment, by drinking health and happinefs to
the people of Cafos. The guefts were beginning to grow merry, when the found of
mufical inftruments made us rife from table.

About twenty young girls, dreffed all in
white, with flowing robes, and plaited locks,
entered the apartment, and with them a
young man who played on the lyre, which he
accompanied with his voice. Several of them
were handfome, all healthy and lively, and
there were among them fome who even rivalled
the two belles I have already defcribed. I muft
own, Madam, that this fcene appeared to
me enchanting. The uniform drefs of thefe
nymphs, the modefty which heightened their
charms, their becoming bafhfulnefs, their joyous
but decent merriment, all contributed to make
me almoft imagine myfelf fuddenly tranfported to the ifland of Calypfo. They began
to range themfelves in a ring, and invited me
to dance. I did not wait for many entrea-

ties.

ties. The circle we formed is fingular from the manner in which it is interwoven: the dancer does not give his hand to the two perfons next him, but to thofe next them, fo that you have your hands croffed before your neighbours, who are thus locked, as it were, in the links of a double chain. This interweaving is not without pleafure, for reafons by no means difficult to underftand. In the middle of the circle ftood the mufician, who played and fang at the fame time, while all the dancers kept exact time in advancing, retreating, or turning round him. For myfelf, I followed where my partners led me, my mind being lefs occupied with the dance than with the charming females who compofed it.

The next day I took a view of the village. It confifts of about a hundred houfes, each of them inhabited by a fingle family: they are all of ftone, built very ftrong: and contain, in general, two or three lower parlours, with a couple of rooms above. Each houfe has its oven, and ciftern, cut out of the rock. The latter are filled during the rainy feafon, and the water is preferved in them pure and limpid. Befides this, a hundred

paces

paces below the village is a fine fpring, which flows the whole year.

I entered feveral houfes, where I found the women employed in fpinning, and embroidering, and fome in making the fine linens which they wear. Their frames are fmall, but well contrived, and they work with a great deal of fkill. I every where met with activity, induftry, and neatnefs. I afterwards paid vifits to feveral · of the girls I danced with the day before, and was received very favouraby. I entered into converfation with them, and inquired why fo many pretty women were to be feen in the ifland, and fo few men, for I had only met with five or fix. They anfwered that, during the fpring, the fummer, and part of autumn, the men were out at fea. " They trade," faid they, " to differ-
" ent iflands of the Archipelago, and re-
" turn from time to time, to bring their
" families the provifions they may ftand in
" need of, but only pafs the winter with
" them. They fow the land in November,
" get in the harveft in March, and, immedi-
" ately afterward, return to fea. The pro-
" duce of the ifland not being fufficient for
                                        " the

" the maintenance of its inhabitants, they
" are forced to feek fupplies from other coun-
" tries, with the affiftance of which, if we
" are not rich, we live at leaft in a comfort-
" able mediocrity. The boys accompany
" their fathers, and become failors : while
" they are abfent, we fpin cotton as you fee,
" and weave a part of it for their clothing
" and our own."

In thefe vifits I could not but admire the
regularity and wifdom of this little republic,
the peace and harmony that reigned among
its members, and, above all, that cheerfulnefs
and content, which was fo vifible in their
countenances. Happy people! faid I to myfelf; ambition and intrigue trouble not your
tranquillity ; the thirft of gold hath not corrupted your manners ; the quarrels, diffenfions,
and crimes with which it hath covered
the earth, are to you unknown. Here no
citizen, proud of his titles, or his wealth,
tramples under foot his humble countrymen ;
no cringing valet flatters the vices of his
mafter ; man is equal to man, nor does the
Cafiot blufh, or abafe himfelf before the Cafiot. Refpect and mutual efteem unite you.
Your enjoyments confift in the pure pleafures
which

which nature offers to all her children, and
your happinefs is founded on the durable bafis
of mediocrity and equality!

The refpect I owe to truth, however, ob-
liges me to confefs that, in a private converfation with fome of thefe handfome Cafiot girls,
I drew a flattering picture of the happy lot of
the ladies of France. I reprefented them as
elegantly dreffed, adorned with gold, filk, and
diamonds; conveyed in fuperb carriages from
fhow to fhow, and from entertainment to entertainment, furrounded by admirers only at-
tentive to give them pleafure, and wholly occupied with their amufements, and a fucceffion of new delights. I had only pourtrayed
the rofes of a life apparently fo delicious,
and my admiring hearers feemed enchanted
with my defcription. They fighed, regretted
their condition, and, defpifing the humbler
plafures to which they were born, could
have wifhed to have been tranfported inftantly
to France. So natural is it to the human
heart to quit the happinefs it enjoys for the
brilliant chimeras of imagination.

Another day I paid a vifit to two fifters
who were faid to be very amiable. Melancholy reigned in their houfe, and fighs efcaped

caped them amid their occupations. The
eldeſt, who was about eighteen, was tall, well
made, and had a very pleaſing countenance.
She had not been at the ball. A deep grief
caſt a veil over her beauty, and her cheeks
had loſt almoſt all their colour. A dying
flame ſhone languidly in her eyes, and tears
ſeemed ready to ſtart. How much was I affected! Her younger ſiſter ſhared in her ſor-
rows, and reſembled a flower which, growing
in the ſhade, receives not the beneficent rays
of the ſun, but languiſhes at its opening. I
could have wiſhed to conſole theſe afflicted
charmers; but I had no claim whatever on
their hearts, and, in ſo ſhort a time, could not
inſpire them with ſufficient confidence to be
permitted to dry up their tears. I knew that
one of them had juſt loſt a huſband, whom ſhe
tenderly loved. I was told that they were the
handſomeſt couple in the iſland, and united
by the pureſt affection; but that, after having
been married only a month, the unfortunate
man was ſhipwrecked, and periſhed in the
ſea. " He is the more to be lamented," added
my informers, " as he had not attained his
" twentieth year. The younger of theſe
" amiable girls, tenderly attached to her ſiſter,
" par-

" participates fincerely in her grief. This,
" however, is not the only caufe of her me-
" lancholy; fhe is fixteen, and not yet mar-
" ried; and, in this country, men are fcarce;
" the fea devours a great number of them,
" and, therefore, many of our poor girls re-
" main without hufbands."

This explained to me the reafon why in
Candia, and in feveral other cities, I have
frequently met with Cafiot girls, who have
voluntarily forfaken their country. Thefe
young females, having neither protectors,
friends, nor relations, are obliged to feek a
maintenance by fervice. Their innocence is
expofed to great dangers, and, frequently, led
aftray by example, or feduced by the tempta-
tions wealth ever has it in its power to offer,
they embrace a life of licentioufnefs and de-
bauchery. I have feen many of them, who
had entirely forgotten the manners of their
ifland, and totally loft that modefty, and in-
genuoufnefs, which conftitute the lovelieft
charm of their countrywomen.

During my ftay at Cafos, a bark arrived,
laden with rice, melons, pomegranates, and
various fruits. Immediately almoft all the
women haftened down the hill with the
greateft

greateft impatience; fome to meet a hufband, others a father, a brother, or a friend. I never witneffed ftronger expreffions of joy and tendernefs; they embraced them with tranfport, preffed them to their bofoms, and thanked Heaven for once more reftoring them to their anxious wifhes. Every token of the moft heartfelt joy, every expreffion of the tendereft love, was lavifhed on both fides. The fcene was indeed moft affecting. Thefe, faid I to myfelf, are the ancient Greeks; fuch was their lively imagination, ever ready to take fire, and fuch the exquifite fenfibility, which diftinguifhed them from all the nations of the earth. This rock has preferved them from the Turkifh yoke, and they have retained their ancient character.

The afternoon of this memorable day was dedicated to pleafure. The Cafiot captain gave a little ball, and I accepted of his invitation. The hall was filled with a number of lively girls, with their treffes perfumed, and dreffed in their handfomeft boddices, their beft embroidered fafhes, and their whiteft gowns. Various rounds, fuch as I have before defcribed, were formed. Two lyres, and fingers placed on a raifed feat, animated the motions of the dancers,

dancers, and pleafure fparkled in every eye.
The young men who had juft arrived took
their places at the fide of their wives or miftreffes, clafped them round the waift in dancing, and felt the palpitation of their hearts,
while joy beamed in every face. The young
Greek females, with downcaft eyes, endeavoured to conceal the pleafure they felt; but
their blufhes, and their heaving bofoms, fufficiently fhewed who were the objects of their
affection. How great the pleafure of this
fimple recreation! Each motion gave a new
fenfation of delight. Our artificial dances may
be infinitely more graceful, elegant, or majeftic;
but how cold are they when compared to this
joyous round! In thofe vanity alone is gratified; in thefe heart fpeaks to heart, by a
look, a fmile, and, above every thing, by the
touch. All-wife Nature has implanted the
means of happinefs within ourfelves. The
rich man flatters himfelf he fhall obtain it amid
the brilliant companies he affembles, and, by
difplaying pomp and magnificence, endeavours to purchafe it with gold. Alas! knows
he not that this inconftant divinity flies the
importunity of oftentation, difdains a bribe,
and contemns the pride and vanity of wealth!

The

The wefterly winds have detained us eight days in the road of Cafos, and I thank Heaven for their continuance. I have vifited countries, on which liberal Nature has lavifhed all her treafures. I have feen others where tyrants have compelled her to refrain her bounties, and every where have found nations unhappy, not by their own fault, not by the fterility of the foil, but by the vices of the government to which they are fubject. In the midft of flaves crouching beneath the Ottoman yoke, I have found a rock, only three leagues in circumference, on which the Turk dares not to fet his foot, and inhabited by a free and happy people. There each father of a family is a fovereign within his own houfe; he decides every difference, and his decrees are laws, which cannot but be equitable, fince they are only dictated by paternal tendernefs. When any difputes arife, the priefts and the old men affemble and decide them; but difputes cannot be frequent among citizens, who are all equal and alike unacquainted with poverty or riches. All the members of this little fociety are employed; and I have feen the handfomeft of their women go down into the valley, to wafh their linen at the

fountain

fountain, as in the days of Homer. They cheer their labours with a fong; nor do they imagine themfelves difgraced by their humble employment. It is only in countries where the rich can purchafe fervice from the hands of the poor, that they blufh to make ufe of their own.

Travellers, who have made obfervations on the character of the Greeks under the Ottoman yoke, juftly reproach them with hypocrify, perfidy, and meannefs. Thefe vices are not inherent in their nature, but are the confequence of the fervitude in which they live. The inhabitants of Cafos are alfo Greeks; but, enlightened, and warmed, by a ray of liberty, they poffefs induftry, fenfibility, and integrity. Send them a Cadi, a Pacha, or a Mouteveli, they will become as perfidious, and corrupt as the reft of their nation. From this obfervation we may be convinced of the firft and moft facred of political truths; that, in general, man is virtuous in proportion as he preferves his liberty and natural rights, and that as he is deprived of thefe, he becomes vicious and degenerate.

I have the honour to be, &c.

LET.

L E T T E R XVII.

To M. L. M.

Candia.

OUR ftay in the road of Cafos is at an
end. The captain, impatient to be gone,
weighed anchor on the firft appearance of good
weather. It feems. as if the wind, wearied
with finding him ftill at fea, had at length determined to conduct him to the place of his
deftination, for it blew right abaft, and carried us rapidly towards Standia; in lefs than
a day we have paffed the further point of the
ifland, and got fafe into the harbour. We
arrived exactly in time, for fcarcely was the
anchor down, before the wefterly wind refumed its fway, and the fea became furious: a
quarter of an hour later, and we fhould have
been forced to return to Cafos, which will not
foon be effaced from my memory.

Dia, now called Standia, is four leagues
diftant from the city of Candia. It is abfolutely barren; we meet with neither vil-

lages

lages nor inhabitants. The briars, thorns, and brambles, that cover the rocks, ferve as food for the wild goats, which are found there in great numbers: they run with fuch fwiftnefs among the precipices, that it is almoſt impoſſible to approach them. We have given chace to feveral without fuccefs.

Standia has three ports at which veſſels touch, that are laden for Candia. From the fummit of the mountain we difcovered the town; but the fea was fo rough that no boat would venture to releafe us from our prifon; the fecond day after our arrival, however, a refolute Turk came off to us in a little ſkiff. He told us that our arrival had been long expected: that they had feen us beating off the coaſt, and were apprehenfive we had periſhed. The bad weather ſtill continued, and detained us on the defert rocks of Standia; but at length, on the fourth day, a boat came for us, and conveyed us to Candia, about two months after our departure from Alexandria.

I have the honour to be, &c.

L E T T E R   XVIII.

To M. L. M.

Candia.

As often, Madam, as the curious inquirer, excited by the defire of knowledge, endeavours to inveftigate the origin of ancient nations, mythology firft prefents him with gods and heroes, for the moft part emblematical. The fabulous hiftory of every celebrated people always precedes their more authentic annals. This is lefs interefting to us, who with all our labours can only conjecture the truth through the veil of allegory, but was of much more importance to the ancients. Though the multitude faw nothing in it but a facred theology, to which they were obliged implicitly to fubmit their reafon, the philofophers, initiated in thefe myfteries, difcovered in them the opinions of learned men on the formation of the univerfe, aftronomy, phyfics, and natural hiftory.

Before we take a furvey of the ifle of Candia, let us firft, Madam, with your permiffion, vifit the ancient *Crete*. The information this will procure us will guide us on

our

our way, and ferve to explain many facts, the origin of which would otherwife be un- known to us. It is only by comparing the paft with the prefent, that we can be enabled to form a juft idea of this famous country. I am aware, Madam, that it is become almoft ridiculous to fpeak of the ancients, and that it is the fafhion, either to extol them to the fkies, or to depreciate them without meafure ; but reafon obferves a juft medium, and weighs men's actions in an equal balance ; fhe makes no diftinction of ages nor of perfons, but admires, or condemns, with impartiality, what- ever merits eulogium or cenfure.

· The .Cretan mythologifts, quoted by Dio- dorus Siculus (*e*), fay, that the firft inhabit- ants of their ifland were the Idean Dactyli, who lived near Mount Ida *(f)* ; they were confidered as magicians, from their poffeffing various kinds of knowledge, and efpecially

(*e*) Diodorus Siculus, lib. v.

(*f*) Other writers make them come from Mount Ida in Phrygia. They are not agreed, why they received the name of Dactyli. Diomedes the grammarian fays, it was given them on account of the fkill with ·which they moved their fingers, or becaufe they invented the metri- cal foot, called the Dactyl, or becaufe they were ten in number, &c.

L

the

the fcience of the facred myfteries *(g)*. Or-
pheus, fo celebrated for poetry and mufic, was
their difciple. They difcovered the ufe of
fire, and the art of working iron and copper
in Mount Berecynthus, near Aptera *(h)*.
Thefe valuable inventions obtained them divine honours. One of them, named Hercules, rendered himfelf famous by his courage and heroic actions. He inftituted the
Olympic games ; and it is only from the fimi-
larity of the name, that pofterity attributed
this inftitution to the fon of Alcmena, who
trod indeed in the fteps of his predeceffor,
and, like him, became immortal.

(*i*) The Idean Dactyli gave rife to the
Curetes.

(g) The name of magician was anciently not odious. It did not convey with it the idea of knavery
and impofture, which has fince been annexed to it.
Thofe were called magicians who, inftructed in the facred
myfteries, underftood the fenfe of allegories, and difcovered natural truths, concealed under the emblems of
fable. The Telchines at Rhodes, the Dactyli of Crete,
the Egyptian priefts, and Mofes himfelf, were accounted
magicians.

(h) Strabo, who makes the Telchines pafs from Crete
into the ifland of Rhodes, fays, that they firft brought
thither the art of working metals.

(*i*) Others confider them as the children of the Earth.
Strabo

Curetes. The latter at firft inhabited the forefts, caverns, and mountains : they afterwards taught men to dwell in houfes, and contributed to civilize them by their inftitutions. They inftrueted them to colleét flocks of fheep, to tame wild animals, and make them fubfervient to their wants, and to profit by the labour of bees, by keeping them in hives. They taught them the ufe of the bow, and formed them to the chace. They forged the fword, and were the inventors of military dances. The noife they made in dancing, armed, prevented Saturn from hearing the cries of Jupiter, whofe education had been intrufted to them by Rhea. Affifted by the nymphs, they brought up the god in a cave of Mount Ida, feeding him with the milk of the goat Amalthea (*k*), and the honey of their bees.

At

Strabo fays, that the name of Curetes was given them from the care they took of the infancy of Jupiter. lib. x.

(*k*) Laétantius, lib. i. cap. 22, fays, " Didymus relates, " that Meliffeus, king of Crete, was the firft who facrificed " to the gods; that he introduced new rites and pompous " ceremonies ; that he had two daughters, Amalthea and " Meliffa, and that they nourifhed the infant Jupiter

L 2   " with

At this period the Cretan mythology places the birth of the Titans, who dwelt near to Cnoffus, where the palace of Rhea was to be feen, their expeditions over the whole earth, their war againft Ammon, who was defended by Bacchus, the nuptials of Jupiter and Juno, celebrated near the river Therenus in Crete, and the gods, goddeffes, and heroes, to whom they gave birth.

The moſt illuſtrious of thefe heroes were Minos and Rhadamanthus (*l*): they are faid to have been the fons of Jupiter and Europa, who had been brought into the ifland upon a bull. Minos having become king, built feveral cities, the moſt confiderable of which were Cnoffus, on the coaſt oppofite Afia, Phæſtus on the fouth fide, and Cydon on the weſt, fronting Peloponnefus. He inſtituted admirable laws, which he feigned to have received from Jupiter, in a cave of Mount Ida.

Rhadamanthus diſtinguiſhed himfelf by the juſtice of his judgments, and by the feverity

---

" with goat's milk and honey." This is the reafon, perhaps, why the poets have faid, that the goat Amalthea fed Jupiter.

(*l*) Diodorus Siculus, lib. v.

with

with which he punifhed offenders. He reigned over feveral large iflands, and almoft the whole coaft of Afia, which fubmitted to his fceptre, on account of the reputation he had acquired for juftice. The mythologifts have made him judge of the infernal regions, to determine on the fate of the virtuous and the wicked, and have decreed him the fame honours as to Minos, the moft juft of kings (*m*).

Thus far I have followed the Cretan traditions, as preferved by Diodorus; but hiftorians are not agreed among themfelves. There are a multitude of opinions concerning the firft inhabitants of Crete. Strabo (*n*), who has learnedly difcuffed them, after feveral pages, fays: " I am not fond of fables, yet I " have entered into a long detail of thefe, " becaufe they have relation to theology. " When we treat of the gods, we ought to " weigh ancient opinions, and diftinguifh them " from fables. The ancients delighted in

(*m*) Rhadamanthus was a juft man, inftructed by Minos, not in the whole art of government, but in the part of the royal adminiftration which concerns juftice ; hence he received the name of the juft judge. Plato de Minoide.

(*n*) Strabo, lib. x.

" throwing

" throwing a veil over their knowledge of
" nature. It is not poffible to explain all their
" enigmas ; but, by placing the numerous al-
" legories they have left us in a full light, by
" examining with attention in what they re-
" femble each other, and in what they differ,
" we may, by comparifon, arrive at truth."

Let us quit mythology, and inquire what
hiftory has left us of greateft certainty, refpecting the different inhabitants of Crete.
This celebrated ifland received its name from
Cres, the firft of its kings (o). He was the
author of many ufeful difcoveries, which contributed to the happinefs of his people (p),
who, in gratitude to their benefactor, and to
preferve the memory of his benefits, immortalized his name, by beftowing it on their
ifland (q).

To

(o) Eufebius in Chron. Cres, a native, was the firft
who reigned in Crete, and gave it his name. It was faid
that he was one of the Curetes who concealed and nourifhed Jupiter.—Ifid. Orig. lib. xiv. c. 6. This ifland
was called Crete, from one Cretes, who dwelt there.—
Cedrenus. Crete received its name from Cretes, who
was king of the ifland.

(p) Diod. Sic. lib. v.

(q) Stephen of Byzantium, who reports the opinions of
the

(r) To diftinguifh the native Cretans from foreigners, they were called Eteo Cretans. Numerous colonies fettled in the ifland from all parts of Greece, invited by the beauty of the climate, and the fertility of the foil. The Lacedemonians, Argives, and Athenians, were the principal ftates who fent colonies thither *(s)*. This made Homer fay, " *(t)* Crete " is a large ifland, in the midft of a ftormy " fea. The foil is rich and fertile. It con- " tains an innumerable people, and is adorn- " ed by a hundred cities. Its inhabitants " fpeak various languages. We there find " Acheans, the brave Eteocretæ, Cydonians, " Dorians, and the divine Pelafgi." The Eteocretans inhabited the fouthern part of the ifland, where they founded the city of Præfus, and erected a temple to Jupiter Dictæus *(u)*.

the ancients refpecting this ifland, fays, it was fo named from *Cores,* or *Cretus,* fon of Jupiter and the nymph Ida, or *Creta,* one of the Hefperides, &c. but he adds, that the beft derivation is from *Cres,* one of its inhabitants. It had many other names, unneceffary to repeat in this place.

(r) Euftat. in Iliad.
(s) Scylax in Periplo. Dicæarchus de Vit. Græc.
(t) Odyff. lib. xix.
(u) Strabo, lib. x.

Cres

·Cres was not the only monarch who reigned over the ifland of Crete; he had fucceffors, but we can obtain little information concerning them from hiftory; we only find the names of fome of thefe kings, and a few events, intermixed with fabulous accounts, which happened under others *(v)*.

Among

(v) The following are the names of thefe kings, as collected by Murtius, in his learned differtation on the ifland of Crete.

Jupiter, the firft.

Cres, who gave name to the ifland.

Ammon, who, after reigning in Lybya, came to Crete, and married the daughter of Cres. He was the prince whom Bacchus defended againft the Titans.

Melisseus, whofe daughters brought up Jupiter.

Jupiter II. who was brought up by the Curetes. After him is a great chafm.

Cecrops.

Cydon.

Apteras, who built the city of Aptera.

Laps, or Lapithas.

Teutamus, who took poffeffion of the ifland at the head of the Dorians and Pelafgians.

Asterius, who efpoufed Europa, carried off by Jupiter, and adopted her children.

Minos I. the adopted fon of Afterius, who died without children. He married Itona, daughter of Lycaftus, and had by her Lycafta.

Lycastus,

Among thefe fovereigns we find two Ju-
piters, and two of the name of Minos.
Writers in general, however, confound thefe,
and attribute actions to one only, which fhould
be fhared between the two. This obfervation
is particularly true of Minos, whom antiquity celebrates as the wifeft of legiflators.
The place affigned him in the infernal
regions is a very unequivocal teftimony of
the glorious reputation he had acquired by
his juftice. " It is not without reafon," fays
Plato, " that Greece has adopted the laws of
" Crete, fince they are founded on thofe
" folid principles which cannot but render
" the people who are fubject to them fiou-
" rifhing and happy *(x)*." One of his laws

LYCASTUS, who efpoufed Ida, daughter of a Corybant,
and had by her Minos the fecond.

MINOS II. who married Pafiphae, daughter of the fun.
He had two other wives and feveral children.

DEUCALION, fon and fucceffor of the fecond Minos, and
different from the fon of Prometheus. He efpoufed Phædra,
fifter of Thefeus.

CATREUS, brother to Deucalion. He built the city of
Catrea.

IDOMENEUS, grandfon of Minos. He, together with
Merion, conducted eighty fhips to the fiege of Troy. (Here
ends this incomplete lift.)

(x) Plato, de Legibus, lib. i.

was

was expreffed in thefe words : *Let the Cretans never drink together to intoxication.* The following was well calculated to check the prefumptuous ardour of youth *(y).* " Let not
" the young men indulge an indifcreet curio-
" fity refpecting the laws ; let them not exa-
" mine whether the legiflator did right or
" wrong to enact them ; but let them ex-
" claim with one voice, *They are good, becaufe*
" *they proceed from the Gods.* If any of the
" old men difcover in them abufes proper to
" be reformed, let him addrefs himfelf to a
" magiftrate, or difcufs the fubject with his
" equals, but never in prefence of young
" people."

(z) Thefe admirable laws were engraven on tables of brafs, and Talos, the minifter of Minos, vifited the towns and cities three times every year, to fee they were properly obferved *(a).*

The king of Crete, well knowing how neceffary the marvellous is to gain credit with the multitude, pretended that he had received

(y) Plato, de Minoide.

(z) Cicero, Tufcul. lib. ii. fays, the laws of Crete given by Minos, or Jupiter, or as the poets tell us, by his advice, are a fource of inftruction for youth.

(a) Plato, de Minoide.

them

them from Jupiter his father, in a cave of Mount Ida. In the fame manner Lycurgus, before he publifhed his laws, repaired to Delphi, and declared that he received them from Apollo. Thus Numa afcribed his inftitutions to the nymph Egeria, and Mahomet his religious effufions to the angel Gabriel.

On the other hand, the ancients defcribe Minos as a prince who was the flave of his paffions, and a barbarous conqueror! Having become enamoured of the nymph Dictynna, who refifted his defires, he purfued her to the extremity of the ifland, and forced her to precipitate herfelf into the fea, where fhe was faved by fome fifhermen, who received her in their nets. He was the firft of the Greeks who appeared in the Mediterranean at the head of a powerful fleet (b). He made a conqueft of the Cyclades, whence he expelled the Carians, and having fettled colonies there, committed the government of them to his fons (c).

(b) Strabo, lib. x. Ariftot. Polit. lib. ii. Diodorus Siculus, lib. v. Plin. lib. vii. cap. 56.
(c) Thucydides, lib. v.

Having

Having learnt, during his ftay at Paros *(d)*, that his fon Androgeus was flain at Athens, he declared war againft Ægeus, and impofed on him the fhameful tribute from which Thefeus delivered his countrymen. He took up arms againft Nifus, king of Megara, made him prifoner, by the treachery of his daughter Scylla, and put him to death, together with Megareus the fon of Hippomenes, who had brought him fuccour. Dædalus, againft whom he was incenfed, defpairing of moving fo implacable a prince, employed all the refources of his genius to efcape from his refentment. He fled into Sicily, gained the protection of king Cocalus, and obtained an afylum at his court. Valerius Flaccus *(e)* has given a truly poetical defcription of this flight: " Thus " Dædalus, become a bird, precipitated him-

---

(d) Apollodorus, lib. iii. Having been informed of the death of his fon, at Paros, while he was facrificing to the Graces, he immediately took the crown from his head, and quitted his flute: he, however, finifhed the facrifice. To preferve the memory of this event, the inhabitants of Paros long facrificed to the Graces, without a crown, and without a flute.

(e) Valerius Flaccus, lib. i.

" felf

" felf from Mount Ida, with refounding wings.
" Near him flew his companion on fhorter
" pinions; they refembled a cloud rifing
" into the air. Minos feeing his vengeance
" fruftrated, trembled with rage; his eyes
" were wearied with vainly following the
" fugitives through the immenfity of fpace;
" and the guards returned to Gortyna,
" with their quivers filled with arrows."
The king of Crete, however, did not fo eafily
give up his prey; he equipped a fleet, purfued
him into Sicily *(f)*, and perifhed before the
walls of Camicus.

It is evident that thefe actions but ill became a juft fovereign, who merited to be
a judge in the fhades, and pronounce the everlafting deftiny of the virtuous and the wicked. We may reafonably conclude, therefore,
that Minos, the legiflator, was a different perfon from Minos the conqueror; that it was
the elder Minos who acquired an immortal reputation for wifdom and juftice; and
Minos the fecond, who conquered the greater part of the iflands of the Archipelago,

(f) Hygin. Fab. 44. Paufanias, in Achaicis.

but who, unable to govern his paffions, tarnifhed his glory by cruelty and revenge.

I fhall fay nothing, here, Madam, of Pafiphae,
Thefeus, Ariadne, or the Minotaur. Their
hiftory is connected with that of the Labyrinth, and will naturally follow, when I fhall
have occafion to mention that famous prifon, which was the work of Dædalus, and
which had nearly become his tomb. Before I conclude this letter, however, I fhall
add a few words concerning Idomeneus, the
laft king of Crete.

I have faid, that this prince, accompanied
by Merion (g), conducted eighty veffels to
the affiftance of Agamemnon. Homer has
immortalized the exploits by which he diftinguifhed himfelf before the walls of Troy.
At his departure, he committed the government of his ftates to Leucus (h) his
adopted fon, and promifed him the hand of
his daughter Clifithera in marriage, if he ruled
with wifdom during his abfence.

This ambitious youth foon forgot the favours that had been lavifhed on him. Having

(g) This Merion was the fon of Molus, uncle of Idomeneus.

(h) Quintus Smyrneus.

gained

gained a great number of partizans, he afpired to the crown, nor would his impatience allow him to wait till a legitimate
marriage placed it on his head. Finding the
king was long in returning, and flattering
himfelf, perhaps, that he would fall in battle,
he refolved to mount the throne.   Mida (*i*),
the wife of Idomeneus, and the princefs
Clifithera, were impediments to his project.
But ambition knows no bounds, and hefitates
not to violate the moft facred laws.   The
ufurper having feduced the people, and
gained over fome of the principal perfons,
murdered thefe unhappy victims in the temple ;
and when Idomeneus, crowned with laurels,
landed on the coaft of Crete, Leucus, who
made all around him tremble at his power,
purfued him with an army, and forced him
to return to his fhips. I know indeed that
the flight of Idomeneus is differently related.
Servius (*k*) fays, that he had vowed, in a
ftorm, to facrifice to the Gods whatever
he fhould firft meet, on his arrival on the
coaft ; that his fon being the firft, he flew

(*i*) Johannes Tzetzes.
(*k*) Servius, in Eneid. lib. iii.

him ;

him (*l*); and a plague happening immediately after, the inhabitants confidered this calamity as the confequence of divine vengeance, and expelled the murderous father; who left Crete, and founded Salentum on the coaft of Meffapia (*m*). This opinion feems to me deftitute of foundation. Hiftory does not inform us that Idomeneus had a fon. If he had male offspring of his own blood, why fhould he have adopted Leucus? Or why have committed to him the government of the ifland, with a promife of his daughter's hand? I fhould rather be inclined to think, that he brought the plague with him in his fhips, from the fiege of Troy, as Herodotus afferts (*n*), and that Leucus artfully availed himfelf of this pretext to procure the banifhment of his lawful fovereign. It fhould feem, however, as if the ufurper did not long

(*l*) Fenelon has followed this tradition, in his immortal work, which has done fo much honour to France.

(*m*) Virgil, Æneid. lib. iii. It is faid, the hero Idomeneus, driven from the throne of his anceftors, has fled far from his country.—Idomeneus of Lyctos (a city of Crete) covers with his troops the fields of Salentum.

(*n*) Herodotus. lib. vii.

enjoy

enjoy the fruit of his crimes; for, immediately after the departure of Idomeneus, we
find the monarchy at an end, and the government become republican.

I have the honour to be, &c.

L E T T E R XIX.

To M. L. M.

IT now remains for me, Madam, to give you fome account of the republic of Crete, which has been honoured with the eulogium of Plato; which Lycurgus took for his model (*o*) in the inftitutions he framed for Lacedæmon, and which was admired and celebrated through all Greece: Strabo

(*o*) " Lycurgus, retiring into Crete, fought the friend-
" fhip of Thales, the poet and legiflator ; from him he
" learnt the metrical rhythmus in which Rhadamanthus
" and Minos delivered the laws they profeffed to have
" received from Jupiter. He next travelled into Egypt,
" and ftudied the inftitutions of that people.   Some
" add, that he repaired to Chio, where he converfed with
" Homer. On his return to his country, he found
" his nephew Charilaus on the throne, and then em-
" ployed himfelf in forming his new code of laws ; but,
" previous to their publication, went to pafs fome time
" at Delphi, after which he declared he had received them
" from Apollo. . . . .   The laws of Lycurgus are entirely
" fimilar to thofe of Crete."   Strabo. lib. x.

has

has thought an account of it not unworthy his
pen, and has preferved its leading features in
his immortal work. You will, doubtlefs, be
ftruck with their fingularity. You will difcover a prodigious difference between the
principles on which this ancient republic was
founded, and thofe of the greateft part of
modern governments. But you will fee with
pleafure a legiflation whofe fole object it was
to fow the feeds of virtue in the heart of
infancy, and to nourifh them in youth ; to
infpire into the ripened man the love of his
country, of glory and of liberty, and to confole old age by the efteem and reverence due
to its wifdom and experience ; you will find
all its inftitutes directed to form faithful
friends, patriotic citizens, and wife ftatefmen.
Do not imagine a multitude of laws and
edicts were neceffary to procure thefe ineftimable advantages. They naturally flowed
from one fingle fource ; the public education of youth under wife regulations.

The examples placed before the Cretans in
their early years, the virtues to which they were
witneffes, the memorable deeds which they
heard recited, and the applaufes beftowed on
them, the honours which rewarded courage and
noble actions, and the fhame and opprobrium

M 2   which

which ſtigmatized vice, were the only ſprings
ſet in motion by their legiſlator, to render
them a warlike, virtuous, and wiſe nation.
I will be bold to add, that the ſame regulations, founded, as they were, on a juſt knowledge of the human heart, would have the
ſame happy effect on the morals of a people under every form of government ; but
morals are what modern governments are
leaſt ſolicitous concerning ; our cold politics
deſpiſe them, and condemn the man who
dares to proclaim their importance. Taxes
are levied on the depravation of manners ;
and the corrupt politician, inſtead of pro-
moting what conſtitutes the true happineſs of
a nation, is wholly occupied in increaſing the
wealth and power of kings.

The government of Crete, immediately
after the flight of Idomeneus, became ariſto-
cratical. The people ſtill poſſeſſed a ſhare
of the power ; but as the nobles were in
poſſeſſion of the principal employments, they
had, by conſequence, the greateſt weight in the
adminiſtration of affairs (*p*). Ten magiſtrates
were annually choſen in a national aſſembly, by
the plurality of voices, who were called *Coſmi*,

(*p*) Plutarch. in Dione.

and

and whofe office was the fame with that of the Ephori at Sparta (*q*). They had the management of war, and all the moft important public bufinefs (*r*). They poffeffed the right of choofing counfellors from among the old men ; and thefe, in number twenty-eight, compofed the fenate of Crete (*s*), and were chofen from among thofe who had paffed the office of Cofmi (*t*), or perfons eminently diftinguifhed by their merit, and unimpeached integrity. Thefe fenators held their dignity for life ; great deference was paid to their opinion, and nothing finally determined without confulting them. The wifdom of the legiflator had intended them for a counterpoife to the ambition of the ten chiefs, whofe power was ftill farther circumfcribed by limiting the duration of their magiftracy to one year.

(*q*) Ariftot. Polit. lib. ii. The Ephori have the fame authority with the Cretan magiftrates, called Cofmi ; only the former are limited to five, and the Cofmi are ten in number.

(*r*) Ariftot. Polit. lib. ii.

(*s*) Hefychius. " At Lacedæmon, at Carthage, and " in Crete, the college of old men is called Geronia." It was compofed of twenty-eight fenators.

(*t*) Strabo, lib. x.

His

His precaution did not end here; as the votes
of the people might be improperly obtained,
and their choice confequently fall upon a perfon unworthy of fo honourable a poſt; he
very wiſely provided, that whoever ſhould
diſgrace the dignity of the Coſmi might
be removed, either in an aſſembly of the
people, or by his colleagues only (*u*). So excellent a conſtitution cauſed Plato to ſay (*v*),
" The republic, which approaches too much
" to a monarchy, and that which admits too
" unreſtrained a liberty, are equally remote
" from the juſt medium. O Cretans ! O La-
" cedæmonians ! ye have avoided theſe two
" rocks, and eſtabliſhed your ſtates on the
" moſt ſolid foundations."

From what I have ſaid, Madam, concerning the Cretan form of government,
you will perceive that nothing was more
ſimple. A free people, conſcious they were
unable to govern themſelves, name magiftrates, into whoſe hands they transfer their
authority ; theſe chiefs, inveſted with regal
power, elect ſenators to aid them with their

(*u*) Ariſtotle.
(*v*) Plato, de Legibus, lib. iii.

counſels,

counfels, which counfellors again can decide
nothing of themfelves; but their office is perpetual, which increafes the refpect paid them,
and enables them to extend their knowledge
and information. The chiefs of the republic
have a powerful motive to incite them to
act worthy the honourable ftation in which
they are placed, as, on the one hand, they are
checked by the fear of difgrace, and on the
other encouraged by the hope of one day becoming members of the national council.

Let us now examine the means employed
by the legiflator to form the manners of the
citizens. All the Cretans were fubject to their
magiftrates, and divided into two claffes, that
of the youths, and that of the men of mature
age (x). The former confifted of young men
who had attained their feventeenth year, and
the fecond of men of riper age (y). The

(x) The firft clafs were called Andreia, and anfwered
to the Pheidicia of the Lacedæmonians. Thefe two
names were alfo given to the public places where the
Cretans and Spartans made their repafts in common,
and where they difcourfed of affairs of ftate; anciently,
thefe affemblies were named, even at Lacedæmon, Andreia.
Ariftotle.

(y) The fecond clafs were called Agelas (company).
This name was given alfo to the buildings where the youths
met together to take their repafts in public.

fociety

society of men made their repasts in common, in certain public edifices, where the chief, the magiftrate, the poor, and the rich, feated together, all eat and drank alike; a veffel filled with wine and water (z), which was paffed from one to the other, was the only drink for the whole company, and the aged men alone had the privilege of demanding an addition of wine. The Cretans were certainly too wife to be unacquainted with the power of beauty, as a woman prefided at each table (a), who took publicly the beft of every thing, and diftributed it to thofe who had fignalized themfelves by their courage in battle, or their wifdom in council. This honourable diftinction, far from caufing jealoufy, excited emulation in every breaft, to render themfelves worthy of the fame reward. Near the place where the citizens affembled (b), two tables, called *the hofpitable*, were prepared, to which all travellers and ftrangers, who prefented themfelves, were admitted; a particular houfe was likewife fet apart for them, where they might pafs the night.

(z) Dofiadas.
(a) Dofiadas.
(b) Dofiadas. Euftathius.

To

To provide for the expences of the ſtate, every citizen was obliged to bring into the common ſtock the tenth part of his revenues; the general diſtribution of which was veſted in the prefects of the cities. " In Crete," ſays Ariſtotle, " a certain part of the fruits " of the earth, the flocks, the revenues of the " ſtate, and the impoſts is confecrated to the " Gods, and the reſt diſtributed to the dif- " ferent claſſes into which the inhabitants " are divided; ſo that men, women, and " children, are maintained at the public ex- " pence."

(c) After dinner, the chiefs were accuf- tomed to converſe together, and to con- ſult on the affairs of the republic; they then recounted heroic actions performed in bat- tle; celebrated the courage of the moſt illuf- trious of their warriors, and exhorted the young men to valour. (d) Theſe aſſem- blies were the firſt fchool of infancy. At ſeven years old, the bow was put into the hands of the Cretan youth, who from that

(c) Doſiadas.

(d) Euſtathius (in Odyſſ.) ſays, the Cretans after dinner confulted on public affairs: They afterwards difcourfed of war, celebrated the exploits of their warriors, and exhorted the young men to imitate their heroic actions.

moment

moment was received into the fociety of the men, which he did not quit before the age of feventeen. There, feated on the ground, and clad in a fimple garment which ferved him the whole year, he attended on the old men, and liftened in filence to their counfels; his youthful heart took fire at the recital of high deeds of arms, and he ardently pant-ed to atchieve the like. (e) He became ha-bituated to fobriety and temperance; and hav-ing inceffantly before his eyes examples of moderation, wifdom, and patriotifm, the feeds of every virtue were implanted in him, even before he knew the ufe of reafon.

He was early inured to arms and to fa-tigue (f), that he might be able to endure heat and cold, to climb mountains and preci-pices, and bear with refolution the blows and wounds he might receive in the gymnafia, or in battle. But his education was not confined to the gymnaftic exercifes; he was taught to fing, in a peculiar kind of air (g), the laws written

(e) Strabo, lib x.

(f) Strabo, lib. x. The laws of Crete, fays Cicero, exer-cifed the youth in hunting, running, and fupporting heat and cold, hunger and thirft.

(g) Strabo, lib. x. fays, that the laws of Crete were written in verfe, the meafure of which was very confined.

in

in verfe, that the pleafure of mufic might imprefs them more deeply on his memory, and prevent him from pleading ignorance, fhould he offend againft them : he next learned hymns in honour of the Gods, and poems compofed in the praife of their heroes. When he had attained his feventeenth year, he quitted the fociety of the men, and entered into the clafs of the youth.

The education of thefe continued on the fame plan; they exercifed themfelves in hunting, wreftling, and fighting with their companions, while martial airs were played on the lyre (*h*), and they were obliged to obferve exact time. Thefe exercifes were not always without danger, as iron weapons were fometimes made ufe of (*i*). But the Pyrrhic dance, invented in Crete (*k*), was that in which the youth were moft ambitious to excel; the dancers wore the warlike drefs, which was

(*h*) Athenæus, lib. xii. The Lacedæmonians charge the enemy to the found of the flute; the Cretans to that of the lyre.

(*i*) Strabo, lib. x.

(*k*) Diodorus, lib. v. Dionyfius Halicarnaff. lib. vii. Pliny, lib. vii. cap. 56. Strabo, lib. x. fays, that this dance was invented in Crete. Nicholas Damafcenus fays that the inventor of it was Pyrrhicus of Cydon.

a fhort

a short and light loose jacket, that descended only to the knee, and was fastened with a girdle that went twice round the waist; they wore also the buskin, were completely armed, and imitated various military evolutions to the sound of instruments. " The Lacedæ-" monians and Cretans," says Libanius (l), " cultivated dancing with the utmost ardour; " they considered it as a necessary exercise " enjoined by the laws; and it was almost as " dishonourable to neglect it, as to quit their " post in the day of battle."

(m) The opulent Cretans, and those of an illustrious birth, were permitted to form societies of young men of their own age, and among these the contention was, who should have the most numerous company. In general, the father of the young man who had collected them was their chief; he was to instruct these warlike youths, to exercise them in running and hunting, and to bestow rewards, or inflict punishments.

(l) Liban. Orat. pro Saltatoribus.

(m) Strabo, lib. x. These companies, as I have said, were called Agelas.

Friend-

Friendſhip was highly honoured among the Cretans; " But," ſays Strabo (n), " their " manner of loving is very extraordinary. " Inſtead of gentle perſuaſion, they em- " ploy violence to gain friends. He who " has a ſecret paſſion for a young man of " his own age, and is deſirous of attaching him " by indiſſoluble ties, forms the projeдt of " carrying him off; which he imparts to " his companions three or four days before " he intends to execute it. The latter can " neither conceal him, nor hinder him from " going out, as that would ſeem to imply " in them an avowal that he did not merit " ſuch excefs of love. On the day appoint- " ed they meet together, and if the raviſher " appears to them to poſſeſs equal or ſuperior " merit to his favourite, they at firſt pre- " tend to oppoſe the intended violence, in " compliance with the law; but afterwards " favour it with joy: if, on the contrary, they " do not judge him worthy of the choice " he has made, they prevent him from exe- " cuting his deſign. This pretended reſiſtance " continues until the young man has con- " ducted his prize to the aſſembly of which he

(n) Strabo, lib. x.

" is

" is a member. They do not confider ·him
" as the moft amiable who furpaffes others in
" beauty, but him who is moft diftinguifhed
" by modefty and bravery.

" The ravifher loads his young friend
" with favours, and accompanies-him where-
" ever he defires; he is followed by thofe
" who have favoured the enterprize, and
" conducts him from feftival to feftival, pro-
" cures him the ·pleafures of the chafe and
" good cheer, and, after endeavouring for
" two months to ' win his heart by every
" poffible means, he brings him back to the
" city, and is obliged to reftore him to his
" parents. ' But, previous to this, he prefents
" him with a warrior's drefs, an ox, and a
" vafe, which are the cuftomary and pre-
" fcribed gifts. Sometimes his generofity ex-
" tends ftill further, and he beftows on him
" fumptuous prefents, to the expence of
" which his companions contribute. The
" youth then facrifices the ox to Jupi-
" ter, and gives an entertainment to thofe
" who affifted in carrying him off. He de-
" clares whether he will accept the friend-
" fhip of him who has been at fo much trou-
" ble to gain his efteem; and if he has reafon

" to

" to complain of any part of his conduct, he
" is at liberty to renounce a friend unworthy
" of the name, and to demand his punifh-
" ment.

" It would be difgraceful," adds Strabo,
" for a handfome young man, of illuftrious
" birth, to be without a friend, as the fault
" would be imputed to his morals. They who
" have been carried off receive public honours.
" They have the privilege of the firft places
" in the public affemblies, and are allowed to
" wear the drefs they owe to affection and
" efteem, during the remainder of their lives;
" which diftinctive mark is a public proof
" they have enjoyed a friendfhip efteemed fo
" honourable.

" When the young men had completed their
" exercifes, and attained the age appointed by
" the laws, they entered into the clafs of men
" of mature age. Being now become members
" of fociety, they had the right of voting in
" the national affemblies, and might be ad-
" vanced to all the employments of the repub-
" lic. At this period they were obliged to
" marry; but before they brought home their
" wives, they waited till they were qualified
" to manage a family." Such, Madam, were

the

the leading features of the Cretan government.
" The legiflator," fays Strabo, " juftly con-
" fidered liberty as the greateft bleffing cities
" can poffefs ; fince that alone fecures the pro-
" perty of the citizens, of which flavery is
" the certain deftruction. The flave poffeffes
" no property, not even that of his perfon.
" It is incumbent on all men, therefore, to
" preferve their liberty, the fureft foundation
" of which is concord ; and we fee it every
" where flourifh, when the feeds of diffenfion
" are deftroyed. Difcord almoft always ori-
" ginates in the thirft of riches, and the love
" of luxury. If for thefe we fubftitute fru-
" gality, moderation and equality, we fhall
" eradicate envy, hatred, injuftice, and the
" paffions moft injurious to fociety."

This is precifely what the Cretan legiflator
effected ; and hence that wealthy, profperous
and powerful republic received fuch well-
deferved encomiums from the moft celebrated philofophers of Greece. But the
greateft honour to Crete was, that her laws
furnifhed Lycurgus with the model of thofe
inftitutions which he eftablifhed at Lacedæmon.

I have the honour to be, &c.

L E T-

L E T T E R XX.

To M. L. M.

THE republic of Crete, which, as you have feen, Madam, was as ancient as the fiege of Troy, ftill flourifhed in the time of Julius Cæfar. We know of no other of fo long continuance. The legiflator, founding the happinefs of the Cretans on liberty, gave them laws and inftitutions fitted to form men capable of defending their freedom (*o*). All the citizens were foldiers (*p*), and all exercifed and expert in the art of war: for we even find that foreigners reforted to Crete, to be inftructed in that art. " Philopœmen," fays Plutarch (*q*), " not enduring to remain inactive, and ar- " dently defirous of acquiring knowledge in " the profeffion of arms, embarked for Crete; " where having exercifed himfelf among that

(*o*) Ariftot. Polit. lib. vii.   In Crete the greater part of the laws had relation to war.

(*p*) Plato, de Legibus, lib. i.   The Cretan legiflator framed both his public and private laws to have a reference to war, becaufe victory affured to the victors the property of the vanquifhed.

(*q*) Plutarch, in Vita Philopœm.

N   " warlike

" warlike people, well verfed in every mi-
" litary art, and accuftomed to lead a frugal
" and auftere life, he returned to the Achæans,
" and fo much diftinguifhed himfelf by the
" knowledge he had acquired, that he was
" immediately appointed general of the ca-
" valry."

On the other hand, the legiflator, perfuaded
that conquefts were ufually only acts of violence and injuftice, which frequently en-
feebled, and almoft always corrupted the morals of the victorious nation, endeavoured to
prevent the Cretans from endeavouring to
fubdue foreign countries. The abundant productions of their ifland were fufficient to fupply every real want, and they had no need of
foreign riches, which, together with commerce, would have introduced luxury, and all
its attendant vices. He knew how to infpire his nation with a difregard for thefe fu-
perfluities, without exprefsly forbidding them.
The gymnaftic exercifes, which furnifhed
fufficient employment for the leifure of ardent
youth; the pleafures of the chace, to which
they were much addicted; friendfhip, which
he had taught them to revere as a divinity;
the public fhows, where all the different claffes
of

of fociety met together, and to which the women were admitted (r) ; the love of equality,
regularity, and their country, with which all
hearts were inflamed ; and the wife inftitutions,
which rendered the whole nation but a fingle
family ; all confpired to attach the Cretans to
their ifland, on which they found the utmoft
happinefs they could wifh, without entertain-
ing any defire to feek abroad an imaginary
glory, or fubject other nations to their power.
From the time the government of this country
firft became republican, till it was attacked
by the Romans, we never find the Cretans
to have attempted any foreign invafion ; an
honour referved exclufively to them among all
the people celebrated in hiftory. Individuals,
indeed, might ferve in the armies of other
ftates : the kings and princes of which, knowing their bravery and fkill in archery, ftrove
who fhould firft induce them to enter into
their pay, as each was defirous of having in
his army a body of Cretan bowmen, fince
the whole world could not produce any more
expert (s). " The arrows of Gortyna," fays
Claudian,

(r) Plutarch, in Vita Thefei.
(s) Claudian, Plutarch. in Pyrrh. Paufanias in Me-
neffiacis,

Claudian, " happily directed, carry certain
" wounds, and never mifs their aim."

But though the numerous and flourifhing
cities of Crete did not unite to enflave the
neighbouring iflands, by drenching them with
the blood of their inhabitants, they were not
wife enough to preferve peace among themfelves. The torch of difcord was frequently
lighted. The moft powerful wifhed to rule
over the others. Cnoffus and Gortyna, fometimes in alliance, attacked and fubjugated the
neighbouring cities, and fometimes . making
war on each other, faw the braveft of their
youth perifh in thefe civil contefts. Lyctos
and Cydon oppofed an unfhaken barrier to
their ambition, and preferved their liberty.
The latter had obtained fuch power (*t*), as
to be able to turn the fcale in favour of whichever fide it declared. Thefe civil wars occafioned the ruin of many cities, and deluged
with blood the country of Jupiter.

To what muft we attribute thefe inteftine
diffenfions? One part of the ifland was occu-

neiliacis, atteft the fkill of the Cretans in the art of fhooting
arrows, and that foreign princes were very defirous to
form bodies of archers, confifting entirely of that nation.

(*t*) Strabo, lib. x.

pied

pied by the Eteocretans, or native inhabitants, among whom were fettled colonies from Athens, Sparta, Argos, and Samos (*u*), who poffibly ftill retained in their hearts the feeds of ancient animofity, and their inveterate hatreds only waited a favourable opportunity to ripen into open violence and revenge. Perhaps too, the ftrongeft, confiding in their fuperiority, were tempted to avail themfelves of their power, and fubftituted force for right ; nor are we to forget that the Cretan youth, trained to military exercifes from their infancy, were ever ready to betake themfelves to arms. Thefe probably are the reafons which fo often hurried to the combat, a people fubject to the fame laws, the fame cuftoms, and the fame religion. Be this as it may, the Cretans, convinced that victory depended on the unanimity of their troops, magnificently adorned the moft beautiful young men of the army ; and made them facrifice to friendfhip, before they engaged in battle (*v*). There are countries where, on like occafions, the commanders

(*u*) Herodot. lib. iii. fays, the Samians, who built Cydon, erected temples there, among which was that of Dictynna.

(*v*) Athenæus, lib. xiii.

ought

ought to be obliged to facrifice to Concord ; and if their facrifice were fincere, it would at once redound to their own glory, and prevent rivers of human blood from being fhed to no purpofe to the ftate.

The love of war did not extinguifh in the hearts of the Cretans that exquifite fenfibility which made them cultivate and encourage the fine arts. " The Cretans," fays Sozomen (x), " difplayed their ' munificence to " Homer, by giving him a thoufand crowns ; " and glorying in a generofity not to be furpaffed, preferved the memory of their donation by a public infcription." In Crete, adds Ptolemy (y), men are ftill more anxious to cultivate their minds, than to exercife their bodies. Therefore, when difcord reigned among them, the voice of wifdom, and the charms of poetry, brought them back to reafon. Thales of Gortyna (z), the inftructor of Lycurgus, was one of their moft celebrated philofophers, poets, and legiflators ; and he

(x) Sozomen. Hift. Ecclef. in Pref.

(y) Ptolem. in Tetrab. lib. ii.

(z) Paufanias, in Atticis; fays, that this Thales was ef Gortyna. Diogenes Laertius afferts, that he lived in the time of Lycurgus and Homer. Strabo, lib. x. feems to confirm this opinion.

fuccefsfully

fuccefsfully applied his knowledge and talents
to reftore concord to his fellow citizens (a).
" His poetry confifted of difcourfes in verfe,
" exhorting the people to unanimity and obe-
" dience to their fuperiors ; he poffeffed the
" art of conveying in the moft harmonious
" metre, the moft folid and beneficial inftruc-
" tion. So great was the effect of his poetry,
" that his hearers, who found their under-
" ftanding, heart, and ears, equally perfuaded
" and charmed, gradually fuffered all their
" animofity to fubfide ; and enamoured with
" the bleffings of peace, which he painted in
" the moft lively colours, forgot their inteftine
" hatreds, and ranged themfelves under the
" ftandard of concord." It is faid that this
fage invented the arts appropriated to the military dances, and the Cretan Pyrrhic (b). Men,

over

(a) Plutarch, in Vita Lycurg.

(b) The Scholiaft on Pindar (Pyth. Od. 2.) fays that
thefe dances were inftituted by the Curetes. Strabo (lib. x.)
is of the fame opinion ; he adds, however, that Thales invented the Cretan Rhythmus. Nicholas Damafcenus, and
Marius Plotius (de Metris), attribute the invention of the
armed Pyrrhic to Pyrrhicus of Cydon. May we not reconcile thefe authors by fuppofing the Curetes to have been the
firft inftitutors of the military dances ; that Pyrrhicus invented

over whom poetry and mufic had fuch power, could not be enemies to pleafure; and we accordingly find it to have been a cuftom with them to mark their happy days by white ftones and their unhappy ones with black (c). At the end of the year, they examined the number of thefe ftones, and only efteemed themfelves to have lived the days denoted by the white ones, as they eftimated the length of life only by its enjoyments. Hence the infcription frequent on their tombs: *He lived, fo many days; he exifted, fo many.*

In minds of fenfibility and generofity, a love of glory is eafily awakened. The Cretans reforted to all the celebrated folemnities of Greece, and bore away the palm in the Olympic, Nemean, and Pythian games (d); others, who were favourites of the Mufes, turned into heroic verfe the oracles of the prophets, and compofed poems to celebrate the great deeds of heroes (e). Several diftinguifhed

vented that particular one which bore his name, and that Thales compofed the airs, or adapted new mufic to them.

(c) Cornutus, on the fecond Satire of Perfius.

(d) Such as Ergoteles of Cnoffus, celebrated by Pindar, Ode xii.

(e) Jophon of Cnoffus put into heroic verfe the oracles of

guifhed themfelves as hiftorians *(f)*. It is faid,
that the moft ancient conteft was that in which
a prize was propofed to the poet who beft
fhould fing a hymn to Apollo, and in which
the victory was adjudged to Chryfothemis of
Crete *(g)*.

Time, however, has annihilated almoft all
their works; and if Pindar had not immor-
talifed fome of thofe Cretans who were victors
in the Grecian games, we fhould not at prefent even know their names. The temple of
Diana, at Ephefus, built by Ctefiphon, and
his fon Metagenes, both Cretans, has not
proved more durable *(h)*. This noble building
was of the Ionic order *(i)*; and to the beauty of

of the Prophets. Paufanias.—Rhianus of Bena wrote feveral
books in verfe, and compofed feveral poems.   Stephanus.

(f) Dictys of Cnoffus accompanied Idomeneus into
Troas, and wrote the hiftory of that famous fiege which
Homer has rendered fo celebrated.   Joannes Tzetzes.——
Lucillus of Tarrha wrote a commentary on the hiftory of the
Argonauts, &c.

(g) Paufanias, in Phocicis.

(h) Pliny, lib. vii. cap. 37. Ctefiphon of Cnoffus was
celebrated for the admirable fkill he difplayed in building
the temple of Diana at Ephefus.

(i) Vitruvius, lib. ii.

the

the marble, the elegance of the architecture, the majesty of the edifice, and the inimitable perfection of the whole, was added a solidity which alone could add value to so grand a design. The names of the artists who built it have descended to posterity, though the marbles, columns, and ornaments, which rendered them immortal, have been disperfed or destroyed, leaving scarcely the slightest trace remaining of one of the seven wonders of the world.

Nations pass away from off the earth, like the monuments of their power, and after a few centuries, with difficulty can we discover, in their descendants, the vestiges of their ancient character. Some subsist longer than others, and we are able almost always to calculate their duration by the wisdom of their laws, and the fidelity with which they are observed. The republic of Crete, established on the solidest foundations, for ten centuries knew no foreign master, and bravely repelled the attacks of every foreign prince who attempted to enslave her. But at length the fatal period arrived when the Romans, elated with their victories, and proud of their power, aspired to the empire of the world, and would no

longer

longer admit of any diſtinction among the
ſurrounding nations, but that of ſlaves or ſub-
jects *(k)*. Florus does not diſſemble that ambition, and the deſire of ſubjecting the famous
country of Jupiter, were the only motives
which induced the Romans to attack Crete.
" Should we inquire into the real cauſe of
" the Cretan war," ſays he, " it muſt be con-
" feſſed, it was entered into only from the
" deſire of ſubjugating that celebrated iſland;
" Crete was ſuppoſed to have favoured Mi-
" thridates, and Rome revenged the pretended
" inſult, by declaring war againſt her. Marcus
" Antonius *(l)* (the father of the triumvir)
" failed on this expedition, perſuaded he ſhould
" make an eaſy conqueſt; but his meanneſs
" and preſumption met with deſerved puniſh-
" ment. The enemy cut off the greater part
" of his fleet, and hung up their priſoners to
" the maſts; after which they returned trium-
" phant into their harbours."

Rome never forgave a defeat. No ſooner

(k) Florus, lib. iii.

(l) Marcus Antonius was appointed to guard all the maritime coaſts of the Roman empire. He periſhed in Crete,
where he loſt his honour.

was the Macedonian war ended, then she
armed for vengeance, and sent Quintus Me-
tellus with a formidable armament against
Crete (*m*). He met, however, with a very ob-
stinate resistance. Panarus and Lasthenes, two
experienced commanders, having assembled
twenty thousand men, of determined courage,
and ardent in the caufe of their country,
withstood for three succeffive years the
arms of the Romans; who were not able to
gain poffeffion of the island, till they had destroyed its bravest warriors. They lost there
a great number of men, and with the utmost
difficulty obtained a bloody victory. The
fortune of Rome, at length, triumphed, and
the first care of the conqueror was, to abolish
the laws of Minos (*n*), and substitute those of
Numa. The fenfible and judicious Strabo (*o*)
complains of this feverity, and fays, that in
his time the Cretan institutions were no longer
obferved, becaufe the Romans had compelled
the conquered provinces to adopt their laws.
Still more effectually to fecure to themfelves

(*m*) Velleius Paterculus, lib. ii.
(*n*) Paulus Diaconus, Hift. Mifc. lib. vi.
(*o*) Strabo, lib. x.

the

the poſſeſſion of the iſland, they ſent a numerous colony to Cnoſſus (*p*).

From that period to the preſent time, Madam, that is to ſay, during a ſpace of nineteen hundred years, the Cretans have ceaſed to be a nation, and have gradually loſt their courage, their virtues, their ſciences, and their arts. This deplorable debaſement can only be attributed to the extinction of their liberty. So true is it, that man is born for liberty, and that, deprived of this ſupport, which he has received from nature to ſuſtain his weakneſs, his genius expires, and his courage languiſhes, till he ſinks to the loweſt point of degradation.

(*q*) The iſland of Crete, together with the little kingdom of Cyrene on the coaſt of Lybia, compoſed a Roman province, which at firſt was governed by a Proconſul, afterwards by a Queſtor and an Aſſeſſor (*r*); and, at length, as we learn from Suetonius, by a Conſul (*s*). This iſland was one of the firſt which received the light of the Goſpel. The Chriſtian faith

(*p*) Idem, ibid.
(*q*) Idem, lib. xvii.
(*r*) Dion.
(*s*) Suetonius, in Vita Veſpaſiani.

was planted there by St. Paul; and his difciple Titus, whom he left to bring to perfection the good feed he had fown, was the firft bifhop. Under the reign of Leo, Crete contained twelve bifhoprics (*t*), all fubordinate to the patriarch of Conftantinople (*u*). Conftantine divided the province of Crete and Cyrene in the diftribution he made of the empire. Leaving three fons, Conftantius, Conftantine, and Conftans; he gave to the former Thrace and the Eaft; to the fecond, the kingdom of the Weft; and to the third, the ifland of Crete, Africa, and Illyria.

(*v*) When Michael Balbus was in poffeffion of the throne of Conftantinople, the revolt of Thomas, which continued three years, caufed him to neglect the other parts of the empire. The Agarenians, an Arab nation, who had conquered the fineft provinces of Spain, took advantage of this opportunity, to fit out a confiderable fleet, and, after having pillaged the Cy-

(*t*) Thefe bifhoprics ranked in the following order, as we fee in the Novel of the Emperor Leo: *Gortyna, Cnoffus, Arcadia, Cherronefus, Aalopotamos, Agrium, Lampa, Cydonia, Hiera, Petra, Sitea, Ciffamo.*

(*u*) Zozim. lib. ii.

(*v*) Conftant. Porphyrogenit. de adminiftrando Imperio, cap. xii.

clades,

clades, they attacked the ifland of Crete, where
they eftablifhed themfelves almoft without refiftance.   To fecure their conquefts, they built
a fortrefs, which they called *Khandak* (*i. e.* an
intrenchment), and which name by the Venetians was foftened into Candia.   From this
citadel the Barbarians made incurfions into
every part of the ifland, fpreading terror and
defolation wherever they came ; and, at length,
made themfelves mafters of all the cities and
towns, except Cydon.   Michael in vain endeavoured to drive them from the ifland ; nor
was the emperor Bafilius the Macedonian more
fortunate ;   they defeated him in a bloody
battle ; but one of his generals, having been
more fuccefsful, impofed on them a tribute.
At the expiration of ten years, the Arabs refufed to pay the fum ftipulated, and it was
referved to Nicephorus Phocas (*x*), who afterwards became emperor, to deliver this beautiful ifland from the yoke of the infidels.   He
landed there with a numerous army, attacked
them with great bravery, and defeated them
in feveral battles ; till at length the Saracens,
no longer daring to keep the field againft this
formidable opponent, fhut themfelves up in

(*x*) Murtius.

their

their fortreffes. Phocas, provided with all the warlike machines neceffary for fieges, took their places of ftrength one after the other, and forced them even in Khandak, their metropolis, and laft ftrong hold. After a campaign of nine months, he entirely reduced the ifland, made the king Curup, and his lieutenant Anemas, prifoners, and reftored to the empire a province which had been in the poffeffion of the infidels during one hundred and twenty-feven years. It remained fubjeft to the emperors of Byzantium till the time of Baldwin earl of Flanders, who, raifed to their throne, magnificently rewarded Boniface, marquis of Montferrat, for the fuccours he brought him, by creating him king of Theffalonica, and adding the ifland of Crete to his dominions. By this nobleman, who was more greedy after wealth than ambitious of glory, it was fold to the Venetians in 1194 *(y)*.

Under the wife laws of this great republic, Crete again began to revive. The people enjoyed the bleffings of a mild government, and, encouraged by their mafters, applied themfelves to commerce and agriculture. Travel-

(y) La Guerra Cretenfe.

lers

lers received from the Venetian governors every affiftance they could defire, for extending and perfecting inquiries beneficial to mankind. Belon, the naturalift, fpeaks, in terms of the higheft gratitude and commendation, of the fervices rendered him by them, and gives an interefting defcription of the flourifhing ftate of the country through which he travelled.

The feat of government was eftablifhed at Candia, where the magiftrates and members of the council refided. The fupreme authority was vefted in the Proveditor General, whofe power extended over the whole kingdom.

Venice had been in the poffeffion of Crete during five centuries and a half, when, at the time that Cornaro occupied the moft important poft, the ftorm began to gather on the fide of Conftantinople. The Turks, for a whole year, had been affembling a prodigious armament, and deceived the Bailli by affuring him it was intended againft Malta. But in 1645, in the midft of profound peace, they fuddenly invaded Crete with a fleet of four hundred fail, having on board fixty thoufand fol-

O   diers,

diers, under the command of four Pachas (z).
The Emperor Ibrahim, who gave orders for
this expedition, had no plea for undertaking
it. He, however, had recourfe to the ufual
arts of eaftern perfidy. To impofe upon the
Venetian Senate, he loaded their ambaffadors
with prefents; ordered his fleet to proceed as
far as Cape Matagan, as if quitting the Archipelago, and pofitively affured the governors
of Tine and Cerigne, that the republic had
nothing to fear for her poffeffions; yet, at the
very moment the Porte was making thefe
proteftations, the fleet failed into the gulph
of Canea, and paffing between that place and
Saint Theodore, proceeded to form a landing
below the river of Platania. Such indeed has
ever been the manner in which the Turks
have acted towards the people they wifhed to
fubjugate. Fraud and force are the two means
they employ to accomplifh their defigns; but
the time is certainly not far diftant, when

(z) The Captain Pacha, by birth a Croat, who commanded the fleet; the Pacha who commanded by land,
and was to conduct the fiege; Haffian Pacha, Beglier Bey
of Romelia, who was the firft that entered the walls of
Babylon; and Amurat Pacha, Aga of the Janiffaries.

they

they will be compelled to reftore their unjuft conquefts.

The Venetians, not expecting this fudden invafion, had made no preparations for defence, and the Turks landed without the leaft refiftance. The little ifland of St. Theodore is but a league and a half from Canea, and only three quarters of a league in circumference. Here the Venetians had erected two forts, one called Turluru, on the top of the fteepeft cliff, and the other named St. Theodore, lower down. It was of the utmoft importance for the invaders to poffefs themfelves of this rock, which might have greatly incommoded their fhips. They loft no time, therefore, in commencing the attack, which they carried on with vigour. The former of thefe fortreffes had neither cannon nor foldiers, and was taken without firing a gun. The fecond had only a garrifon of fixty men, but they defended themfelves to the laft extremity; and when the Turks entered it, they found only ten foldiers remaining, whofe heads were barbaroufly ftruck off by order of the Captain Pacha.

Mafters of this important poft, as well as of the Lazaret, a rock fituated half a league

from Canea, the Turks blockaded the city by
fea, and furrounded it with lines of circum-
vallation by land. General Cornaro was thun-
der-ftruck, on learning that the enemy hád
made a defcent. The whole ifland contained
only a body of three thoufand five hundred
infantry, and a fmall number of horfe; and
he knew that the befieged town had only a
thoufand regular troops for its defence, and a
few citizens able to bear arms. He fent inftant advice of his diftrefs to Venice, and took
his poft at the harbour, that he might be more
at hand to fuccour the befieged. He threw
about two hundred and fifty men into the
town, before the enemy could get their lines
completed, and often attempted, but in vain,
to introduce new reinforcements. The Turks
approaching the body of the place, had carried a half moon, which covered the gate of
Retimo; and availing themfelves of their numerous artillery, continued daily to batter the
wall in breach. The befieged bravely returned
their fire, and made them pay dearly for a few
doubtful fucceffes. General Cornaro endeavoured to arm the Greeks, and efpecially the
Spachiots, who boafted of their bravery. He
formed a battalion of them; but their days

1   of

of prowefs were no more: the moment they faw the enemy, and heard the thunder of the artillery, they fhamefully took to flight, nor was it poffible to make a fingle man of them ftand fire.

While the Senate of Venice were deliberating on the means of faving Candia, and bufied in fitting out a fleet, the Mahometan generals lavifhed the blood of their foldiers, to bring their enterprize to a glorious termination: they had already loft twenty thoufand warriors in the different engagements; but they had defcended into the fofies, and dug under the ramparts thofe frightful cavities, in which the powder confined burfts with an horrible explofion, and overturns forts of the greateft folidity. They played off one of thefe mines under the baftion of St. Demetrius, which blew up a great part of the wall, and fwallowed all its defenders. The affailants inftantly mounted the breach, fabre in hand, and, profiting by the general confternation, made themfelves mafters of that poft. The befieged, recovered from their fright, fell upon them with unexampled intrepidity. About four hundred Venetians rufhed on two thoufand Turks, already in poffeffion of the wall, and pufhed them with

with fo much ardour and obftinacy, as to make prodigious flaughter, and force the remainder into the ditches. In this extremity every body fought; the monks carried the mufket; women, forgetting the delicacy of their fex, appeared in the midft of the defend- ants, either to affift in fupplying them with arms, or to wield them themfelves againft the enemy; and feveral of thefe glorious heroines loft their lives.

During fifty days the place held out againft the whole forces of the Turks; and even at the laft moment, if the Venetians had fent a fleet to its fuccour, the kingdom of Candia would have been faved. They could not, undoubt- edly, be ignorant of the following fact: The north wind blows full into the gulph of Ca- nea, and when ftrong, the fea runs very high. It is then impoffible for any fquadron, how- ever numerous, to form in line of battle to wait an enemy. Had the Venetians fet fail from Cerigne with this favourable wind, they would have reached Canea in five hours, and entered the harbour in full fail, without firing a fhot, or the poffibility of being oppofed by a fingle Turkifh veffel, which could not move without endangering their fafety on the coaft,

and

and dafhing to pieces on the furrounding fhoals. Inftead of executing fuch a plan, fuggefted by the very nature of the fituation, they fent a few galleys, which not daring to double Cape Spada, coafted along the fouthern fhore of the ifland, and failed of effecting the purpofe intended.

The garrifon of Canea, defpairing of fuccours which had been long delayed, feeing three breaches open, by which the infidels might eafily mount to the affault, overcome with fatigue, and covered with wounds, reduced to five hundred men, whom it was neceffary to difperfe over walls of half a league's circumference, every where undermined, at length demanded a capitulation. They obtained the moft honourable conditions; and after two months glorious defence, which coft the Turks five and twenty thoufand men, marched out of the place with all the honours of war. The citizens who did not choofe to remain had permiffion to withdraw; and the Turks, contrary to their cuftom, executed the convention with tolerable fidelity.

The Venetians, after the capture of Canea, retired to Retimo; and the Captain Pacha proceeded to lay fiege to the Caftle of La Sude,

Sude, fituated at the entrance of the bay, on a rock about a quarter of a league in circumference. He raifed batteries, and endeavoured, but without effect, to make a breach in the ramparts. Defpairing to carry it by force, he left troops to continue the blockade, and marched towards Retimo. This town, without walls, was defended by a citadel, built on an eminence that commanded the harbour, into which General Cornaro had retired. At the approach of the enemy, he drew his men out of the citadel, and waited for them in the open field. During the action he expofed his perfon without referve, and fought in the ranks to encourage his foldiers. A glorious death was the reward of his bravery ; but his fall was followed by the lofs of Retimo (a).

The Turks, by landing frefh troops in the ifland, introduced the plague, which almoft conftantly accompanies their armies. This dreadful diftemper made a rapid progrefs from day to day, and, like devouring flame, exterminated the greateft part of the inhabitants (b). The remainder, terrified at its ra-

(a) Etat général de l'Empire Ottoman, *troifiéme partie.*
(b) Idem.

vages,

vages, efcaped into the Venetian ftates, and left the ifland almoft a defert.

In 1646 commenced the fiege of Candia, of a much longer duration than that of Troy. Were a fertile and brilliant imagination, like that of Homer, to collect into one poem the extraordinary events of this celebrated fiege, pofterity would be prefented with noble deeds of arms, magnificent fcenes, and heroes not inferior to thofe of the Iliad. Memorable actions are not wanting in the hiftory of nations. Every age produces new ones ; but a genius, like that of the father of poetry, does not arife in many ages. It would be inconfiftent with my intention, in thefe letters, to enter into long details. I fhall confine myfelf, therefore, to a curfory defcription of the principal events which occurred during the fiege of Candia. The Turks, in 1648, had made but little progrefs before that place: they were frequently defeated by the Venetians, and fometimes compelled to retire to Retimo. At this period Ibrahim was folemnly depofed, and his eldeft fon, only nine years of age, placed on the throne, under the name of Mehemet IV. But the Sultan, in the receffes of his prifon, ftill continuing an object of in-

quietude

quietude and alarm to the authors of the revolution, he was ftrangled on the 19th of Auguft of the fame year. The young emperor, whofe advancement to the throne was thus effected by the murder of his father, was himfelf, in the end, precipitated from it, to pafs the remainder of his days in the obfcurity of a dungeon (c). The whole Ottoman hiftory is nothing but one continued tiffue of fuch murders and treafons; but how important are its leffons for all defpots!

In 1649, Uffein Pacha, who continued the blockade of Candia, receiving no fuccours from the Porte, was obliged to raife the fiege, and fly to Canea. The Venetians now kept the fea with a ftrong fquadron, and attacked the Turkifh fleet in the bay of Smyrna; burnt twelve fhips, two gallies, and killed fix thoufand men. But the infidels, fome time after, having found means to land an army in Candia, recommenced with ftill greater fury the fiege of that city, and having gained poffeffion of an advanced work, which greatly incommoded the befieged, reduced them to the neceffity of blowing it up.

(c) After a reign of thirty-feven years, Mehemet IV. was depofed, and confined in a prifon.

From

From 1650 to 1658, the Venetians, continuing mafters of the fea, waited every year for their enemies at the ftraits of the Dardanelles, and defeated their numerous fleets in four fea-fights, in which they funk a great number of their caravelles, took many others, and fpread confternation to the very walls of Conftan-tinople, which was filled with tumult and dif-order. The Grand Signior in difmay, not thinking himfelf in fafety, abandoned his capital with precipitation.

Thefe glorious fuccefies raifed the hopes of the Venetians, and deprefled the courage of the Turks. They converted the fiege of Candia into a blockade, in which they fuffered confiderable lofles. In 1659, the Sultan, to drive the Venetian fleet from the Dardanelles, and fecure a free paffage for his fhips, or-dered two new caftles to be built at the en-trance of the ftraits. He commanded the Pacha of Canea to renew the fiege of Candia, and make every effort to obtain poffeffion of that important fortrefs. In the mean time the re-public of Venice, profiting by the advantages already gained, made feveral attempts upon Canea, which city, in 1660, being vigoroufly prefled, was on the point of furrendering,

when

when the Pacha of Rhodes, haftening to its fuccour, threw into it a reinforcement of two thoufand men. He fafely doubled the point of Cape Melec, in fight of the Venetian fleet, which, lying becalmed off Cape Spada, was unable to make the fmalleft motion to give battle to an inferior enemy, and rob him of his conqueft.

Kiopruli, the fon and fucceffor of the Vifir of that name, who had fo long upheld the declining fortune of the Ottoman empire, knowing that the people murmured loudly at the length of the fiege of Candia, and dreading a general revolt, which muft have proved fatal to him and to his mafter, left Conftantinople about the end of 1666, at the head of a formidable army. Having eluded the vigilance of the Venetian fleet, which was waiting for him off Canea, he effected his landing at Palio Caftro, and formed his lines round Candia. He had under him four Pachas, and the flower of the Ottoman forces. Thefe troops, encouraged by the prefence and promifes of their commanders, and feconded by a numerous train of artillery, performed prodigies of valour. All the out-works were entirely deftroyed, and nothing remained to the befieged but

but a fimple line of walls, which, continually
fhaken by the cannon, were falling into ruins
on every fide; yet, though it will with difficulty be believed by pofterity, they ftill held
out for three years, againft the whole forces
of the Ottoman empire. At length they were
about to capitulate, when the hope of fuccours, fent from France, again revived their
valour, and rendered them invincible. Thefe
fuccours arrived on the 26th of June, 1669,
under the command of the Duke de Navailles,
who brought with him a great number of
French noblemen, who came to try their arms
againft the Turks.

The day after their arrival the impatient
French made a general fally. The Duke de
Beaufort, admiral of France, put himfelf at
the head of the forlorn hope. He marched
the firft againft the infidels, and was followed
by a numerous body of infantry and cavalry.
They rufhed headlong upon the enemy, attacked, forced them in their intrenchments,
and would have obliged them to abandon their
lines and artillery, but for an unforefeen event
which checked their courage. In the midft
of the action a powder-magazine blew up.
The moft advanced loft their lives. The

French ranks were broken, and feveral of their leaders, among whom was the Duke de Beau-fort, were never feen more. The foldiers took to flight in confufion. The Turks pur-fued them, and it was with the greateft dif-ficulty that the Duke de Navailles regained the walls of Candia. The French accufed the Italians of having betrayed them, by directing them to fally fooner than they fhould have done, and reimbarked, in fpite of all the entrea-ties of the governor. Their departure decided the fate of the city : as only five hundred men remained for its defence. Morofini capitu-lated with Kiopruli, to whom he gave up the whole ifland of Crete, excepting Sude, Gra-buge, and Spina Longa. The Grand Vifir made his entry into Candia on the 4th of Octo-ber, 1670, and remained there eight months, to repair the fortifications.

The three fortreffes, left by treaty to the Venetians, remained long in their poffeffion ; but at length fell fucceffively into the hands of the enemy. Thus, after upwards of thirty years war, after facrificing more than two hundred thoufand men, after deluging the ifland with rivers of Mahometan and Chriftian

blood,

blood, the Porte is at prefent in undiflurbed poffeffion of Candia.

This, Madam, is a feeble fketch of the hiftory of Crete, from the diftant ages of antiquity to the prefent æra. As we are about to make a tour in the ifland, I fhall next fpeak to you of its commerce, government, population, and whatever I imagine you will think moft interefting.

I have the honour to be, &c.

L E T T E R XXI.

To M. L. M.

YOU have now, Madam, fome acquaintance with the Cretans; I have laid before you a fketch of their hiftory, and we will next proceed to make an excurfion into the ifland they inhabited, and vifit its antiquities.

Elated with having been the birth-place of Jupiter, and proud of her hundred cities, Crete long continued more powerful than the other iflands of the Mediterranean. At prefent her glory is eclipfed. Time has not fpared a fingle one of all her cities, of which we fee nothing but the ruins. That we are about to quit is the modern capital, and has given its name to the ifland. As it is fituated on the fame fpot where ancient Heracleum formerly ftood, and is the refidence of the great officers of the Ottoman government, it merits a particular defcription.

" The ifle of Dia," fays Strabo (d), " is " fituated opofite to Heracleum, the fea-port

(d) Strabo, lib. x.

" of

" of Cnoſſus. It is only three leagues and a
" half diſtant from the coaſt." This deſcrip-
tion is exaɕt, and perfeɕtly correſponds with
the poſition of Candia, and the diſtance between that city and the iſle of Dia, now called
Standia. The following paſſage confirms alſo
the opinion of thoſe who aſſert, that the capital of Crete is built on the ruins of Heracleum (e). " Cnoſſus, ſituated within land,
" at the diſtance of twenty-five ſtadia from
" the north ſea, has for its port Heracleum."
Twenty-five ſtadia are equivalent to a league,
and it is at this diſtance from Candia, to the
ſouth-eaſt, that we find the village of Cnoſſou,
where the ruins of that once celebrated city are
ſtill to be ſeen.

There is no doubt, therefore, that the
modern Candia, the *Kandahk* of the Arabs,
now occupies the ſcite of the ancient Heracleum. You have read, Madam, the principal occurrences of the memorable ſiege this
city ſuſtained againſt the whole forces of the
Ottoman empire. The Turks have repaired
the ravages of war. The walls, which ſur-
round it, are more than a league in circum-

(e) Strabo, lib. x.

P   ference,

ference, well preferved, and defended with
deep ditches, but covered by no out-work.
It is, however, fafe from an attack on the fide
of the fea, as fhips cannot approach for want
of water.

Candia is the feat of the Turkifh government. The Porte ufually fends thither a Pacha
with three tails. Here alfo the principal officers, and different corps of the Ottoman foldiery, are affembled. This city, fo rich,
populous, and commercial, under the Venetian government, is greatly fallen from its
ancient grandeur. The harbour, which is a
handfome bafon, where fhips are fheltered
from every wind, is daily filling up, and is
now only capable of receiving boats and fmall
veffels, lightened of a part of their cargo.
Thofe freighted by the Turks at Candia are
obliged to proceed almoft in ballaft, to wait
for their loading in the ports of Standia, whither it is brought to them in fmall barks.
Thefe difficulties, which the governors do not
endeavour to remedy, are very detrimental to
commerce, which accordingly has extremely
declined.

Candia, greatly embellifhed by the Venetians,

tians, is divided into ftrait ftreets, and decorated with well-built houfes, a handfome
fquare, and a magnificent fountain, but contains
within its extenfive walls only a fmall number of inhabitants.   Several quarters of the
town are almoft deferted.   That of the market
is the only one in which we perceive activity
or affluence.   The Mahometans have converted the greateft part of the Chriftian temples
into mofques.   They have left, however, two
churches for the Greeks, one for the Arme-
nians, and a fynagogue for the Jews.   The
Capuchins have a fmall convent, with a chapel,
in which the French vice-conful hears mafs;
for at prefent he is the only perfon of that nation who refides at Candia, the French merchants having retired to Canea.

To the weft of Canea ftretches a chain of
mountains, defcending from Mount Ida, the
point of which forms the promontory of Dion.
Before we arrive there, we find on the fea-
fhore *Palio Caftro*, a name the modern Greeks
give to all ancient places.   Its fituation correfponds with that of Panormus, which lay to
the north-weft of Heracleum.

The river to the weft of Candia was anciently called the Triton, and near its fource

Minerva

Minerva was born of Jupiter *(f)*. A little further is the Loaxus; and about a league to the
eaſt of the city the river Ceratus flows through
a delightful valley, which, according to Strabo,
paſſed at a ſmall diſtance from Cnoſſus. Beyond is a river, I imagine to be the Therenus,
on whoſe banks, according to the fables of
antiquity, Jupiter celebrated his nuptials with
Juno *(g)*. In the ſpace of more than half a
league, round the walls of Candia, we do not
meet with a ſingle tree. The Turks, during
the ſiege, cut them all down, and deſtroyed
the gardens and orchards which environed the
town. The country beyond abounds in corn
and fruit-trees, and the adjacent hills, covered
with vineyards, yield the malmſey of Mount
Ida, worthy of a place at the tables of epi-
cures. This wine, little known in France, is

(f) Diodorus Siculus, lib. v. Tradition ſays, likewiſe,
that Minerva was born of Jupiter in the iſland of Crete,
near the ſources of the Triton, whence is derived the epithet
Tritogenes.

(g) Diodorus Siculus, lib. v. It is ſaid, that the nuptials
of Jupiter and Juno were celebrated in the diſtrict of Cnoſſus,
near the river Therenus. We ſtill ſee there a temple,
where the prieſts of the country imitate yearly, in a public
feſtival, the ceremonies which tradition ſays were obſerved
at theſe nuptials.

perfumed,

perfumed, of a very agreeable flavour, and in high eftimation in this country.

To-morrow, Madam, we fhall leave Candia. Our company will confift of twelve travellers, among whom are a French vice-conful, a conful, who is to enter on his office at Canea, fome young merchants, janiffaries, and others who travel from curiofity. We are all armed with mufkets, piftols, fabres, and fwords. In a country where every thing is decided by force, this mode of travelling is the fafeft. The Mountaineers and Turks have a great refpect for the arms of Frenchmen; and the only method of being under no apprehenfion from their violence is, to appear well provided with the means of defence. We fhall not take the fhorteft road, as we defign to vifit the moft remarkable places in the ifland.

I have the honour to be, &c.

L E T T E R XXII.

To M. L. M.

LEAVING Candia, Madam, we directed our courfe towards Gortyna, and foon arrived at the ruins of Cnoffus, called by the modern Grecks *Cnoffou*. This was the royal city of Minos, who eftablifhed there the feat of his empire, and there gave thofe wife and admirable laws fo juftly boafted by antiquity. This city was a league and a half in circuit (*h*), and long continued one of the moft celebrated of the ifland. United with Gortyna, it gave law to (*i*) almoft all Crete; but falling afterwards into misfortunes (*k*), Gortyna and Lyctos profited by its decline, and Cnoffus was for a time ftript of almoft all its fplendour; but foon repairing thefe loffes, recovered part of its ancient power, and refumed its ftation among the moft flourifhing cities of Crete. The Romans, to fecure their conqueft, eftablifhed there a numerous colony. At length,

(*h*) Strabo, lib. x.
(*i*) Polybius, lib. iv.
(*k*) Strabo, lib. x.

" in

" in the thirteenth year of the reign of
" Nero (*l*), the whole island suffering by a
" violent earthquake, Cnossus was totally de-
" stroyed." (*m*) The lightning, during this
tremendous calamity, did not proceed from
the clouds, but from the earth, and the sea
retreated seven stadia (*n*). Several tombs burst
open, in one of which was found the work
of Dictys of Crete, containing the events of
the Trojan war.

From that time the lofty Cnossus, humbled
in the dust, has never risen from her ruins, but
heaps of stones, ancient walls half demolished,
the remains of edifices, and the name of *Cnoffou*, which the spot it stood on still retains,
enable us to assign, with certainty, its ancient
situation. These ruins were, no doubt, much
more considerable before the building of Candia: because, as they were so near, it may
well be believed the Venetians made use of
them, as materials for the ramparts and houses
of that capital.

Leaving Cnossou on our left, we continued
our journey. As soon as we had reached the

(*l*) Septimius in Epist. ad Arcad.
(*m*) Philostratus in Vita Apollonii.
(*n*) Suidas.

lofty

lofty hills, which range along the foot of
Mount Ida, on the eaft, the country prefented
the moft agreeable profpects. At different
diftances we difcovered vallies clad with verdure, fmall villages, fituated on the banks of
rivulets, environed with beautiful orchards,
and interfperfed here and there with tufts
of branching trees, which crowned the hil-
locks.

We were about four leagues to the fouth-
eaft of Candia, and employed in climbing a
very fteep path, when our guides apprifed us
that we were paffing near the *tomb of Jupiter.*
We laboured up the mountain to view this
ancient monument, but faw nothing but a
heap of ftones, half eaten away by time, which
the inhabitants of the country call the tomb of
Jupiter.

Both the fables and hiftories of antiquity
agree that a Jupiter died, and was buried in
the ifland of Crete. The third Jupiter, the fon
of Saturn (*o*), was born there, and his tomb
is

(*o*) Cicero de Natura Deorum, lib. iii. Arnob.
lib. iv. The third Jupiter, fon of Saturn, was buried
in the ifland of Crete. (Theophilus, lib. i.) Jupiter,
fon of Saturn, who was king of Crete, has a tomb
in

is ftill fhewn there *(p)*. Jupiter having ended his days in Crete, his relations and friends, in obedience to his laft commands, erected a temple and a tomb to his memory. This temple ftill fubfifted in the days of Plato ; but time, or earthquakes, have deftroyed it. This philofopher, who was well acquainted with the places he defcribes, fpeaks of it thus *(q)*. " The road, which leads from Cnoffus to the " cavern and temple of Jupiter, is very plea- " fant. We continually meet with alleys of " large tufted trees, whofe foliage fhelters us " from the fcorching beams of the fun. If " we proceed ftill further, we find woods " of cyprefs-trees, of furprifing height and " beauty ; by the fide of which are delight- " ful meadows, where travellers may repofe, " and converfe."

From all thefe authorities we may conclude,

---

in that ifland. (Pomponius Mela, lib. ii. cap. 7.) We fee in Crete a tomb, where, it is almoft impoffible to doubt, that Jupiter was buried. The inhabitants fhew the remains of the infcription, which proves the fact. (Chryfoftom, in Epift. Pauli ad Titum.) The Cretans poffefs the tomb of Jupiter, on which we read this infcription : *Here lies Zan, who is called Jupiter.*

(p) Cedrenus.

(q) Plato de Legibus, lib. i.

that

that a man, called Jupiter, who, by great actions, merited well of his fubjects, and on
whom divine honours were beftowed, died
in the ifland of Crete ; that a temple was
erected to him, which has been deftroyed by
time ; that his tomb was fhewn with an infcription on it, until the time of the Roman
Emperors, and that at prefent there is to be
feen, about three leagues from Cnoffus, an
eminence, commonly called Mount Icarus, on
the top of which the inhabitants of the country point out a heap of ftones, which they
call the tomb of Jupiter. As for the facred
cavern, in which he was brought up, and to
which Minos repaired every ninth year, to
converfe with his father, and receive his laws,
it may be prefumed not to have been far
diftant from this place (r), but we did not
fee it.

As

(r) The ancients almoft always join together the cavern
and the tomb of Jupiter. Plato fays, the cave and temple of
Jupiter : becaufe in his time the fepulchre was embellifhed
with a temple. Minutius Felix fays, " Jupiter reigned in
" Crete. . . . . We ftill fee his cave and tomb." The conftant mention of the tomb and cavern together, feems to in-
dicate that thefe monuments were not diftant from each other.

The

As we defcended the hill, we met with a village wedding, on its way to the neighbouring hamlet. A great number of Greeks, mounted on horfes and mules, compofed the efcort of the bride, who was furrounded by a company of handfome girls. They were all decked out in their beft array, and their long white veils fell gracefully on their fhoulders : the men wore fine coloured fafhes, and all appeared extremely merry. We thought it a neceffary piece of French politenefs to falute the bride, and drawing up in a line, as fhe paffed, gave her a general difcharge of mufketry. Thofe among the Greeks who had arms, returned the compliment, and we feparated with mutual expreffions of refpect.

We now defcended into the plain, where, though it was the month of November, we found the heat confiderable. We were to fleep at the convent of St. George, from which we were ftill three leagues diftant, and in our road had to pafs feveral ranges of hills, which form the bafis of Mount Ida on the eaft. The

The ancients place the facred cavern at the foot of Mount Ida. Plato defcribes it as on one fide of Cnoffus. The fituation of Mount Icarus fufficiently correfponds with thefe indications.

country

country prefented a great variety of the moft picturefque profpects. Sometimes, from the fummit of a hill, we difcovered an immenfe horizon, terminated by mountains which concealed their heads in clouds; and prefently ftraying along the bottom of profound vallies, adorned with fruit-trees, and flowering fhrubs, we feemed as if imprifoned by the vaft and fteep declivities on each fide. At length, after having continued afcending a long time, we perceived at a diftance the monaftery of St. George, the fight of which gave us no little pleafure, and we redoubled our pace. It was evening when we entered the court. The monks, at firft, were alarmed at our number; and the fuperior, according to cuftom, concealed himfelf. But we had a perfon with us who was perfectly acquainted with the Greeks and their fubterfuges. He addreffed himfelf to fome of the fathers, telling them, that we had with us the French conful, who was going to Canea, and who, as he had great influence with thofe in power in that country, was able to render effential fervices to their bifhop, and all the convents in the ifland. They did not fail to convey this information to the fuperior, who inftantly came

to

to receive and compliment us, and immediately all the doors were thrown open to our company.

We had travelled feven computed leagues, equal to ten French ones, and our horfes were much tired. As foon as we had alighted, feveral children came to take them by the bridle, and walked them about for a quarter of an hour, before they put them into the ftable. This cuftom is conftantly obferved in Crete : they never fhut up the horfes when in a fweat, but always make a rule of walking them about fome time in the open air. . Hence the Cretan horfes are ftrong, healthy, and fcarcely ever tire. They boldly climb the fteepeft rocks, and defcend the fame into the vallies, without ftumbling. The traveller's life depends on the furenefs of their footing : for he frequently paffes along narrow paths on the edge of dreadful precipices, where a fingle falfe ftep would infallibly be his deftruction.

While fupper was preparing, one of the monks earneftly requefted us to vifit his cell. He was a lover of good wine, which indeed might be feen in his countenance, and he regaled us in the beft manner he could with his beloved liquor. It is true, he had but one

cup,

cup, but that was large and deep; he circulated it brifkly, and feemed highly pleafed with the encomiums we beftowed on his wine.

The monks of Saint George poffefs extenfive lands on which they feed numerous flocks, and which produce corn, barley, wine, oil, wax, and honey, in abundance. The Turks have left them thefe lands, on condition of their exercifing hofpitality towards all travellers, which they commonly do with a tolerable good grace. Both riders and horfes are lodged and fupplied with provifions. Thefe houfes are of great ufe in a country where there are neither inns nor caravanferas: for without them, the traveller would be obliged to carry with him a load of baggage, and every neceffary of life. The monks cultivate their fields themfelves, and owe what they enjoy to the labour of their hands.

A magnificent repaft (*) was ferved up to us: the middle difh was a roafted pig, round which were excellent mutton, pigeons, and very fine poultry; the reft of the table was

(*) The French word is *ambigu*. An ambigu is an entertainment confifting of both meat and fruits. T.

I   covered

covered with plates of pomegranates, almonds, grapes, frefh olives, and honey. This honey, as tranfparent as cryftal, was delicious ; as highly perfumed as the flowers themfelves, as delicate as the fineft fweet-meats, and equally grateful to the fmell and tafte. The fuperior fet before us moft exquifite wines ; red, white, and orange-coloured, the produce of the hills round the monaftery, on which we alternately beftowed the higheft commendations.

After fupper we were conducted to a fpacious hall, where, notwithftanding the hardnefs of our beds, we perfectly well enjoyed the pleafures of repofe. To fhew refpect to the French conful, they had allotted him a feparate apartment, and placed two full decanters by his bed-fide. In the morning, he wifhed to wafh his mouth, and pouring out fome of the fuppofed water, found it to be white wine. He took the other decanter, and filled his glafs, but this proved to be pure brandy. No doubt, thefe good monks are accuftomed to make libations to the god of fleep, or to confole themfelves for his rigours with the bottle.

I have the honour to be, &c.

L E T T E R XXIII.

To M. L. M.

OUR intention being to vifit Gortyna and
the Labyrinth; we fet out early in the
morning, from the monaftery of St. George,
and after thanking our hofts, who politely
furnifhed us with provifions for our breakfaft, directed our courfe toward the fouthern
part of the ifland, and continued defcending for, two hours from the convent into
the plain. The journey was lefs fatiguing
than the preceding day. We travelled through
a beautiful country interfperfed with villages,
and furrounded with olive and almond trees.
The declivities of the hills on the right and
left prefented us with charming landfcapes.
This whole diftrict appeared rich and populous; but the time of harveft and the
vintage being over, we met with but few inhabitants, who were fhut up in their houfes,
occupied in domeftic labours.

After

After fome hours travelling, a little path, lined with verdant turf, and watered by a limped ftream, which meandered through the valley, invited us to halt. We fpread out the provifions of the good monks, and breakfafted at the foot of a plane-tree. Our journey had fharpened our appetites, and we found our repaft delicious. The water of the fountain was cool and pure, and a few bottles of wine rendered it ftill better. Our breakfaft was very cheerful and agreeable, but foon over; we re-mounted our horfes, and continued our journey.

Our way lay over a level ground, in-clofed between two chains of mountains, the fides of which were furrowed by the channels of limpid ftreams. Numerous flocks of goats and fheep were feeding on thyme, or browfing on the leaves of wild fhrubs. Here a cottage, furrounded with vineyards, fhewed itfelf on the fummit of a rock; and there another lay concealed in the obfcurity of a thicket. Our eyes were amufed on every fide with the agree-able and variegated profpeffs, and we made a great progrefs in our journey without per-ceiving it.

The fun had run half his courfe; and we had been feven hours on horfeback, when

Q   we

we arrived at a large town, the inhabitants of which have not the beft of characters. They are accufed of a difpofition to rob travellers; but, confiding in our arms, we refolved to afk for a dinner. We were very indifferently received in feveral houfes, and the forbidding appearance of thofe who lived in them made us go on further, till, at length, we knocked at a door, where we found the inhabitants better inclined. We did not find, indeed, the fplendid table of our rich monks. Eggs, olives, honey, and bad cheefe, were all they offered us; and for thefe we paid generoufly. When leaving this villanous place, many of the inhabitants infulted us with ill language; but the fight of our mufquets levelled at them, and the drawn fabres of our janiffaries, foon filenced them.

We now entered the plain of Meffara, which is feven leagues in length, and extends as far as the fea on the fouth fide of the ifland. It is the moft fertile in corn of any in the kingdom of Candia; the foil here is excellent, and the crop never difappoints the expectation of the hufbandman. A ftrait and good road here fhewed us we approached Gortyna ; the ruins of which we foon difcovered, and fpent feveral hours in examining.

The origin of Gortyna is uncertain; the opinions of authors varying on the fubject. We know, however, that it is of the higheft antiquity. Homer fpeaks of it, as of a power-ful city defended by walls. It was a flou-rifhing place when Lycurgus travelled into Crete. Some fay it was founded by Gor-tynus, fon of Tegetes (*t*). Plato tells us, it was built by a colony from Gortyna, a city of Peloponnefus ; and feveral ancient writers affert that Taurus, who carried off Europa, and who reigned in Crete, founded this celebrated city (*u*).

(*t*) Stephanus Byzantius. Gortyna received its name from the hero Gortynus. It was alfo called Lariffa, Crem-nia, and at length Gortyna. (Paufanias in Arcadicis.) It is related that Cydon, Catreus and Gortynus, fons of Tegetes, paffed into the ifland of Crete, and gave their names to Cydon, Catrea, and Gortyna. But the Cretans reject this account, and fay that Cydon was the fon of Mer-cury, and Acacallidis the daughter of Minos ; that Catreus was the fon of Minos, and Gortynus, of Rhadamanthus.

(*u*) Plato de Legibus, lib. iv.

How-

However well or ill founded thefe different accounts may be, Gortyna, fituated in a plain of vaft extent, watered by numerous rivulets, fertile in corn, barley, olives, and all kinds of productions, became one of the moft confiderable cities of the ifland. It was only five leagues diftant from the fea, on the fouth-fide, on which it had two harbours (v); Lebena, where was a famous temple (w), and Metalla, fituated at the extremity of the cape fo called. The people of Gortyna knew how to avail themfelves of thefe advantages, and became exceedingly powerful. They united their arms with thofe of the Cnoffians to fubdue the neighbouring cities, and greatly extended the limits of their territory. Their walls were more than two leagues in circumference; but

(v) Euftathius in Dionyfium. Gortyna was built by Taurus, who carried off Europa the Phœnician, and who reigned in Crete. (Chron. Alexand.) Taurus founded, in the ifland of Crete, a city which he called Gortyna, from the name of his mother, the grand-daughter of Jupiter. (Cedrenus.) Taurus built in Crete the city of Gortyna, fo called after his mother's name.

(w) Strabo, lib. x. Gortyna has two ports on the Lybian fea; Lebena, from which it is only four leagues diftant, and Metella, fituated two leagues beyond.

2

having

having been deftroyed by time, the magiftrates began repairing them, but finifhed
only eight ftadia, leaving the reft of the town
open (*x*).   Strabo attributes the rebuilding
thefe walls *(y)* to Ptolemy Philopater; but
adds, that he did not complete them, and
that they remained unfinifhed.

Gortyna contained feveral temples, among
which the moft remarkable were thofe of
Apollo (*z*), Jupiter (*a*), and Diana (*b*).   The
firft was held in great veneration by the
people of Greece, who, in the time of a
plague, fent thither deputies to confult its
oracle (*c*).   Menelaus, going in purfuit of
Helen, facrificed in the fecond a hecatomb
to Jupiter; and Hannibal, dreading left the
avarice of the Gortynians might tempt them
to deliver him up to his enemies, in order
to obtain his treafures, the report of which
had preceded his arrival, depofited, in prefence

(*x*) Phranzes, Chron. lib. i.
(*y*) Strabo, lib. x.
(*z*) Stephan. Byzant.   In the middle of Gortyna was
the temple and altar of Apollo.
(*a*) Photius Biblioth. Hift. lib. v.
(*b*) Æmilius Probus.
(*c*) Antonius Liberalis, metamorph. 25.

of

of the people, veſſels filled with lead, and
covered with gold and ſilver, in the temple
of Diana, declaring that he confided to them
his fortune. Shortly after, however, he took
an opportunity to eſcape into Aſia with his
riches encloſed in brazen ſtatues ; but the implacable vengeance of Rome purſued him
every where. The Lethe ran near Gor-
tyna *(d)*. Strabo (*e*) aſſures us that he croſſed
it. This city having undergone frequent
revolutions, the river may have, at ſome
period, flowed round its walls, and, at others,
through the city ; for it is certain that, at
preſent, ruins are diſcoverable beyond this
river, which is now only a tolerably large
rivulet. It was called Lethe, becauſe Har-
monia, the daughter of Venus, forgot her
huſband Cadmus on its banks *(f)*. Geographers reckon ſeveral rivers of this name.
Strabo enumerates four (*g*).

The

(d) Solinus. The river Lethe runs near Gortyna, where
Taurus carried off Europa.

(*e*) Strabo. The river Lethe runs through the city of
Gortyna.

(*f*) Vibius Sequeſter, de Amnibus.

(g) Magneſia was ſituated on the Meander, where the
river

The ruins of Gortyna cover a vaſt extent of ground, and enable us to form ſome idea of its ancient magnificence. Such of its monuments as ſtill ſubſiſt, are not of the higheſt antiquity. One of the moſt remarkable is a gate built with large bricks, which have been formerly covered with freeſtone; thoſe of the ſides and arch-way have been detached, yet it ſtill does, and muſt long continue to ſubſiſt. This edifice is of a conſiderable thickneſs, and preſents an extenſive front. It cannot be ſuppoſed more ancient than the time when Ptolemy Philopater undertook to rebuild the walls of Gortyna. Beyond this gate, we find a large open ſpace, in form nearly a parallelogram, on each ſide of which is a double row of pedeſtals. The baſes of the marbles are buried, and the tops alone appear above the ground. The order in which they are ranged gives reaſon to conjecture they were part of the portico of a temple. At different intervals we meet

river Lethe falls into it; another river of the ſame name runs near Gortyna; a third bathes Tricca, a city of Theſſaly; and we find a fourth Lethe in the weſtern part of Africa.

with

with heaps of rubbifh, and columns of marble, and of granite, buried up to the middle
of their fhafts. The capitals lie near them,
broken off; but feveral of them have none.
Near the farther end of thefe ruins, on
the banks of that beautiful river, where Har-
monia forgot Cadmus, we enter a church,
one fide of which is deftroyed. Its architecture is fimple, without colonnades;
and it is about one hundred and twenty
feet long, by fixty wide. This is probably the ancient cathedral founded by Titus,
the difciple of Saint Paul. Some confiderable ruins, fituated at a little diftance, may
be the remains of the palace of the archbifhop.

These ruins do not appear fuitable to what
might be expected from the grandeur and
magnificence of Gortyna. But we muft confider that the fineft marbles have been carried
off, that we fee, in adjacent villages, ancient
columns employed in making gates for the
Turkifh gardens, and that the greateft part
of its ornaments are buried under the earth,
which is confiderably raifed. If the ground
were dug into, and proper refearches made,
we fhould certainly find ftatues and valuable
anti-

antiquities. At prefent, the hufbandman paffes his plough over them, and covers with
his harveft the ruins of the palaces and temples of Gortyna. Such, Madam, is the deftiny of ancient cities. They are the work
of man, and perifh like himfelf. Thofe
which, in ages paft, were the ornament, or
terror of the world, Thebes, Memphis and
Babylon, are now no more. Can you imagine that Paris, that noble city, which contains within itfelf all the arts, and innumerable inhabitants, will exift for ever? Can
you doubt that the curious traveller fhall
one day wander amid heaps of rubbifh, in
fearch of the fituation of her temples and her
palaces? Let us confole ourfelves: that period
is ftill very remote.

We quitted the plain of Gortyna to vifit
the Labyrinth. The road leading to this memorable place is rough and fteep; but, after
an afcent of near an hour, we, at length,
reached the entrance. We had brought with
us the thread of Ariadne, that is to fay, four
hundred fathoms of twine, which we faftened to the gate, where we ftationed two
janiffaries, with orders to fuffer nobody to
enter. The opening of the Labyrinth is
natural,

natural, and not wide. When you have advanced a little, you find a confiderable fpace ftrewed with large ftones, and covered with a flat roof cut out of the folid mountain. To difcern our way amid this gloomy abode, we each carried a flambeau. Two Greeks bore the clew, which they unfolded or wound up as occafion required. At firft we loft ourfelves in different alleys without an opening, and were obliged to meafure back our fteps, but at length difcovered the true paffage, which is on the right as we enter; we arrive at it by a narrow path, and are obliged to creep on our hands and feet for the fpace of an hundred yards, the roof being extremely low. At the end of this narrow paffage the ceiling rifes fuddenly, and we were able to walk upright, in the midft of the impenetrable darknefs that furrounded us, and the numerous ways which ftruck off on each fide, and croffed each other in different directions. The two Greeks we had hired trembled with apprehenfion; the fweat poured down their faces, and they refufed to advance, unlefs we took the lead.

The alleys through which we paffed were in general from feven to eight feet high; in

width

width they varied from fix to ten, and fometimes more. They are all chiffeled out of the rock, and the ftones, of a dirty grey, are ranged in horizontal layers. In fome places, huge blocks of ftone, half detached from the roof, feem ready to fall on your head, and you muft ftoop in paffing them, not without fome danger of their falling. This havock has, no doubt, been occafioned by earthquakes, which are fo frequent in Crete.

Thus did we continue wandering in this maze, of which we endeavoured to difcover all the windings, and as foon as we had got to the end of one alley, entered into another. Sometimes we were ftopped fhort by a paffage without an opening, and at others, after long circuits, were aftonifhed to find ourfelves at the crofs-way from which we had fet out. Frequently, after encircling with our cord a great extent of rock, we were obliged to wind it up, and return the way we came. It is impoffible to defcribe to what a degree thefe paffages are multiplied and crooked; fome of them form curves which lead you infenfibly to a vaft empty fpace, fupported by enormous pillars, whence three or four paffages ftrike off that

conduct

conduct to oppofite points ; others, after long windings, divide into feveral branches : thefe again extend a great length, and, terminated by the rock, oblige the traveller to trace back his way. We walked with precaution in the doublings of this vaft Labyrinth, amid the eternal darknefs that reigns throughout it, and which our torches could hardly difpel. Thus fituated, the imagination raifes up phantoms ; it figures to itfelf precipices under the feet of the curious, monfters placed as centinels, and, in a word, a thoufand chimeras which can have no exiftence.

The precaution we had taken of proceed-ing with the thread of Ariadne, and of faf-tening it at different diftances left it fhould break, allowed us to advance farther than Belon, Tournefort, and Pocock, were able to do for want of fuch affiftance. We obferv-ed, in feveral parts of the middle avenue, the cyphers 1700 written with a black pen-cil, by the hand of the celebrated French botanift. An extraordinary circumftance which he remarks, and which we admired no lefs than he had done, is the property poffeffed by the rock of prefenting the names engraven on it in relief. We faw feveral

of

of them, wherein this fort of fculpture had arifen to the thicknefs of two lines (the fixth part of an inch). The fubftance of this re-lief is whiter than the ftone (*h*).

After ftraying for a long time in the fright-ful cavern of the Minotaur (*i*), we arrived at the extremity of the alley which Tourne-fort followed. There we found a wide fpace, with cyphers cut in the rock, none of which were of an earlier date than the fourteenth cen-tury. There is another fimilar to this on the right; each of them may be about twenty-four or thirty feet fquare. To arrive at this place we had run out almoft all our line, that is to fay, about twenty-four hundred feet, without mentioning our various excurfions. We re-mained three hours in the Labyrinth, con-tinually walking, without being able to flatter · ourfelves with having feen every thing. I believe it would be impoffible for any man

---

(*h*) Several of us engraved our names deeply at the end of 1779. At the time of preparing thefe letters for publica-tion, I am informed that the hollow is already filled with this white fubftance, which projects about a line (the twelfth of an inch) above the names.

(*i*) The reader will fee in the following letter why I give it this name.

to get out of it, if left there without either clew or flambeau ; he would lofe himfelf in a thoufand windings : the horrors of the place, and the intenfe darknefs, would fill him with confternation, and he muft miferably perifh.

On our return, we examined a winding we had not before noticed ; it conducted us to a beautiful grotto, rifing into a dome, wrought by the hand of nature. It has no ftalactites, nor indeed is a fingle one to be found in the whole extent of the cavern, as the water does not filtrate through the roof. Every thing is dry; and, as the air is never renewed, the fmell is extremely difagreeable. Thoufands of bats, the dung of which lies in heaps, inhabit this gloomy abode. They are the only monfters we difcovered. We came out with a great deal of pleafure, and breathed the external air with a kind of rapture. Night now began to come on, and the road was not very eafy to be found ; we haftened, therefore, to defcend the mountain, and entered a neighbouring farm, where we were very hofpitably entertained by a Turk.

I have the honour to be, &c.

L E T-

L E T T E R XXIV.

To M. L. M.

SEVERAL authors, Madam, among whom are Befon (*k*) and Pocock (*l*), pretend that the Labyrinth, which I have been defcribing, is no more than a quarry, from which ftones were brought to build the city of Gortyna. M. Tournefort *(m)* has fatisfactorily confuted this opinion ; he has proved that the ftone of this cavern is too foft to be fit for building, and that it would have coft enormous fums to convey it acrofs the fteep mountains that lie between the Labyrinth and the city. It muft have been much more natural for the inhabitants to procure their ftone from the mountains in the vicinity of Gortyna. Had the Labyrinth been

(k) Obfervations de plufieurs Singularités et Chofes memorables trouvées en Gréce, &c.

(l) Defcription of the Eaft.

(m) Voyage du Levant.

but

but an ordinary quarry, why leave at the entrance a channel a hundred yards long, fo low as not to be acceffible but by creeping, and from whence ftones could not be brought until broken in pieces? This would have been to double both labour and expence to no purpofe. It is much more probable, adds M. Tournefort, that nature has produced the Labyrinth, and that the paffage at the entrance has not been altered, to fhew pofterity what was the ftate of thefe fubterranean channels before they were enlarged by the hand of man. It is evident, that nothing more has been attempted than merely to render them paffable, fince only thofe ftones have been cleared away which have obftructed the paffage; all the others have been left, and are ranged in order along the walls.

But for what purpofe was this Labyrinth intended? Is it of great antiquity? And was it there the Minotaur was confined? Thefe are queftions which, I believe, have never been anfwered. Let us endeavour, if poffible, to refolve them. The difcovery of truth, obfcured by the lapfe of time, gives

plea-

pleafure to the reader, and amply recom-
penfes the labour of inveftigation.

In the firft place, it is certain that the
immenfe cavern, the windings of which I have
defcribed, is not the Labyrinth formed by
Dædalus, on the plan of that of Egypt (*n*).
All the ancient writers atteft, that the famous
work of that celebrated architect was fituated
at Cnoffus. " It was agreed," fays Paufanias,
" to fend to the Minotaur of Crete feven vir-
" gins and feven boys, to be thrown into the
" Labyrinth built in the city of Cnoffus (*o*)."
" As foon as Apollonius arrived at Cnofius,
" he vifited the Labyrinth *(p)*," &c.

(q) John Tzetzes very fatisfactorily defcribes
this famous edifice, and informs us of the
ufe for which it was intended. " Dædalus,
" the Athenian, made for king Minos a pri-
" fon, from which it was impoffible to efcape.

(*n*) Diodorus Siculus, lib. i. It is faid that Dædalus,
travelling into Egypt, was ftruck with admiration at
the fight of the Labyrinth conftructed with wondrous
art, and that he formed a fimilar one for Minos king of
Crete.

(*o*) Paufanias in Atticis.

(p) Philoftratus, in Vitâ Apollonii.

(*q*) Johannes Tzetzes.

R   " Its

" Its numerous windings were in the form
" of a fnail, and it was called the Labyrinth."
Philocorus (*r*) afferts, after the unanimous
teftimony of the Cretans, that " the La-
" byrinth was a prifon contrived more effec-
" tually to prevent the efcape of male-
" factors."

Such then was the plan of that celebrated
work of antiquity, conftructed on the model
of that of Egypt. It was a prifon wherein
Thefeus and his companions were to end their
days, or live deprived of honour. But love
and courage extricated them from their danger. This Labyrinth fubfifts no longer. It
was indeed already deftroyed in the days
of Pliny. Let us therefore proceed to confider that which is ftill exifting.

Permit me, Madam, to go fomewhat further back, in order to throw a little light on
a few obfcure facts, mingled with fo many
fables. By collecting the various opinions of
ancient authors, perhaps, we may be able to

(*r*) Plutarch, in Thefeo.

remove

remove the veil which conceals truth. You know that Androgeos, fon of Minos, went to Athens, and that Ægeus, at his return from Trœzene (s), celebrated what were called the Panathenaic games, to which all Greece repaired. The Cretan hero entered the lifts, vanquifhed all the combatants, and was publicly crowned (t). This prince entered into a friendly alliance with the Pallantides, who made pretenfions to the throne. Ægeus, dreading the confequences of this friendfhip, had him affaffinated near Œnan in Attica, when on his way to a facred folemnity.

(u) Minos foon appeared at the head of a naval armament, to demand vengeance for the death of his fon ; and, after a long and bloody fiege, during which Athens was ravaged by the plague, Ægeus, incapable of defending himfelf any longer, demanded of the king of Crete what fatisfaction he required. That prince infifted on his fending him, every fe-

(s) Apollodorus, lib. iii.
(t) Diodorus Siculus, lib. iv.
(u) Apollodorus, lib. iii.

R 2   venth

venth year (*v*), feven boys and feven girls, to be delivered to the Minotaur. Thefe unhappy victims were abandoned to him, and he carried them off in his fleet. At the ftated time he again appeared with a number of fhips, and was fatisfied in like manner.

Thefe children were chofen by lot, and the parents of thofe on whom the fatal chance fell, murmured loudly againft Ægeus. They were filled with indignation, on reflecting that the author of the mifchief fhould alone efcape the punifhment (*x*); and that he fhould raife to the throne a natural fon (*y*), while he deprived them of their legitimate children. They were even ripe for a revolt. But when the time for fending the third tribute arrived,

(*v*) Diodorus, lib. iv. fays, that they were fent every feven years. Apollodorus fays, every year. Plutarch (in Vitâ Thefei) afferts, that this tribute took place only once in nine years. Thefe opinions, though they vary refpecting the number of years, all confirm the fact.

(*x*) Plutarch, in Vitâ Thefei.

(*y*) Hygin. Fab. xxxvii. Neptune and Ægeus, fons of Pandion, had amorous commerce, in the fame night, with Æthra, daughter of Pytheus, in the temple of Minerva. Thefeus fprang from this union. Ifocrates fays, he was called the fon of Ægeus, but that Neptune was really his father.

1

Thefeus,

Thefeus, whom feveral gallant actions had already raifed to the fame of a hero, and who, in the bloom of youth, united every endowment of mind and body (z), was determined to put an end to thefe murmurs. He voluntarily offered himfelf to be one of the victims, refolving to perifh, or free his country from an odious tribute ; and departed, after facrificing to Apollo at Delphi, who directed him to take Venus for his guide (a).

Let us now endeavour to difcover the true meaning of the fable of the Minotaur. Taurus was the name of one of the principal men of Crete, who was a native of Cnoffus (b). His valour, and other great qualities, no doubt, recommended him to Minos, who made choice

(z) Servius ad Æneid, lib. vi. Thefeus was as beauteous as brave. (Ifocrates) I may fay to the praife of Thefeus, that, being born in the time of Hercules, he fo comported himfelf as to merit a like glory. Not only did they bear the fame arms, but they applied to the fame exercifes of body and mind, as became two heroes of the fame blood.

(a) Plutarch. Thefeus having confulted the Delphic Apollo, before his departure, the oracle told him to take Venus for his guide.

(b) Ifaac Tzetzes ad Lycophron. Taurus was a native of Cnoffus, a city of Crete, and general of the army that carried off Europa.

of

of him to command an expedition againſt Phœnicia. " Taurus," adds Palæphatus, " a " citizen of Cnoſſus, made war on the Ty. " rians. Having overcome them, he carried " off ſeveral young women from their city, " among whom was Europa, daughter of " king Agenor. This it was that gave riſe " to the fable of a bull having ſeized Europa, " and carried her away. The poets, fond " of the marvellous, added, that ſhe was ra- " viſhed by Jupiter in the form of a bull."

The conqueror lived at the court of Minos : he had returned laden with the ſpoils of Tyre, and as he poſſeſſed the advantage of a fine perſon, the renown he had acquired by his military exploits, rendered him ſtill more handſome in the eyes of Paſiphaë, the daughter of the Sun, and wife of the king of Crete. She became enamoured of him, and finding means to gratify her paſſion (*c*), had a ſon by him. Minos having diſcovered " that this " child could not be his, but that he was the " fruit of the amours of Taurus and Paſiphaë, " would not, however, put him to death, but " confined him to the mountains, to ſerve the " ſhepherds. In theſe ſolitary abodes he grew

(*c*) Palæphat. de Fab.

" wild

" wild and fierce, and lived by robbery, and
" stealing sheep from the flocks. Having
" learnt that Minos had sent soldiers to take
" him, he dug a deep cavern, which he made
" his place of refuge. At length the king of
" Crete sent to the son of Taurus such cri-
" minals as he wished to punish with death."
His ferocity, and this employment, no doubt,
procured him the name of Minotaur, and induced poets and painters to represent him as
a monster, half a man, and half a bull. An
ingenious emblem, which had reference at
once to his birth, his character, and his odious services.

Theseus having landed in Crete, endeavoured to calm the anger of Minos, who had
fallen in love with *(d)* Pæribea, one of the
seven Athenian virgins. He convinced him,
that he was the son of Neptune, and endeavoured to mitigate the rigour of his fate.
The prince, almost disarmed, treated him at
first very favourably, and permitted him to
mix with the combatants in the public games.
The Athenian hero excited universal admiration (*c*) by his address and courage, and en-

(*d*) Plutarch, in Vitâ Thesei.
(*e*) Ibid.

chanted

chanted every heart with the gracefulnefs of his perfon *(f)*.

In Crete, women were permitted to be pre-fent at the public fhews *(g)*; and Ariadne faw Thefeus engage with, and overcome, the moft renowned warriors of her country; but while fhe admired the bravery and graces of the youthful hero, love ftole into her heart, and inflicted one of his deepeft wounds. It is probable fhe confefled her paffion to the con-queror; and that, to fulfil the precept of the oracle *(h)*, he profited by her declaration. It is natural to fuppofe alfo, that Minos, in-formed of this intrigue, confidered it as a new offence, and refolved to fhut him up in the Labyrinth of Cnoflus, that he might be for ever buried in the horrid obfcurity of that tremendous prifon. This conjecture is ren-dered more than probable by the following

(f) Servius, Euftathius, and Hyginus, agree in inform-ing us, that Thefeus united the utmoft gracefulnefs of perfon with a lofty ftature, ftrength, and courage.

(g) Plutarch (in Vitâ Thefei) fays, Thefeus was admitted to the public games of Crete; that he vanquifhed the warri-ors who entered the lifts againft him; and that Ariadne faw, and fell in love with him.

(h) Apollo, as we have feen, had commanded him to fa-crifice to Love.

paflage.

paſſage (*i*). " Theſeus arriving at the gate
" of the Labyrinth, encountered Deucalion
" and the guards, and put them to death."
So deſperate an action determined Minos no
longer to keep any meaſures with his enemy,
and he ſent him to Taurus, with orders to put
him to death (*k*).

You recollect, Madam, that Taurus was the
executioner of Minos; that he dwelt in a
profound cavern, in which he deſtroyed the
priſoners condemned to death. The ancients
aſſert, that the name of Labyrinth was given
alſo to this gloomy abode, in which art
aſſiſting nature, had formed new paſſages,
and contrived a multitude of windings, from
which it was almoſt impoſſible to eſcape.

" The Labyrinth of Crete (*l*) was a cavern
" dug out of a mountain." Cedrenus adds
theſe remarkable words (*m*): " The Minotaur
" fled to a place called the Labyrinth, and
" concealed himſelf there, in the depth of a
" cavern."—" (*n*) The Labyrinth of Crete,

(*i*) Plutarch, in Vitâ Theſei.
(*k*) Palæphat. de Incredibilibus.
(*l*) Auctor. Etymologic.
(*m*) Cedrenus.
(*n*) Euſtathius, in Odyſſ.

" that fubterraneous cavern, with a thoufand " windings, contained an inhabitant."

Thefe teftimonies, Madam, remove all doubt. They accurately defcribe the Laby- rinth I vifited; its fituation in a mountain, its winding paffages, fufficiently prove it con- tained an inhabitant. This could be no other than the fon of Taurus, who, in order to efcape the emiffaries of Minos, dug a cavern in the mountain. This horrid place was his abode, and, in part, his work; and here the monfter performed the bloody executions commanded by the king. The following facts will clearly demonftrate thefe affertions. But let us return to Thefeus.

(*o*) Condemned to fuffer an ignominious death by the hand of the executioner of Minos, the Athenian hero departed from Gor- tyna; and, ignorant of the deftiny that await- ed him, muft have fallen, but for Love, who watched over his life. Ariadne, alarmed, in- formed him of the fnare laid for him. She defcribed to him the windings and dangers

(*o*) Minos, getting his enemy Thefeus into his power, fent him to be flain by Taurus. Ariadne, informed of this defign, fent him a fword, with which he flew the Minotaur. Palephat. de Incredib.

of

of the Labyrinth (*p*); gave him the thread by which he might direct his steps; taught him the method of making use of it, and sent him the sword that was to shed the hateful blood of the Minotaur.

It should seem as if Theseus had procured secret friends in the island, and that, by his address, his courage, or the good offices of his mistress, he had gained the guards, who attended on Taurus, and assisted him in his executions: for, as soon as he arrived at Gortyna, all of them, " forsaking the Mino-" taur (*q*), pretended to take to flight. The " monster, suspecting he was betrayed, fled. " into the place called the Labyrinth." These words clearly prove, that he escaped into the gloomy cavern I have before mentioned; which was a place of refuge, perhaps his fortress ; for there he put his victims to death.

(*p*) Plutarch, in Vita Thesei. Theseus arriving in the island of Crete, Ariadne fell desperately in love with him. She bore him a son, and taught him how to escape from the winding passages of the Labyrinth; and he slew the Minotaur.

(*q*) All the guards forsaking the Minotaur of Gortyna, pretended to take to flight. The Minotaur, suspecting treachery, took refuge in the place called the Labyrinth. Cedrenus.

Claudian,

Claudian, to diftinguifh this cavern from the
famous edifice built by Dædalus at Cnoffus (r),
calls it, " the Labyrinth of Gortyna, the ufual
" abode of the Minotaur."

The retreat of the executioner of Minos
might have been a feint. He might wifh to
draw his enemy into a cavern, with all the
avenues of which he was well acquainted, and
where it would have been eafy for him to
kill him, by attacking him at an advantage.
But Thefeus had the thread of Ariadne, her
fword, and his own undaunted courage. He
purfued the Minotaur through the winding
alleys of his den, came up with him, and put
him to death.

As foon as he had executed his defign, he
fled precipitately on board a veffel (s), taking
with him his miftrefs, and the young victims
he had faved. The remainder of the hiftory

(r) Claudian, in Sext. Conf. Honorii. It forms different circuits, which are neither inferior to the art with
which the Labyrinth of Gortyna, the ufual abode of the
Minotaur, is built, nor the windings of the river
Meander.

(s) Plutarch, in Vita Thefei. He flew the Minotaur, and
immediately haftened on board his fhip, carrying with him
Ariadne, and the young Athenians.

of

of Ariadne and Thefeus is well known; not to mention that it is foreign to my fubject.

This is what appears.to me moft probable concerning the Labyrinths of Crete. One of them, fituated at Cnoffus, was an edifice built by Dædalus (*t*), and which, on account of its various windings, deceived thofe who got bewildered in it, and prevented their return. It was in the form of a fnail, and of vaft magnitude, as well as great ftrength. Minos converted it into a royal prifon; but the criminals, confined there, were only deprived of their liberty.

The other, near Gortyna, and called by the ancients the Labyrinth of Gortyna, ftill fubfifts, and has been treated of in the preceding letter. It was partly the work of the fon of Taurus; but the firft fketch of it was given by nature. He indeed rendered the paffages more fpacious, and excavated new ones. In this cavern he deftroyed thofe who were fent to him by the king to be put to death. Thus have we vifited the gloomy habitation of a man, who, from the ferocioufnefs of his character, merited to be transformed into a monfter.

(*t*) Apollodorus, lib. iii.

There

There were feveral other fimilar labyrinths, more or lefs complicated. Near Nauplia, fays Strabo (*u.*), we fee caverns, in which labyrinths have been formed, and which are called the Cyclops.

I have the honour to be, &c.

(*u*) Strabo, lib. viii.

LETTER XXV.

To M. L. M.

LET us now, Madam, purſue our journey. The Turkiſh farmer, who had received us ſo kindly at our coming out of the Labyrinth, offered us the beſt entertainment in his power. But our bed was the carpet on which we ſupped, and we laid ourſelves down, booted as we were. In the morning, therefore, we were ſoon dreſſed, and we ſet out at ſun-riſe, after ſatisfying our hoſt, who accepted what we thought proper to give him.

For ſome hours, our way lay along the plain, and we had an eaſy and pleaſant road; but when we had arrived at the high lands, it became extremely rugged. We travelled along the ſides of the hills which terminate Mount Ida, to the ſouthward. Two chains of theſe hills formed, between us and that mountain, a double amphitheatre, above which it reared its majeſtic head. We could perceive large clouds, of a ſhining whiteneſs, ranging themſelves around its ſummit, and circling it with

a ſilver

a filver crown, which, illumined by the fun, fhone with a wonderful fplendor. Thefe clouds, obeying the law of attraction, after encompafling for fome hours the head of the mountain, fell in imperceptible drops on all the furrounding objects, and intirely difappeared; others fucceeded, and were diffipated in the fame manner.

This attractive power, univerfally diffufed, which forces the clouds towards the tops of lofty mountains, is the origin of fprings, fountains, ftreams, and all the rivers on the globe. In the higher regions of the air, where the rifing vapours are condenfed by cold, the water of the clouds is converted into hail and fnow; but if they attain only a moderate height, where the cold is not very great, they fall in mifts, rains, and copious dews. When the hills are covered with forefts, the fprings and rivulets become more numerous, as the leaves of trees poffefs the peculiar property of attracting the humidity diffufed throughout the atmofphere. To procure water for a dry country, nothing more would be neceffary than to plant foreft-trees on the hilltops. When we find the ancients beftowing the name of rivers on the Glaucus and the
Xanthus,

Xanthus, which run through Afia Minor, and
are now little more than inconfiderable brooks,
we are tempted to fufpect them of exaggera-
tion. But if we reflect that the hills, where
thefe rivers arife, are at prefent ftript of their
trees and foil, and no longer oppofe a barrier
to the paffage of the clouds, though formerly
crowned with lofty forefts, they attracted them
around their tops, and drew from them all
their moifture, we fhall find no difficulty in
believing that the Glaucus, the Xanthus, and
many other at prefent infignificant rivulets,
might anciently, when fed with more copious
fupplies, well deferve the appellation of rivers.

While we were journeying round Mount Ida,
we perceived the fummit gradually overcaft,
and foon after vanifh inveloped in a thick
mift; nor was it long before we again perceived the naked top whitened with heaps of
fnow, and the fides covered with the glittering
mantle of winter. We, however, who were
lefs elevated by twelve hundred fathom, enjoyed a delightful temperature. The fky was
clear and ferene, and the fun moved through
the azure vault in all his majefty and fplendor.
In the deep vallies on our left, myrtles and
laurel rofes fkirted the channels of the tor-

S   rents.

rents. Trees, in their brighteſt verdure, adorned the foot of the mountain; and, in the
month of November, we found groves, as green
and pleaſant as in the middle of ſpring.

Mount Ida begins near Candia, and ſtretches
from eaſt to weſt, as far as the White Mountains. It extends from the northern to the
ſouthern ſea, and is the higheſt in the iſland.
In manyi parts of it, the ſnow lies all the year.
From its ſummit we may diſcover the ſea of
Crete, and that of Lybia. The eye wanders
over an immenſe horizon, and diſcerns many
of the ſcattered iſlands of the Archipelago,
ſuch as Cytherea, Milo, and Argentiera. If
we confine our attention to the view of the
objects before us, they appear as in an immenſe
perſpective, and preſent proſpects highly varied,
and aſtoniſhingly rich and beautiful.

In ſummer, when the ſnows are melted,
vaſt plains, ſituated on the declivity of the
mountain, afford excellent paſturage for the
flocks. On that part of it oppoſite to Candia
are foreſts, conſiſting chiefly of maple and
green oak. The ſouthern ſides abound with
the ſtrawberry tree, privets, and rock-roſes.
The eaſtern brow is beautified with cedars,
pines, and cypreſſes; but on the weſt, its

perpendicular

perpendicular fides prefent nothing but piles
of rocks, impoffible to fcale. It is enriched
with an infinity of other plants, which would
delight the botanift, fuch as the true me-
lilot, the yellow-flowered marjoram, &c.
Abundant ftreams flow on every fide from its
fummits. Some rufh in torrents into the vallies, while others water the plains, which produce luxurious harvefts, or, diftributed by art,
maintain fecundity in the innumerable fruit-
trees, which grow round the villages. The
hill-fides, expofed to the powerful rays of the
fun, are clothed with vineyards, which produce exquifite wines ; and the olive-trees every
where conftitute the principal riches of the
country.

The diverfity of landfcapes, which conftantly charmed the eye, made us forget the
dangers to which we were expofed. For the
fpace of a league we rode along the flope of
a very high hill. On one fide, the ground
was as perpendicular as a wall, and on the
other was the channel of a torrent, two hundred feet deep, through which the water
rufhed, over the large flint-ftones, with a
violent noife. The path at laft grew fo narrow,
that when once fairly entered, it was impof-

fible

fible to difmount, but at the rifk of throwing
both ourfelves and our horfes into the abyfs
below. I can affure you, Madam, that, in
many places, the road was not more than a
foot and a half wide, though on the brink of
a tremendous precipice, which no one could
look down without fhuddering. We were
now convinced of the excellence of our horfes,
not one of which fo much as made a falfe
ftep. They feemed to feel the danger, trod
with caution, and examined where to put
their feet. In a wet place, however, mine made
a fmall flip, and tottered for a moment on
the brink of the precipice; but I kept my feat
firmly, and he recovered himfelf. We defcended from thefe heights by fo fteep a valley, that the rider's back was againft the
crupper of the horfe. But at length, after
ten hours ride, we arrived, in perfect fafety, at
the monaftery of Afomatos.

It was night, and our Janiffaries entering
firft, the fuperior thought the convent was
attacked by a body of Turks, and ran and hid
himfelf. But we had with us, as I have before faid, an interpreter, who was perfectly
acquainted with the manœuvres of thefe
monks; and who, after making diligent fearch,

at

at length difcovered his hiding-place. He
complimented him on the part of the French
conful, who had juft arrived; made him a
proffer of his good offices at Canea, and, by
alternately addreffing his vanity and felf-in-
tereft, completely gained his confidence and
favour. At firft we had been conducted into
the apartment ufually allotted to ftrangers,
where we muft have flept upon the floor, and
been contented with a meagre repaft; but ap-
pearances were greatly changed when we had
made the mafter our friend. He came in perfon
to congratulate the conful on his fafe arrival,
and invited us into a fpacious hall, in the
midft of which a table was fpread. We held
a converfation with him for fome time; and
our adroit interpreter, difcovering our hoft's
weak fide, flattered his vanity, and gave him
great hopes from the power and influence of
the conful. Nor was this labour thrown
away: we were quickly fupplied with every
thing we could wifh, and, including meat,
vegetables, and fruits, had not lefs than forty
difhes on the table. This was a charming
fight to hungry men, who had travelled the
whole day without eating; nor did we remain
idle fpectators. The fuperior honoured us
with

with his prefence, and heartily encouraged us
to fatisfy our appetites. He gave a private
key to a deacon, who ftood behind his chair,
who directly left the room, and foon returned with feveral bottles of old wine, the
odour of which was of itfelf a perfume. To
enliven the company, the good father drank
feveral glaffes to our healths, and infifted on
our returning the compliment. Towards the
end of our feaft, he was in fuch high fpirits,
that, thinking to amufe us, he propofed his
priefts fhould chant the *Kyrie eleifon.* We accepted his propofal; and immediately a number of children, deacons, and fub-deacons,
made their appearance, and, on a fignal given,
began the *Kyrie eleifon.* They fang through
their nofes, and produced fo frightful a noife,
that it was with the utmoft difficulty we could
refrain from laughing; but at length they
concluded their difcordant jargon, and we
clapped our hands in applaufe. We were
now in hopes that this entertainment was
ended, but he begged us to go through the
fame ceremony in French. On this, a young
man in our company ftruck up a lively fong,
and we all joined chorus. The fuperior, and
his brethren, were delighted with the fpright-

linefs

linefs of our *Kyrie cleifon*; but affirmed, their mufic was more folemn and majeftic; to which we readily fubfcribed.

Pardon me, Madam, for taking up your time with fuch trivial incidents; but nothing can, fometimes, better defcribe the character of the people we vifit. The Greeks, notwith-ftanding the contemptible ftate of debafement to which they are reduced, ftill retain a pride and vanity, that can only be equalled by their ignorance. By flattering thefe, you may obtain every thing; but if their foibles are not humoured, they become implacable enemies, and you are in no fmall danger of feeling the effects of their perfidious refentment. The ignorant fuperior of Afomatos wifhed to difplay his uncommon talents, and excite our admiration, by mingling his wretched voice with thofe of the priefts, giving them the pitch, and chanting with them the *Kyrie eleifon*; and the good cheer, choice wines, and excellent beds, we here met with, we entirely owed to a little well-timed complaifance, and the incenfe we offered to the vanity of our hoft.

I have the honour to be, &c.

L E T.

L E T T E R XXVI.

To M. L. M.

THE monaftery of Afomatos, Madam, is
fituated at the foot of Mount Ida, on the
fouth fide, and is fo near, that large pieces
of rock, that in many places hang over, feem
ready to fall upon it, and bury it under their
fragments. The other fide of the convent is
much more pleafing, and prefented us with
the agreeable profpects of orchards of jubjub
trees, with ripe fruit, and orange, lemon, and
almond trees. Thefe Monks poffefs large
plantations of olives, arable lands, and excellent vineyards on the hill-fides; and their
fields are fertilized by numerous rivulets.
Afomatos would be a delightful place, if it were
a little farther from the mountains.

We got on horfeback about feven in the
morning, and gave extravagant thanks to the
fuperior, who came to wifh us a good journey.
Our intention was to breakfaft at Arcadi, the
handfomeft monaftery in the ifland; and as it

was only three leagues diſtant, we expected to reach it in good time; but the roads were dreadful. We continued aſcending for an hour and a half, before we came to the top of the firſt chain of heights, that run parallel with Mount Ida, and on which Arcadi is built. We met with ſteep paths, cut out of the rock, and our horſes were obliged to clamber up ſteps of marble and granite, without ſlipping or ſtumbling, otherwiſe we muſt have been daſhed to pieces on the ſtones, or tumbled head-long into the torrents. I do not exaggerate the horror of the roads we had to paſs. The firſt time one unaccuſtomed to ſuch ways travels in Crete, he imagines his life in danger at every ſtep; but more experience ſoon relieves him from his fears: for there is no place ſo dangerous and dreadful, but it may be eaſily paſſed with the mules and horſes of the country.

We were repaid for our fatigues by the beauty of the proſpects which every where preſented themſelves to our view. We traverſed whole woods of ſtrawberries and privets, which never loſe their verdure. Firs, of a prodigious height, rear their heads amid the ſnow, and are the haunts of herds of

wild

wild goats. In the vallies, the courfe of the waters is traced by tufts of myrtle, fome branches of which were in flower, and mingled the verdant luftre of their foliage with that of the laurel rofe. The fheep were feeding on the brow of the rocks, and the cottages, furrounded with clumps of trees, formed landfcapes the eye was never wearied with admiring. Sometimes thefe profpects were fufficiently near to difcriminate every object, and at others, diftant and obfcure, prefented only light fhades, pleafingly fketched in the horizon.

After a fatiguing fourney of three hours, we arrived at the convent of Arcadi, where the fuperior received us politely, and ordered breakfaft to be prepared. This monaftery, fituated in Mount Ida, poffeffes very extenfive tracts of land, which are carefully cultivated by its numerous monks; and the oil, wine, corn, and wax, produced on them every year, amount in value to confiderable fums. The good fathers live much at their eafe, and are very hofpitable to travellers.

The apartments of this monaftery are built round a large court, in which is a handfome church, whither the Greeks of the neighbourhood

bourhood repair to divine fervice. Among
this numerous body of monks there are but
few priefts; the greater part of them do not
enter into holy orders, but ferve in quality of
brethren, and are employed in the moft fatiguing labours of agriculture. We vifited the
cellar, in which Tournefort (*u*) fays, he
reckoned a hundred cafks of wine; but we
faw only forty barrels full; thefe, however,
were very large. Into this cellar the fuperior defcends, at the end of every vintage, to
blefs the new wines, and the following is the
form of his benediction (*x*): " O Lord God,
" who loveft men, look down on this wine,
" and on thofe who fhall drink it. Blefs our
" cafks, as thou didft blefs the well of Jacob,
" the pool of Siloam, and the drink of thy
" holy apoftles. O Lord, who didft con-
" defcend to be prefent at the wedding of
" Cana, where, by changing of water into
" wine, thou manifeftedft thy glory to thy
" difciples, fend now thy holy Spirit on this
" wine, and blefs it in thy name. Amen."

After a plentiful breakfaft, we defired to
fee the library of the convent, of which we

(*u*) Voyage du Levant.
(*x*) Idem.

had

had heard fo much from the good monks. It was, as they faid, the moft valuable, numerous, and complete, in the ifland. We expected, therefore, to have found fome literary treafures, or at leaft the beft authors of ancient Greece. They conducted us into an apartment, where we faw about two hundred old volumes, ranged on fhelves, and covered with duft, which did not feem to have had the honour of a vifit for many a day. They confifted, in general, of books of devotion, fermons, and controverfial divinity. After turning over a great number, without finding any thing that merited attention, except a manufcript Homer, which they would not fell, we went to return our thanks to the fuperior, and fet out for Retimo.

Leaving the monaftery, we continued defcending for an hour to reach the plain. When there, we found a fmooth and level road, that lay through a country which, from its verdure and fecundity, may be compared to the county of Avignon, except that its trees and plants are different. It is impoffible to tire on a journey, when we travel through a fine country; we then congratulate ourfelves that we are on horfeback, and,

and, therefore, enabled to command a more
extenfive horizon, and lofe nothing of the
fituations, landfcapes, and beauties of nature.
When the temperature of the climate is mild,
we enjoy too the ferenity of the heavens, the
purity of the air, the coolnefs of the winds,
and exquifite perfumes exhaled on all fides
from the odoriferous plants. Shut up in a
carriage, the traveller lofes all thefe advantages; and we find, throughout the eaft, there
is no other mode of travelling but on horfes,
mules, or camels. Litters are only for the
women, who are condemned, by the jealoufy
of the men, to live in imprifonment, even
when on a journey.

A rich Jew merchant, fettled at Retimo,
quietly carried on his commerce there, by
virtue of a firman of the Porte, obtained for
him by the French conful. As it was his
intereft to keep well with his fucceffor, he
made great preparations to receive him. As
foon as he knew we were coming, he fent
the new conful a horfe, fuperbly caparifoned,
and we made a pompous entry into the town.
We alighted at the merchant's houfe, where
we found every conveniency we could defire.
That we might enjoy the coolnefs of the
evening,

evening, fupper was ferved up under a portico, open on one fide to the court-yard, and
on the other, to a garden full of orange-
trees. This was abfolutely a luxurious ban-
quet, in which our hoft difplayed a generofity,
and profufion, which I have not often feen.
The firft courfe confifted of three roafted lambs,
two of which were ftuffed. Thefe were followed by three turkeys: and fix partridges,
fix fat pullets, fix pigeons, and a dozen quails,
formed the third courfe. The table was then
covered with fruits, fweet-meats, almond and
piftachio tarts, and a variety of other de-
licacies. A long ride over fteep hills had
fharpened our appetites, and we did honour
to every difh ; efpecially as we did not
want for good wine. I here drank, for the
firft time, the *vin de loi* (*y*), which is but little
known in France, though it well deferves to
be fo.

To render the entertainment complete, a

(*y*) The name the French give to a white wine made
by the Jews at Retimo. The grape grows on the hill-
fides, expofed to the hotteft rays of the fun. This wine
excites a generous warmth in the ftomach, and has a
delicate fragrance and flavour, not refembling any of our
wines in France.

virtuofo

virtuofo of the country was fent for; this
was a Turk, who played on the violin during
part of the entertainment. Thefe men do not
know a fingle note of mufic, but play intirely
from memory, and often from imagination;
and execute every air, and every idea, which
may happen to occur. Sometimes he played
a feries of gay, lively, and light tunes, which
were very pleafing; but more frequently, his
mournful and melancholy mufic, imitating the
plaintive accents of the romance, excited in
the mind a more profound feeling. This
mufical *improvifatori* was, in fome refpects,
truly aftonifhing; his performance was greatly
varied, and fome of his paffages, which were
extremely tender, compelled, if I may ufe the
expreffion, both the heart and the ear to liften
to his melodious tones. He was very celebrated at Retimo; and I am of opinion that
even at Paris he would not have been heard
without pleafure.

With our hoft's good will we fhould have
paffed the night at table; but as we were to
fet out the next day, we were fhewn up ftairs
at midnight, to very neat apartments, where we
found foft and convenient beds, which feemed

to invite fleep. The God was lavifh of his favours, and fhedding his falutary balm on our wearied limbs, infufed through us the warmth of a new life.

I have the honour to be, &c.

LETTER XXVII.

To M. L. M.

RETIMO is the ancient *Rhitymnia* of Stephen the geographer. Ptolemy calls it *Rhi-
tymna*. It is a handfome town, fituated at the
entrance of a rich and fertile plain. It is not
large, and fcarcely contains fix thoufand inhabitants. A citadel, built on a rock, which
projects into the fea, would be fufficient for
its defence, were it not commanded by a
high hill, from which it might be battered
with artillery. The harbour, which is nearly
choaked up, is only capable of receiving barks
and fmall veffels. The Turks never trouble
themfelves to prevent or repair the ravages of
time, and behold with unconcern the moft
ufeful works become heaps of ruins. Their
harbours, therefore, are every where filling
up, and the commerce they attracted deferts
them, to feek more commodious fituations.
The French had formerly a vice-conful at
Retimo, to which place the fhips of Marfeilles
came to take in oil; but, for a long time paft,

T   they

they have not been able even to approach the town, and the government have withdrawn an officer, who now can be of no ufe.

It is neverthelefs much to be wifhed that the port of Retimo may be reftored. The plains around it abound in various productions; and oils, cotton, fafíron, and wax, are extremely plentiful; all which different branches of commerce would become ftill more extenfive, could the inhabitants convey their produce to a foreign market. Their gardens produce the beft fruit in the ifland. Their pomegrantes, almonds, piftachio-nuts, and oranges, are excellent. Here we find the apricot-tree that produces the *mich mich*, a fruit of an exquifite fragrance, and yielding a delicious juice. It is a kind of alberge, but more mellow and fmaller than that of France.

Five leagues from this town, an immenfe country opens between the weftern extremity of Mount Ida and the firft chain of the White Mountains. In this large valley is the village of Marguarites, the moft populous of any in the ifland; which contains about ten thoufand Greeks, who cultivate the rich adjoining plains, and would carry their oils, grain, and other commodities, to Retimo, if

they

they had a harbour. This village, or rather town, is about two leagues diftant from the northern fea, and not far from the road to Candia. Clofe to it flows a fmall river, which falls from the mountains in cafcades. The charming temperature, and varied productions of this beautiful country, invited the Venetians to fettle there. They had built country houfes in this diftrict, where they paffed a part of the year; feveral of which are ftill to be feen; but it is with regret we find them occupied by ignorant Greeks, or barbarous Turks. Nothing remains but the ruins of thofe gardens which art defigned, and nature delighted in decorating with a perpetual fucceffion of flowers and fruits. The Greeks of Marguarites, inftructed, no doubt, by their ancient mafters, have preferved the art of extracting an agreeable liquor from the olive. In any other part of the country, the thick and coarfe oil would never fuit the palate of a Frenchman accuftomed to that of Provence. The oil made at Marguarites, which is manufactured with more care, is very good, and retains a tafte of the fruit, and an agreeable flavour. This rich valley, and large village, are the appenage of the Sultana Walida, who fends thither

an

an officer to collect their tributes: the Pachas of Retimo and Candia have here no authority.

We quitted Retimo, laden with prefents from the Jew merchant, who gave us a ftock of provifions for our journey. On leaving the town, we had two leagues bad road, cut out of the rock. Defcending from thefe heights, we coafted the fea-fhore for three leagues; and, though our horfes feet funk into the fand, we got forward very faft. When we had gained the back of the White Mountains, the point of which forms to the north the promontory of Drepanum, we were obliged to keep continually climbing up fteep rocks, and defcending into deep vallies. This was a very fatiguing part of our road, but we re. frefhed ourfelves on a verdant grafs plat, which owed its frefhnefs to a neighbouring fpring, while the branches of a few olive-trees fheltered us from the fun. We had recourfe to the provifions of the good Hebrew, and did not fpare them. We had been informed, that in a houfe to which our guides were to conduct us, the French conful had prepared a fupper for his fucceffor, and this flattering profpect rendered us lavifh of our ftock; which

imprudence

imprudence we had afterward reafon to re-
pent.

We now once more cheerfully mounted
our horfes, and rode fix leagues through
frightful roads: we had forfaken the ufual
route, wandering, we fcarcely knew whither,
among the mountains, and were a hundred
times on the point of falling head long from
the precipices. We croffed a river, where our
horfes were almoft obliged to fwim; and, to
complete our misfortunes, night was coming
on, and we could hardly fee our way. When
the darknefs was ftill more increafed, we
were forced to commit the care of our lives
to the fagacity of the animals we rode on.
At length, however, we arrived, at the wifhed-
for village, and entered, in high fpirits, the
houfe where we thought we were expected;
but the French conful, who was old and ava-
ricious, had not kept his promife, but, contrary to the received practice of his brethren,
had totally forgotten us; and, as the inhabitants were all in bed, we could get no kind
of provifions. After long fearch, however,
we did, at length, procure a few olives, eggs,
and fome very bad bread; with which neceffity compelled us to be content. While
we

we were making this forry repaft, our tanta-
lizing memory continually upbraided us with
the ſupper of the night before.   In this difagreeable fituation, you may fuppofe, the old
conful was not without his ſhare of our bene-
dictions.   We all of us lay down with our
boots and clothes on, on mats, the floor, or
wretched mattraffes, as we could, and endeavoured to find, in the enjoyment of fleep, the
only remedy for our misfortunes.

I have the honour to be, &c.

L E T T E R XXVIII.

To M. L. M.

THE houfe where we had paffed the night was only two leagues from Palio Caftro, fituated at the extremity of Cape Drepanum. Murtius (z), in his map of ancient Crete, places here the Mufeum, where was decided the famous conteft between the Syrens and the Mufes; and lays down Aptera at a little diftance from it toward the mountains. Other authors have imagined that the fituation of that city is pointed out by fome ruins ftill remaining at Palio Caftro: but both thefe opinions are without foundation; fince Strabo precifely afcertains the fituation of Aptera, by placing it at four leagues diftance from Cifamus, which ferved it as a harbour; and as the latter town was at the bottom of the bay formed by the capes Spada and Sufa, upwards of twelve leagues from the promontory of Drepanum, it is impof-

(z) Murtius, Differtation on the Ifle of Crete.

fible

fible that Aptera fhould have been fituated near that Cape.

The hardnefs of our beds, Madam, not allowing us a long fleep, we rofe before daybreak, and fet out at three in the morning. We quitted our quarters without regret, and thought only of reaching Canea, from which we were diftant five leagues. At about a mile and a half from the village, we had a deep river to crofs, and it was ftill quite dark, but our guides taking the lead, we followed them. To regain the great road which we had left the day before, we traverfed a hilly country, where fcarcely any thing like a beaten path was to be found. We followed each other in a line, and very flowly. The darknefs caufed the hills to feem to us of a dreadful height, and a valley had the appearance of an abyfs. But thefe illufions were prefently diffipated. Day-light appeared, and we began to diftinguifh objects, and foon after the fun rofe above the mountains. The fight of that glorious luminary awakened our drowfy fenfes, and difpelled the phantoms of night. His refplendent beams now enlightened the cliffs of a rock,

and

and now gilded the foliage of the trees on the hills, or the fummit of a tower. By degrees the whole plain received his rays, and the magnificent fcenery of nature was fully difplayed. In this glorious moment, how is man reanimated to new enjoyment, while he contemplates, in delightful ecftafy, the wonders of creation ! The pleafure produced by the fight of the rifing fun, is univerfal, and extends to every creature ; the birds fill the air with their melody ; the cattle low in the plain ; the bleating lambs fport around their mothers ; the inhabitants of the waters play upon the furface ; and all animals exprefs, in their peculiar manner, the lively joy they feel.

When we had reached the main road, we difcovered the bay of La Sude, and the caftle which defends the entrance ; while beyond it appeared the craggy rocks of Cape Melec. We defcended into the plain that leads to Canea, and a league from that town the vice-conful came to receive us. A beautiful horfe, richly caparifoned, was brought for the new conful ; and ranging ourfelves in two lines, we entered the walls of the ancient Cydon. The Turks, as a token of rejoicing, poured coffee under the feet of our horfes.

We

We arrived at the gate of the Confular-houfe, and thus terminated our journey, in which we had vifited the moft curious places in the ifland. I have fince feen many others that merit particular defcriptions, and which I fhall endeavour to defcribe to you in the courfe of the following letters.

I have the honour to be, &c.

LETTER XXIX.

To M. L. M.

THE city of Canea, Madam, is the ancient Cydon, or Cydonia. Strabo points out pre-cifely its fituation (*a*). " Cydonia," fays he, " is feated on the fea fhore, on the fide oppo-" fite to Laconia." Diodorus agrees with this geographer, in the pofition he affigns to the cities built by the ancient Minos (*b*). " Cnoffus is fituated on the fide oppofite Afia. " Phæftus on the fouthern fhore, and Cydon " on the weft fide of the ifland, facing Pelopon-" nefus." This correfponds exactly with the prefent fituation of Canea; and Geography informs us of no other confiderable town on that fide. The Cydonians poffeffed an ex-cellent harbour, which they fhut in with a chain; and the entrance of the port of Canea is extremely narrow, and confequently would

(*a*) Strabo, lib. x.
(*b*) Diodorus, lib. x.

be

be very eafy to defend by fuch a contri-
vance.

The origin of Cydon is uncertain (c).
Stephen of Byzantium fays, " it was firft
" called Apollonia, becaufe Cydon was the
" fon of Apollo." (d) Paufanias attributes
its foundation to Cydon, fon of Tegetes, who
paffed into Crete. (e) Herodotus afferts, that
it was built by the Samians, and that they
erected the temples it contained. (f) Alexander, in the firft book of the Cretans, fays,
it received its name from Cydon, fon of
Mercury. You perceive, Madam, that this
diverfity of opinions precludes all certainty;
yet may it not be wholly unimportant to endeavour to afcertain, with precifion, the foun-
der of this city.

We know that Cydon was poffeffed of great
power (g), and fuccefsfully carried on a war
againft the combined arms of the Cnoffians
and Gortynians. (h) This was the largeft

(c) Stephen Byzant.
(d) Paufanias in Arcadicis.
(e) Herodot. lib. iii.
(f) Scholiaft. in Apollonium, lib. iv.
(g) Liv.
(h) Phranzes, lib. i. cap. 36.

city

city in the island, and inclined the scale in
favour of the party whose cause it espoused.
It sustained several celebrated sieges (i). Pha-
lecus, prince of the Phocians, passing into
Crete with a fleet and a numerous army,
besieged it both by sea and land, and lost before its walls his army and his life. Me-
tellus, having subjugated the island, turned all
his forces against Cydon; and, after a very
vigorous resistance, at length rendered it
subject to the Romans.

Cydon was built on the scite of the modern Canea, and extended half a league beyond it, on the side of St. Odero, where we
still see, on the sea shore, remains of ancient
walls of a very solid construction. Canea,
built by the Venetians, is only two miles in
circumference. It is surrounded on the land-
side by a simple range of walls of great thick-
ness, and defended by a deep and wide ditch,
cut out of the rock. By deepening it a little more, the sea might be made to flow
round its ramparts, on which cavaliers are
raised, the better to command the plain. It

(i) Pausanias in Phocicis.

has

has but one gate, that of Retimo, covered with a half-moon, which is the only outwork. The town is better defended toward the fea. On the left of the harbour are four batteries, one above the other, mounted with heavy brafs cannon, on which are the arms of Venice. The firft of them is on a level with the water. The right fide is defended only by a great wall, built on a ridge of low rocks, which are dangerous to approach. At the extremity is an old ruinous caftle ; below which the Venetians had erected fuperb arfenals roofed with ftone. Each of thefe vaults has fufficient length, height, and width, to admit the building of a fhip of the line. The ground here has a declivity ; and the extremity of thefe noble arfenals is on a level with the fea, fo that nothing was more eafy than to launch their veffels. The Turks fuffer this magnificent work to go to ruin.

The town of Canea is well laid out ; the principal ftreets are as ftraight as a line, and the fquares are decorated with fountains. It poffeffes no remarkable edifices. The greateft part of the houfes have only one ftory, and are built with terraces : thofe which are round

round the harbour, are ornamented with galleries, which afford a moft charming profpect. From the windows we may difcover the great bay formed by the capes Melec and Spada, with all the veffels entering or leaving the port. The harbour admits fhips of two hundred tons burthen; and, if deepened, would afford good anchorage to the largeft frigates. The entrance is expofed to the violent north winds, which fometimes drive the waves over the ramparts; but as it is narrow, and the bottom good, veffels well moored are in no danger.

Canea contained five or fix thoufand inhabitants when Tournefort travelled in Crete; but fince the ports of Gira Petra, Candia, and Retimo have been choaked up, the merchants have retired to Canea, which, it is eftimated, now contains about fixteen thoufand fouls.

I have the honour to be, &c.

LETTER XXX.

To M. L. M.

THE Turks who inhabit Candia, Madam, are not fo implicitly fubmiffive to the orders of the Grand Signior as thofe of the other provinces of the empire. We are almoft tempted to believe that the air they breathe infpires them with a republican fpirit : they mutually fupport each other againft the tyranny of the Pachas, and refufe to bow their necks to the yoke of defpotifm. Inrolled as janiffaries at their birth, they compofe the principal foldiery of the ifland, and it would be dangerous to drive them to revolt. When their governors have been guilty of oppreffion, they have been known to have recourfe to arms, and demand vengeance. Of this we have juft feen a remarkable example : the Pacha of Canea had a kind of deputy, who, like the reft of thofe in office, made ufe of every means to amafs wealth, and drew on himfelf the deteftation of the people. The Greeks did not dare to murmur, but fubmitted in filence to be the victims of his injuftice. The Turks were not fo patient; they brought their complaints before the governor, and informed him of the tyranny and extortions of his minifter; but either becaufe he had a real friendfhip for him, or was a fharer in his plunder, he would not liften to them; when on a fudden, on the 6th of January, we heard a great tumult in the town. The janiffaries ran through the ftreets fabre in hand, crying, To arms! And as, in fuch circumftances, foreigners are always in danger from a licentious populace, we kept ourfelves fhut up in the confular-houfe, waiting the event.

The houfe of the officer of the Pacha, which was a fpacious building lately finifhed, was oppofite to ours, on the other fide of the harbour. This was prefently filled with upwards of five hundred perfons, pillaging and deftroying every thing that fell in their way. Some tore out the fafhes, and threw them upon the quay: others mounted on the terraces, broke down the parapets; while fome were returning loaded with furniture. A

U   great

great number of them were diligently fearching
to difcover the object of public hatred; and in
lefs than two hours the whole houfe was emptied,
and half demolifhed.

An enraged multitude always proceeds to
exceffes, which no one can forefee. The foldiers took poffeffion of a high fort · which
commands the town, whence they could
thunder on the caftle of the Pacha, againft
which they pointed feveral heavy pieces of
cannon, and after leaving a guard at this
poft, proceeded in a body to demand juftice,
refolved, in cafe of refufal, to bury their
governor under the ruins of his palace. The
whole town followed with dreadful fhouts,
which, reaching the ears of the Pacha, who was
an old warrior, rendered refpectable by many gallant actions, he had himfelf conveyed
in an arm-chair into the middle of his court-
yard; and when he faw the ftorm approaching, and that the furious populace were preparing to break down the gates, ordered them
inftantly to be thrown open. At the fight
of this venerable old man, who had a long
white beard, the mutineers were ftruck filent,
and the moft daring among them feemed
motionlefs with aftonifhment. At length,

none venturing to fpeak, " Well, my good
" people," faid the governor, " what do
" you afk of me?" They all cried out,
" We muft have the head of your deputy."
" He is fled," replied the Pacha; " but if
" you find him, I abandon him to your ven-
" geance; return to your duty, lay down
" your arms, and let every man go peace-
" ably home." This firmnefs awed even the
moft riotous; and a rebellion, which might
have had fatal confequences, was appeafed
in an inftant, by the courage and prudence
of a fingle man. He had however concealed
his favourite, and, in the night, fent him on
board a fhip, which immediately fet fail for
Conftantinople. After his departure, things
returned to their ufual channel, and peace
was once more reftored within the walls of
Canea. This revolt had occafioned us no
little uneafinefs; for had the inhabitants proceeded to extremities with their governor,
they would not have fpared the French merchants, and the lofs of property would have
been the leaft of their misfortunes.

Some time after, we were witneffes to another fcene, lefs alarming, indeed, but which
will enable you to form an idea of the man-

ner

ner in which the Greeks are treated in this
country. They are not permitted to enter a town on horfeback. This honour
is referved to their archbifhop, and Europeans. The bifhop of Canea attempted to brave
this tyrannical law; and one evening returning from the country, with feveral Monks,
did not difmount; but, paffing the guards,
galloped on to his houfe. The janiffaries, ftationed at the gate, confidered this action as
an infult. The next day, they related to
their companions the affront put upon the True
Believers, and came to the refolution to burn
both the bifhop and his priefts. They immediately procured combuftibles, which they
carried to his houfe, uttering a thoufand
imprecations; and thefe unhappy ecclefi-
aftics were on the point of fuffering a cruel
death, when the Pacha; apprized in time,
diverted the rage of the multitude, by iffu-
ing a firman, proclaimed through all the
ftreets of the town, by which every Greek,
of whatfoever condition, was forbidden to
fleep within the walls of Canea. This order was rigoroufly obeyed, and every evening
thefe wretched flaves were to be feen igno-
minioufly ftealing out of the gate of Retimo,

to

to feek an afylum in the neighbouring country. The working-men and the poor, unable to hire apartments, were obliged to take fhelter in the crevices of rocks, or lay under ' trees on the bare ground. The women were not included in this prohibition, but were permitted to remain in their houfes; an exception which does great honour to Turkifh gallantry, but which furnifhed a fubject for many witticifms. However, when this nightly exile had continued two months, the hufbands began to talk of making their peace; and as money here is the remedy for every evil, they joined their purfes, and having raifed a large fum, obtained a revocation of the order, after paying very dearly for the pride of their bifhop.

I have the honour to be, &c.

L E T T E R XXXI.

To M. I. M.

WHEN we travel through differ-
ent countries, Madam, or even through diftant provinces of the fame kingdom, the
change of air is perceived by us in a very
fenfible manner. This impreffion indeed is
greater or lefs, according to the greater or
lefs degree of fenfibility of every individual;
nor does it wholly depend on the accidental
circumftances of cold or heat. We feel, in
refpiring the vital element, an odour, a tafte,
a favour, which vary according to circumftances, and the varieties of climates and feafons. Thefe fenfations produce pleafure, or
an uncomfortable feeling, as they are fuitable or contrary to the actual ftate of our
conftitution; nor are we to efteem this extraordinary: the exhalations from the earth,
waters, plants and flowers, incorporate with
the

the atmofphere, and compofe the air we breathe. Every man of underftanding, therefore, who has any regard for his health, ought not to be indifferent concerning the choice of his habitation, fince on it, in a great meafure, depends the prefervation of that moft valuable blefling.

The inftant I landed on the coaft of Alexandria, I inhaled a fiery air, with which I was nearly fuffocated; I felt a moift and debilitating heat, which rendered me languid, and deprived me of all ftrength of body, or vigour of mind. I concluded it was impoffible I could live in fuch a country; but a copious perfpiration prefently taking place, the violent heat of my blood diminifhed, and I foon found myfelf greatly relieved.

In the beginning of fpring, when the orange-trees round Damietta were in flower, and filled the atmofphere with their fragrance; when heat, as yet only moderate, left the body in poffeffion of its energy and activity, I tafted, in the moft lively manner, the charms of fo delicious a temperature, breathed with rapture a frefh and perfumed air, and every pulfation of the heart was an enjoyment. This

pleafure,

pleafure, though every moment repeated, never produced fatiety.

In the fame places, when, in the month of July, the hufbandman had turned up the mud of the morafles to plant his rice, the atmofphere became loaded with exhalations which op-preffed the breaft, and obftructed refpiration. The faces of the inhabitants were difcoloured; ficknefs became general; and had not the northerly winds, which prevail at that feafon, chafed away the malignant vapours, and the earth been very foon covered with harvefts, the moft violent diftempers would, no doubt, have enfued.

In fact, fo large a river as the Nile flowing through, and periodically inundating Egypt, cannot but render the air humid, which hu-midity moderates the heat of the fun, and renders the country habitable. The air there is very falutary to the lungs; diforders of the breaft are unknown (k); and Galen, who

---

(k) I have faid, that afthmatic diforders are not known in Egypt. This is true with refpect to the inhabitants, and perfons coming from Europe, Afia, and the northern coafts of Africa; but the Abyflinians, and Nubians, who inhabit a much hotter climate, become fometimes afth-matic

who ftudied at Alexandria, and was well acquainted with the nature of the climate, fent thither all his patients with pulmonary complaints, and they commonly found the cure they fought.

Among all the countries, in which I have refided, there is none whofe temperature is fo healthy, and fo agreeable, as that of Crete. The heats there are not exceffive; and violent cold is abfolutely unknown in the plains. By the obfervations which I made at Canea, during a whole year, I found that, from the month of March to the beginning of November, the thermometer only varied from 20 to 27 degrees (of Reaumur's fcale ( )) above the freezing point. This variation is not confiderable; befides that, in the hotteft days of fummer, the atmofphere was refrefhed by the fea-breezes. The winter, properly fpeaking, begins only in December, and ends in January. During this fhort feafon, fnow never falls in the plain, and rarely do you fee the furface of the water frozen. The

matic at Grand Cairo. Thefe facts have been certified to me by phyficians who have refided forty years in the country.

(*l*) From 77 to 93 of Fahrenheit.

t   weather

weather is more commonly as fine as in the beginning of June in France. The name of winter is given to thefe two months, from the heavy rains, the cloudy fky, and very violent north winds, which happen at this time of the year ; but thefe rains are highly ufeful to agriculture, fince the winds drive the clouds towards the high mountains, where the refervoirs of water are formed by nature to fertilize the country, and the inhabitant of the plain fuffers nothing from thefe tranfient variations.

No fooner is the month of February paft, than the earth is adorned with flowers and harvefts. The reft of the year is almoft one continued fine day. We never experience, as in France, thofe cruel returns of piercing cold, which, coming fuddenly after the heats, nip the opening flowers, deftroy the fruits of the year, and are fo prejudicial to delicate conftitutions. The fky is continually bright and ferene, and the winds are mild and temperate. The glorious luminary of day runs his majeftic courfe through the azure vault, and ripens the luxuriant fruits of the hills and plains. Nor are the nights lefs beautiful : a delicious coolnefs then prevails, and the air,

lefs

lefs charged with vapours than with us, difcovers a greater number of ftars to the obferver. The blue vault of heaven fparkles
with gold, diamonds, and rubies, which feem
to dart forth brighter fires. Nothing can be
more magnificent than this fpectacle, which
the Cretans enjoy for ten months of the year.

To the charms of fo delightful a climate, are
added other advantages which enhance their
value. The ifland of Crete has hardly any
marfhes. The waters there are never ftag-
nant, but, flowing from the fummits of
the mountains in innumerable ftreams, form
delightful fountains, or fmall rivers, which
lofe themfelves in the fea. The elevation of
the ground, whence they take their rife, caufes
them to have a rapid courfe, and they form
neither lakes nor ponds. For this reafon, infects cannot depofit their eggs in them, which
would be carried to the fea; and the inhabitants are not tormented, as in Egypt, with
thofe clouds of gnats that fill the houfes, and
of which the fting is fo painful. For the
fame reafon, alfo, the air is not loaded with
thofe dangerous vapours which rife from the
marfhes in wet countries.

The hills, and rifing grounds, are clothed
with

with various species of thyme (*m*), savoury, serpolet, odoriferous rock-roses, and a variety of balsamic plants. Myrtles and laurel roses border the rivulets which meander through the vallies. On every side the country presents you with groves of orange, lemon, and almond trees. The Arabian jessamine blooms in the gardens, which in the spring are decorated with beds of violets. Vast fields are covered with saffron; wild dittany, which has a very fragrant smell, lines the crevices of the rocks : in a word, the mountains, valleys, and plains, exhale on all sides aromatic odours, which perfume the air, and render it delicious to respire. Clouds, ice, and snow, are afflicting objects, which throw a mournful veil over the face of nature; they present to the eye gloomy images, and excite in the mind melancholy reflexions, and painful feelings in the heart. Nay, not unfrequently, they are injurious to health, and produce a general indisposition. But a clear sky has an effect the very reverse. The sight of an unclouded sun inspires man with joy. His

(*m*) We find in the island of Crete three sorts of thyme, one with a white flower, the other red, and the third blue. All of them are very odoriferous.

genial

genial warmth revives him, and infufes that
lively cheerfulnefs, which fprings from. the
confcious feeling of the happinefs he enjoys:
In this ftate of mind every object acquires
new beauty. He contemplates with more
pleafure the luxuriance of the harvefts, and
admires with greater enthufiafm the beauteous
tints of the flowers ; he finds a double fweet-
nefs in their perfumes ; and, delighted with
his own exiftence, feems to communicate, to
every thing around him, the happinefs he
enjoys. The youth begins to be animated
with a new life, and feels himfelf foftly attracted towards another felf; his heart palpi-
tates with inquietude and delight, and the
tender paffion of love fires all his fenfes.
While the aged man, now fafe in the harbour, recollects the tumultuous ftruggles of
his younger days, and feeling himfelf revived
by a fudden warmth, would be ready to en-
counter them anew, did not prudence and
nature foon calm the temporary effervefcence
of his paffions.

In thefe countries, Madam, we are more
fenfible of the truth of fuch reflexions. It is
certain, that in this delightful climate man
is lefs fubject to difeafes, enjoys more pleafures,

fures, and has infinitely more means of being happy than in the northern regions, where the cold is extreme ; or even in our climates, where the winter, though not fo long, is fometimes very fevere.

I have the honour to be, &c.

LETTER XXXII.

To M. I. M.

THE beauty of man, Madam, his powers, and his health, depend, in general, on the climate he inhabits, his food, and the nature of his occupations. In Crete, the Turk, who is not tormented by ambition, or the thirſt of wealth, whoſe mind is never occupied by the chimeras of intrigue, who knows not envy, which debaſes the ſoul, nor exhauſts himſelf in the purſuit of the ſciences, to which we too often ſacrifice our health; the Turk, I ſay, who lives on wholeſome and ſimple aliments, and paſſes his days amid the flowery fields he cultivates, and in the boſom of his family who obey and revere him, grows and riſes into a Coloſſus. The ſalubrity of the air he breathes, the ſweet temperature he enjoys, the delightful ſcenes perpetually before his eyes, and the peaceful life he leads, all con-tribute to ſtrengthen his body, and preſerve his vigour even beneath the ſnows of age. Hither the ſculptor, devoted to his art, and

emulating

emulating the ancients, fhould come in fearch
of models. He would fee young men of eighteen or twenty, five feet fix, or eight inches
high (*n*), who poffefs all the graces peculiar
to their time of life. Their mufcles have ftill
a little plumpnefs, which will foon affume a
bolder character ; their cheeks, gracefully
rounded, difplay an animated carnation, and
their eyes are full of fire ; their chin is
covered with a light down, never violated by
the razor ; their air is full of grace and dignity ; and their whole carriage, and every
gefture, befpeaks health and vigour.

In men arrived at maturity, the features
and outlines are more developed. Their legs
are naked ; and when their robes are lifted
up, the mufcles appear boldly prominent :
their arms exhibit thofe figns of ftrength
which were vifible in thofe of the ancient
Athletæ : their fhoulders are broad, their chefts
full, and their necks, never ftraightened by
the ligatures, which, from infancy, confine
thofe of the Europeans, retain all the beautiful proportions affigned to that part by nature : no tight breeches, or garters, bind
their legs below the knee ; that part of their

(*n*) About fix feet Englifh.

leg,

leg, therefore, is never diftorted or contracted, nor is the knee too prominent. In a word, all their limbs, unaccuftomed to the fetters which confine our motions, and which habit alone could render fupportable, preferve their natural form, and that admirable fymmetry which conftitutes male beauty. When they ftand erect, all parts of the body properly fupport each other. When they walk, they move with an air of dignity, and bodily ftrength and firmnefs of mind difplay them-felves in every gefture. Their majeftic eye announces that they are accuftomed to com-mand. Pride and feverity may fometimes be apparent in their looks, but meannefs never.

The Mahometans, who inhabit the ifland of Crete, are fuch, Madam, as I have here pourtrayed them. They are, in general, from five feet and a half to fix feet high (*o*). They refemble the ancient ftatues ; and, in fact, fuch were the men the artifts of antiquity took for their models. It is not, therefore, wonderful they fhould have furpaffed us, having a more beautiful nature from which to copy. One

(*o*) French meafure, anfwering to from five feet eleven inches to fix feet five Englifh.

X day,

day, as I was walking with an officer in the
environs of Canea, he exclaimed, at the fight
of every Turk that paffed, Oh! were I only
permitted to choofe here feven hundred men,
I fhould have the fineft regiment in France!

In a country where the men are fo remarkable for bodily ftrength and dignity of
afpeft, you may juftly conclude, Madam, that
the women cannot be wanting in beauty and
the graces. Their drefs does not prevent the
growth of any part of the body, but is accommodated to thofe admirable proportions
with which the Creator has decorated the moft
lovely of his works. All are not handfome ;
all do not poffefs charms ; but fome of them
are extremely beautiful, particularly among
the Turks. In general, the Cretan women
have a luxuriant bofom ; a neck gracefully
rounded ; black eyes full of fire ; a fmall
mouth ; a nofe perfectly well made, and
cheeks which health tinges with the fofteft
vermillion. But the oval of their faces is different from that of the women of Europe, and
the character of their beauty is peculiar to
their nation. I will not attempt a parallel
between the two. Whatever is beautiful deferves our homage, though delicacy of fentiment

ment fhould ultimately fix the tafte of a man
of juft feeling.

During the firft year or two of my travels
in the eaftern countries, accuftomed as I had
been to the elegant head-drefs of the ladies
of France, their curls, and different coloured
powder, I could not endure the black hair of
the oriental women, and their drefs feemed to
me to give them a harfh and forbidding air.
So difficult is it for reafon to difengage itfelf
from the fetters of habit, that I long continued the flave of this prejudice. But, after
more mature reflection, their long black locks,
artificially plaited, without either powder or
pomatum, and which neither fpoil their drefs,
nor foil the furniture of their apartments, appeared to me well calculated to heighten their
beauty. Their ebon colour feemed to give
more luftre to the fairnefs of their complexions,
and' the glow of their cheeks. The rofe-
water, with which they wafh their hair, exhaled an agreeable perfume; and I was delighted with the natural beauty of their treffes.
I then changed my opinion, and could not
help wifhing the European women would not
fpoil one of their moft charming ornaments
with the colours of art, fo much inferior to

thofe

thofe of nature. How.. much more lovely
would the fair beauty appear, adorned with
the pale gold of her flowing locks ! · How
would the dark hair of the brunette, arranged·
with art, fet off the rofes of her cheeks !
Thefe, Madam, are the; obfervations of a
traveller, who, by comparing the different
cuftoms of nations, has been able to banifh
his prejudices, and is convinced that nature
alone is truly beautiful ; but he fets little value
on, and entreats your excufe for, the reflections
in which he has here ventured to indulge.

You muft not be furprifed, Madam, that
I have not mentioned the Greeks who ·in-
habit the ifland of Candia, who partake with
the Turks the advantages of a ferene fky, a
pure air, and happy temperature. They en-.
joy, indeed, in common with them, thefe precious bleffings ; but they are ‚ oppreffed by
tyrants. They live in perpetual anxiety and
apprehenfion, and frequently· terminate their
miferable lives in defpair. Excepting the
Spachiots, who are lefs expofed to · tyranny,
thefe unfortunate beings have neither the lofty,
ftature, nor the ftrength, nor the beauty of the
Turks. The ftamp of fervitude is vifible in
their faces; their looks are crouching, and
their

their features diftorted by knavery and meannefs. Such is the character of thofe Cretans,
who were once fo jealous of their liberty;
thofe experienced and intrepid warriors, who
were courted by all nations; and thofe friends
to the arts, which they cultivated amid their
fhady groves. At prefent, cowardly and indolent, they live in debafement, and we may
read in their degraded countenances, that *they
are flaves.*

I have the honour to be, &c.

L E T T E R XXXIII.

To M. L. M.

THE iſland of Candia, Madam, does not produce, like Egypt, a multitude of reptiles. Very few ſerpents, and thoſe only ſmall ones, are to be found in it. Belon, the naturaliſt, reckons three ſpecies, the *ophis*, the *ochendra*, and the *ephloti*. The firſt is not venomous; but I can ſay nothing of the others, only I never heard of any accidents from their bite.

The ancients affirmed, that this beautiful country contained no noxious animal *(p)*. Pliny excepts the tarantula *(q)*, which Belon calls *phalangion* (*r*). They aſſert its poiſon is mortal. It is a ſort of ſpider, almoſt an inch long, with a ſcaly coat. It hollows out, in the ſides of little eminences, a pretty deep

(*p*) Antigonus Ariſthius, Hiſt. cap. x. It is ſaid, that the iſland of Crete breeds no animal which can cauſe the death of man.

(*q*) Pliny, lib. viii. cap. 58.

(*r*) Obſervations de pluſieurs Singularités et Choſes memorables trouvées en Gréce, &c.

hole,·

hole, which it covers with a ftrong web of
crofs threads glued together. This little paffage, at the bottom of which it lodges, is
clofed externally by a valve, that prevents
the rain from penetrating; and which it opens
when going in queft of infects, and clofes
again when it re-enters. If two of thefe
tarantulas are fhut up in a glafs phial, they
fting each other, and die foon after. I am
not acquainted with the effect of their bite
on the human body, but I was an eye-witnefs
to the experiment I have juft mentioned.

The quadrupeds of the ifland are not
mifchievous; we neither meet with lions,
tigers, bears, wolves, nor even foxes; in
fhort, no dangerous animal. The wild
goats are the only inhabitants of the
forefts which cover the high mountains,
and have nothing to fear but the gun of the
hunter. Hares are found on the eminences
and in the plains. The fheep feed in fafety
on the various fpecies of wild thyme. They
are folded every evening, and the fhepherd
fleeps in peace, free from the dread of feeing
death and havock fpread among his flock by
wild beafts.

It is a happinefs for the Cretans, that they

are

are neither troubled with mufquitos, nor have any thing to apprehend from the poifon of ferpents, or the ferocity of wild beafts. The young and lively maiden may dance upon the grafs, without finding, like Eurydice, a viper concealed under the flowers. The ancients afcribed thefe fignal advantages to the birth of Jupiter. " The Cretans," fays Ælian (s), " celebrate in their fongs the bounties of Ju-" piter, and the favour he has granted their " ifland, his native and nurfing land, of being " free from every noxious animal, and of not " even nourifhing thofe which may be brought " into it."

Among the medicinal plants of Crete, dittany holds the firft rank. It is aftonifhing how highly the ancients have extolled its virtues. Theophraftus (t), who gives us the received opinions of his time, fays, " Of all " the known plants, which the earth has pro-" duced, dittany is the moft precious." The father of medicine, the celebrated Hippo.

(s) Ælian. de Natura Animalium, lib. v.

(t) Theophraftus adds, in another place, Dittany poffeffes beneficial and extraordinary virtues in a great number of cafes, and efpecially in the labour of women.

crates,

crates (*u*), ordered an infufion of it to be given in feveral diforders of women, and efpecially during the pains of a difficult labour. For this reafon the ftatue of Diana was, according to fome writers (*v*), crowned with dittany.

I fhall not here repeat, with feveral authors (*w*), that the wild goats, when wounded by the arrows of the hunter, freed themfelves from them by eating this precious plant; that it poffeffed the virtue of healing them, even when the arrows were poifoned (*x*); and that its odour was fo powerful, as to drive away venomous reptiles, and deftroy, if it only touched them (*y*). Thefe accounts are evidently exaggerated; but, on the other hand, we are, poffibly too indifferent to the real utility medicine might derive from this plant. Its leaf is extremely balfamic, and the flower diffufes

(*u*) Hippocrates de Nat. Mulierum : Give, as a drink, dittany of Crete, of the weight of an obolus, infufed in water. He adds (de Morbis Mulierum), lib. i. Give dittany of Crete in wine. De Fœtus Mortui Exfect. If you have any dittany of Crete, drink an infufion of it.

(*v*) Scholiaft. in Euripid. Hippolyt.

(*w*) Plutarch, de Sol. Anim.

(*x*) Cicero, de Natura Deorum, lib. ii.

(*y*) Diofcorides.

a de-

a delicious fragrance. The inhabitants, at prefent, apply it with fuccefs on many occafions.
An infufion of the dried leaf, with a little fugar,
yields a liquor more pleafing to the palate, and
more finely flavoured than tea.   It immediately
removes languor of the ftomach, and reftores it
after digeftion.

(z) Dittany is peculiar to the ifland of Crete,
and is to be found in no other country.   It
grows in the crevices of the rocks, and at the
foot of precipices.   Pliny has not fufficiently
difcriminated it in his defcription (a).   " Dit-
" tany," fays he, " has flender branches, re-
" fembles penny-royal, and is hot and rough
" to the tafte; its leaves only are made ufe
" of; it has neither flower, nor feed, nor
" ftalk."   Virgil knew it better, and his
defcription is more conformable to truth (b).
" His mother gathers dittany on Mount
" Ida of Crete.   This plant bears fhagged
" leaves, which are crowned with purple
" flowers.   The wild goats find in it a

(z) Pliny, B. xxv. ch. 8.   Dittany grows only in the
ifland of Crete.   Theophraftus (Hift. Plant.) fays the fame
thing : Dittany is peculiar to the ifland of Crete.

(a) Pliny, lib. xxv. cap. 8.

(b) Æneid, lib. xii.

" remedy,

" remedy, when wounded by the winged
" arrows."

In a country where the air is extremely,
pure, diforders are not frequent; we find no
epidemical difeafes in the ifland of Candia.
Fevers are, indeed, frequent there, in the fummer; but they are not attended with danger,
and the plague would never make its appearance, had not the Turks deftroyed the Laza-
rettos eftablifhed by the Venetians for performing quarantine. Since then it has been
brought, from time to time, by the fhips from
Smyrna and Conftantinople. This dreadful
diftemper perpetuates itfelf for want of pre-
cautions, vifits fucceffively the different provinces, and, as both the heats and colds are
moderate, fometimes continues its ravages here
for eighteen months together.

But a malady which, though lefs dangerous
than the plague, has fomething even more
hideous in its fymptoms, infects this beautiful
country: I mean the leprofy. This diforder
had its ancient feat in Syria, whence it has
paffed into many iflands of the Archipelago.
It is contagious, and is inftantly communicated by the touch. The unhappy wretches,
who are attacked by it, are confined to little
huts,

huts, built on the fides of the highways, from which they are not allowed to come out, or to converfe with any perfon. They have ufually round their cottages a fmall garden, that fupplies them with vegetables and poultry, with which, and the alms they receive from paffengers, they drag on a miferable life in torment. Their bloated fkin is covered with a fcaly cruft, full of red and white fpots, which occafion intolerable itchings. They intreat relief in a hoarfe and hollow voce, at the very found of which you fhudder, and their words are fcarcely articulate, as the diforder is internally deftroying the organs of fpeech. Thefe wretched fpectres gradually lofe the ufe of their limbs, and live till, the whole mafs of blood becoming corrupted, death is the confequence of putrefaction. No fight can be more melancholy, or more fhocking than that of a leper; no torments comparable to thofe which he endures. It would be an act worthy of a humane phyfician, to endeavour to difcover a remedy for this dreadful and contagious diftemper.

The rich are not attacked by this malady, which is confined to the lower clafs of people,

and

and is particularly frequent among the Greeks, who obferve ftrictly their four Lents, and live during that whole time on nothing but falt-fifh, boutargo (c), pickled olives, and cheefe, and drink copioufly of the heavy and heating wines of the country (d). It is poffible this diet may inflame and thicken their blood, and, at length, be the caufe of a leprofy. I am led to fufpect this, from obferving, that it never manifefts itfelf among fuch of the Turks as are rich enough to procure animal food the whole year, with rice and vegetables; nor even among the Greeks who inhabit the mountains, and eat frequently of fallads, fruits, and milk.

You perceive, Madam, this terrible diforder is not to be dreaded by perfons in eafy cir-cumftances. During a whole century that the French have been fettled in Canea, not one of them has ever fuffered from it; and as it appears to originate from the wretched nutriment of the Greeks; by obliging them to change their manner of living, this difeafe might poffibly be eradicated. Our anceftors

(c) The roe of fifh falted and fmoaked.

(d) Thefe wines are of a very hot quality, and coft only three farthings a bottle.

brought

brought it with them into France, at their return from the Crufades, and difcovered the
method of cure. It is, therefore, little to
be doubted, but the Cretans, under the regulations of a wife government, might be able
entirely to banifh it from the ifland.

I have the honour to be, &c.

L T T T E R XXXIV.

To M. L. M.

A RESIDENCE of fixteen months in Crete, has given me an opportunity, Madam, of attaining a more perfect knowledge of this fine ifland, than travellers, in general, can pretend to, who have only taken a hafty view. At a diftance from all the entertainments and diverfions which amufe the Parifian, I have endeavoured, in my leifure hours, to difcover fituations where I might enjoy the beauties of the country. I wifh, Madam, to prefent you with the defcription of one in particular, to which I frequently repaired, attracted by the pleafing profpects it afforded; but let me entreat you to remember, that the more faithful I fhall be, the more will the fcenes I fhall depict be fufpected of the marvellous. I am not afraid, however, you fhould think them imaginary; the places I am about to defcribe, really exift; I myfelf have feen and felt their beauties in different

feafons

feafons of the year. May they caufe you to forget, for a moment, the rich gardens of Montreuil, and for a while fix your attention on the banks of the Platania!

Quitting Canea, and following the fea-fhore to the fouth-weft, we leave on the right the Lazaret, a low rock, where the Venetians obliged veffels to perform quarantine, before they were admitted into the harbour. A league further on is the rock of Saint Theodore, on which not a ftone remains of the two forts by which it was defended, when attacked by the Turks. This little ifland, and that of the Lazaret, were anciently called *Leuces*, and are famous for the conteft the Syrens dared to maintain againft the Mufes, with whom they difputed the palm of vocal and inftrumental mufic; but being overcome, threw themfelves into the fea.

Coafting the gulph, we difcover to the weft a long chain of mountains, which follow its windings, and terminate in a point at Cape Spada, formerly the promontory of Dictynna. Thefe are a branch of the white mountains, to which Strabo gives the name of Corycus. About the middle of this chain is the temple of Dictynna, erected by the ancient Cretans,

I   on

on the fpot where fhe caft herfelf into the fea, to avoid the purfuit of Minos (c).

Let us continue our expedition, regardlefs of the fables of antiquity. We approach the river of Platania, and the foreft of the fame name; we are now three leagues from Canea. To the weft we have the fea, and the hills with which it is furrounded, and to the eaft a thick wood. Between the fhore and thefe trees is a fandy foil, a quarter of a league in width, interfperfed with beautiful laurel-rofes. Nothing can be more lively than the verdant luftre of their leaves; nothing more magnificent than the purple flowers with which they are crowned. But the fun beats hot on the fands; the fhade invites; let us repofe under its covert.

Heavens! what a delightful fcene! what verdant, what beautiful foliage! A vaft foreft of plane trees, few of which are lefs than feventy feet high! they are larger than our elms, and no lefs majeftic. How they unite their fraternal arms! How do they mutually fupport and defend each other againft tempefts and hurricanes! All hail to the ancient foreft

(c) Murtius, Differtation on Crete.

Y   of

of Platania! Every tree has vines planted round it, whose shoots, four inches in diameter, rise like the ropes which secure the masts of a ship. In this rich and productive soil they shoot with an astonishing vigour, and, growing to the height of the planes by which they are supported, crown them with their verdant tendrils, and adorn them with their fruit. Each tree, thus decorated, forms a large arbour, impenetrable to the rays of the sun. Seated under this magnificent canopy, the traveller sees clusters of grapes pendent over his head, many of which are two feet in length. They are of various species ; and by the side of a yellow cluster, we frequently admire the purple, the violet, the rose, and the muscadine of a deeper, or lighter hue. These grapes, which embellish the Platanus with their beauteous varieties, have a very large berry, and ripen two months later than those which grow on the hill-sides ; but they adorn the tables of the inhabitants till the month of December, and are of an exquisite flavour. I know no place more delightfully pleasant than this forest. In spring, innumerable birds resort thither, to build their nests : the nightingale, the goldfinch, and the

blackbird, ,

blackbird, feek its fhades, where they woo in peace their little loves, and make the echoes refound with their melodious warbling.

Clofe to the edge of this wood flows the river of Platania. It is not deep, and the pure fand, which forms its bed, is eafily difcoverable through its tranfparent waters. The foliage of the plane-trees, and the clufters with which they are hung round, are reflected in this cryftal mirror. Sometimes, taking its way between two rows of trees, its darkened ftream glides in filence under the thick overhanging branches; then, fuddenly efcaping from its prifon, the face of heaven is again imaged in its peaceful waters. It was in this limpid ftream, fays the fable (f), that Europa, fatiated with the favours of Jupiter, went to bathe her beauteous body, while her nymphs danced in chorus, and chaunted hymns to Love. No place can be imagined more favourable to the tendereft of paffions; nor any where the heart overflows more with pure enjoyment, or feels more the want of another felf to participate its delights. O thou ! who, feated beneath the flowery fhades of Bourbon,

(f) Murtius, Differtation on the Ifle of Crete.

Y 2   fang

fang Eleonora, whofe darling name has attracted the admiration of diftant nations, come to Platania; come to admire and paint the charms of this retreat; and, if you would render it immortal, here love, here celebrate another divinity! Acknowledged fongfter of the Graces, beloved poet of Apollo, remember that this is the ancient country of the Mufes; here refide, and you will imagine yourfelf in the bofom of your native land.

Let us penetrate into the thickeft of the wood. What profound filence! what gloomy majefty! Darknefs here reigns amid the clearnefs of the day. Here is the habitation of obfcurity, peace, and coolnefs. They have fled the burning hills, where the fhepherd, from the depth of his grotto, warbles forth his ftrains, and have taken refuge under this impenetrable foliage. But why does a fecret fhuddering feize on the mind? Is this then the temple of the deity? And is the foul awed by his facred prefence? Or, rather, does it dread fome undifcovered enemy? Yet does it experience a kind of pleafure in what fo agitates its feelings. Is this agitation then neceffary to make us more fenfible of our exiftence?

Let us continue to ftray under the arbours

of

of Platania, and afcend toward the fource of.
the river. For the fpace of a league we perceive almoft always the fame richnefs of foil,
and the fame delightful landfcapes. In fome
places the two hills, which embrace the foreft,
widen, and afford diftant views of eminences,
clad with vineyards ; cottages built on their
fummits ; and perpendicular rocks, which feem
ready to rufh into the valley. The goat,
which fports on the brink of the precipices,
is browzing on the leaves of the fhrubs which
grow on them, and feems fufpended over the
abyfs.

We are now at the extremity of the foreft.
Before us opens a plain, three leagues in circumference, bordered on every fide with lofty
hills. Above rife the White Mountains, which
hide their frozen heads in the clouds. From
every point of the horizon, narrow and deep
valleys terminate in the plain, to which they
convey the tribute of their waters. Their
courfe is marked out by the laurel-rofes, the
beautiful flowers of which decorate the fides
of the valleys with a brilliant red ; they are
fo many fuperb garlands, hung by nature to
the fummits of the hills, and which, fufpended
in long folds, reach to the very foot of the
defcent.

defcent. Thefe wreaths of rofes form a charming contraft with the furrounding verdure,
and never can the eye be wearied with admiring them.

Let us now turn our attention to another
principal ornament of this delightful fcene.
You have, Madam, handfome myrtles in your
gardens, but they languifh under a foreign
fky. One part of the year they are fhut up
in hot-houfes, for their delicacy is unable to
fupport the froft. The pots or boxes in
which they are confined, will not permit
them to receive fufficient nourifhment to become vigorous, or to difplay their odoriferous
flowers; but what they efpecially want is the
fun they love; his genial heat is indifpenfable
to their perfection. Hither, Madam, muft
you come to view in perfection the beautiful tree fo dear to the fon of Cytherea. In
the place I am defcribing, and which I fhall
call the plain of myrtles, you may fee them
ten feet high, and covered with bloffoms
from the ground to the very tops. Their
fnow-white flowers, bordered within with a
purple edging, appear to peculiar advantage
under the verdant foliage. Each myrtle is loaded with them, and they emit perfumes, more
                                    fweet,

sweet, more exquisite, than those of the rose itself; they enchant every sense, and the soul is filled with the softest sensation. Sometimes, in this immense plain, we find them growing in thick groves; to walk in which is most delightful. In other places they are seen scattered here and there; but wherever we turn our eyes, we can never be wearied with admiring the beauty of their foliage, and inhaling the delicious odours of their flowers. Twenty times have I reposed under their shade, and as often have I tasted a new delight. The ancients certainly were in the right, when they consecrated the myrtle to love, since it surpasses in beauty every other shrub or tree.

A rivulet traverses the whole extent of this plain; but it has but little water, except during the winter. Its banks are adorned with laurel-roses, which grow best in a moist soil. The vivid colours of their blossoms, which are seen through the interstices of the flowery myrtles, form a picture worthy of the ablest pencils. But the pleasure of the eye is not equal to that communicated by their delicate odours. You leave them, to seat yourself at

the

the foot of the myrtles, which, on a clofer examination, appear more charming.

Every part of the ifland of Crete, Madam, is not fo pleafant and beautiful, as that I have here defcribed. The myrtle and the laurel-rofe grow every where in the valleys; but I never faw thefe beauteous fhrubs collected in fuch abundance as in the plain which ter-minates in fo picturefque a manner the foreft of Platania. If you do not find, in modern poets, defcriptions fimilar to mine, it is not their fault, but that of the country they have before their eyes. The happieft imagination could never form fuch pictures as I have pre-fented you, without having feen the originals; it muft have recourfe to foreign ornaments, at the expence of the moft effential beauty. The ancients, on the contrary, depict fcenes, which, to thofe who have not travelled, feem no bet-ter than the dreams of a brilliant imagination. Yet, on vifiting the countries they inhabited, we fee, with pleafure, that, ftudying after the fineft models, they have copied with fidelity the genuine beauties of nature. They have, indeed, allowed themfelves fome licence in the difpofition of their ornaments, by collect-

ing

ing in one landfcape all the charms to be found in many; but they have, neverthelefs, taken care not to lofe fight of probability, by ftationing each object in the place it ought to occupy, and imagining nothing but what is poffible. The moft frequent error of thofe who have not well examined nature, is to unite incoherent beauties, and diftort what they mean to embellifh.

I know not, Madam, what may be the fate of the defcriptions I now fend you; but I fketched them near the banks of the Platania, and in the plain of myrtles. There I now enjoyed the fhade of the plane-tree, while the purple clufters hung over my head; now inhaled the delicious odours of the blooming myrtle, and now contemplated with rapture the beautiful flowers with which the laurel-rofe adorned the valleys. Charmed with the fcenes, breathing a pure and balmy air, I have endeavoured to defcribe, in this filent retreat, the fentiments and emotions of my foul, and the reflections refulting from the fight of fo many delightful objects.

I have the honour to be, &c.

L E T T E R XXXV.

To M. L. M.

I AM now going to introduce you, Madam, to one of the moſt amiable Turks in the iſland, nor can I ſuppoſe you will be diſ-pleaſed with your new acquaintance. Iſmael Aga, one of the wealthieſt land proprietors in Canea, is a man of about ſeventy years of age, of a majeſtic ſtature, a fine face, and ſtill exhibits in his features the marks of ſtrength and vigour. He has had the command of ſeveral of the Grand Signior's caravelles, and paſſed ſome time at Venice; he has travelled through Egypt, and viſited, according to the religious cuſtom of the Mahometans, the tomb of his Prophet. His travels have entirely diveſted him of that pride, with which ignorance, and the preju-dices of their religion, inſpire the Turks, nor does he, like them, deſpiſe ſtrangers; but, on the contrary, takes pleaſure in, and courts their
ſociety.

fociety. Having invited us to fpend fome time at his country houfe, he fent horfes for us, and ordered his fons to fhew us the way. We accordingly fet out from Canea at eight in the morning, croffed that beautiful part of the country covered with olive-trees, which extends to the foot of the White Mountains, and having rode through the whole length of the delightful plain of myrtles, arrived about noon at his houfe, fituated a league beyond it, on the declivity of a hill. Ifmael received us with friendfhip, but without any of thofe demonftrations of joy and pleafure which ceremony lavifhes in other countries. You are welcome, faid he, with an air of cool fatisfaction; and immediately conducted us to the place of entertainment.

The heavens were clear and ferene, but the atmofphere was heated by a burning fun, to which we had been four hours expofed: nothing could now be fo defirable to us as coolnefs; and our wifhes were amply gratified. The table was fpread in the garden under the fhade of orange-trees. Six of thefe beautiful trees, planted in a circle, united their branches, which had never been mutilated by the fheers, and formed over our heads a

roof

roof impenetrable to the rays of the fun. In the middle of a very hot day, we enjoyed, in this arbour, which nature had fo profufely embellifhed, a delicious coolnefs. On every fide, flowers hung in garlands over the guefts, and formed a crown for each. The brightnefs of their colours, their exquifite odours, the beauty of the foliage, gently agitated by the zephyr, every thing confpired to make us imagine ourfelves fuddenly tranfported to fome enchanted grove. To complete the whole, a beautiful ftream, which defcended from the adjoining hills, paffed under the table, and contributed to preferve the plea. fantnefs and coolnefs of our arbour; on each fide of us we beheld it gliding over a golden fand, and winding its cryftal ftream through the garden, in which a great number of fmall canals had been dug to convey its waters to the orange, the pomegranate and almond trees, which repaid the moifture they received with intereft, in flowers and fruits.

The table was now ferved; the Aga had endeavoured to provide for us fuitable to our taftes; we were prefented with all the utenfils common in France; and our hoft himfelf

conformed

conformed to all our cuftoms. Knowing that
we were ufed to take foup, he fupplied us
with a great difh of roaft-meats covered
with a delicious jelly. Round this were bartavelles almoft as large as our hens, and with
a *fumet* which excited the appetite: there
were befides excellent quails, a tender and delicate lamb, and hafhed-meat dreffed with
rice, and perfectly well feafoned. The wine
correfponded with the excellence of the reft.
of our entertainment; we were ferved with
vin de loi (g), malmfey of Mount Ida, and
a fort of perfumed red wine, equally agreeable
to the fmell and the tafte. Our good pa'riarch,
wifhing to imitate his guefts, and take his
glafs in defiance of the Prophet, had fent
away his fervants, and his children. Lay-
ing afide the Turkifh gravity, which never
condefcends to fmile, he chatted with much
vivacity, and frequently aftonifhed us by the

(g) The wine made by the Jews is called *Vin de Loi.*
or wine of the law, and is little known in France; it is rather
bitter, but leaves an agreeable flavour in the mouth, and excites a gentle warmth in the ftomach.

The Malmfey of Mount Ida is more unctuous, more agreeable to the palate, and not lefs fragrant.

pene-

penetration of his understanding, the aptnefs of his replies, and the juftnefs of his ideas. When the difhes were removed, we were prefented with Moka coffee, and pipes. Do not be too much fhocked, Madam, the pipes made ufe of here are of jafmine, and the part applied to the mouth, of amber; their enormous length entirely takes away the pungency of the tobacco, which, in Turkey, however, is mild; and, being mixed with the wood of aloes, produces a vapour neither difagreeable nor incommodious, as in other countries.

We repofed ourfelves agreeably under the fhade, and enjoyed the delicious fragrance of the orange flowers; our hoft was extreme-ly focial, and took the lead in the conver-fation. No offer was here made to fhine, by thofe flafhes we call wit, to ornament fplendid nothings in gaudy colours, or to diffeminate agreeable fcandal. To attempt this would only have been to lofe time. Ifmael would have underftood nothing of our jargon. We were obliged to content ourfelves with liftening to folid obfervations, and return-ing anfwers according to the dictates of reafon, and found fenfe. As foon as the great

heat

heat was over, he called his fons, and ordered them to attend us on a fhooting party; we defcended into a plain where we found plenty of quails, and had the pleafure of killing many without fatigue.   The darknefs, which now advanced over the hills, brought us back to the houfe; and, as the nights at this feafon are as clear and fine as the days are beautiful, we fupped in the arbour of orange-trees.   Rarely do we enjoy this luxury in France;   the night air has always a degree of chilnefs that makes us fhudder, or a copious dew falls injurious to health.   In Crete, during the Summer, you are not expofed to thofe inconveniencies, which though trifling, interrupt the enjoyment of the company.   The fky was without a cloud, the coolnefs agreeable, and the air fo calm, as fcarcely to difturb the light of four large wax-tapers, which illumined the foliage in a thoufand different ways,   and the varied reflections of which produced lights and fhades of an admirable effect.   Here the leaves fhone upon, affumed a brilliant yellow, and there a deep verdure, while in fome places the whitenefs of the flowers, fufpended in feftoons, was heightened by a golden
ground;

ground; further on, the opening of two leaves left a paffage for the refplendence of a ftar, which fparkled like the diamond. The condenfation of the air had collected the fragrant perfumes of the flowers and fhrubs, and every fenfe was delighted. The luminous corufcations which played upon the foliage, and the contraft of light and fhade, which continually varied its form and colours, produced a fcenery fo delightful, that this flowery canopy extended over our heads appeared to me more beautiful by night, than amid the fplendor of day. Perhaps, too, the delicacy of our good cheer, the excellence of the wine, and the novelty of the decorations, might give new vigour to imagination, and that enchantrefs might take a delight in ftill further embellifhing fo voluptuous an abode.

The Turks do not referve in their houfes feparate apartments for every perfon of the family; the women only have diftinct chambers; the men fleep together in fpacious halls, on matraffes fpread on the carpetting, and provided with fheets and a blanket. Agreeable to this ancient cuftom, ftill obferved by the orientals, we were fhewn into a large room, round
which

which our beds were placed upon the ground. Only two centuries ago, it was ufual, even in France, for the whole family to pafs the night in the fame apartment : fince that time, our manners have undergone a great change; they have infinitely more delicacy and convenience, nay, perhaps decency ; but are they more focial ?

The day had fcarcely begun to break, when the fervants came to awaken us ; for the Mahometans rife with the dawn, to repeat the morning prayer, and to enjoy the firft rays of the fun, and the delicious coolnefs diffufed throughout the air. When we came down from our chamber, breakfaft was waiting for us ; we drank moka, fmoaked the odoriferous tobacco of Latakia, and, accompanied by the fons of the Aga, and two game-keepers, made an excurfion to fhoot partridges. I have only feen one fpecies of that bird in this ifland ; the bartavelle, which inhabits the mountains, where it multiplies prodigioufly ; its colours are more lively, and it is much larger than our red partridge, and excellently well tafted : we found innumerable coveys of thefe birds on all the hills. Our morning was fatiguing, but very fuccefsful. Fre-

Z

quently, after ftraying over eminences covered
with briars, we defcended into a valley over-
fpread with myrtles and laurel-rofes. The
game retires into fuch places during the
violent heat of the fun, and we fprung partridges, quails and hares, from the midft of
thefe flowery thickets.

On our return to the Aga's, an excellent
dinner, the malmfey of Mount Ida, and our
delightful arbour, made us forget all our
fatigues. His women paid us a gallant attention, by the prefent of a large cake made
with their own hands ; it was compofed of
flour, perfumed honey, frefh almonds, and
pounded piftachio-nuts, mixed with a little
rofe water: this paftry was very light, and
we all allowed it to be excellent.

During the whole time we paffed at the
feat of Ifmael Aga, we experienced from him
nothing but the utmoft politenefs ; he made
us no great compliments, but he ftudied our
taftes; and we were fure of finding on our
table the difhes to which we feemed to give
a preference. One morning rifing before my
companions, and walking among the neighbouring orchards, I perceived this venerable
muffulman ftanding near a fountain contiguous

to

to the houfe: he was wafhing his face and hands, and chaunting the firft chapter of the Koran, that is to fay, one of the fineft hymns ever addreffed by man to the Supreme Being (*b*). He feemed intirely abforbed in the adoration he was paying to his Creator; and I conceived a favourable opinion of a man, who fulfilled, with fo much dignity, the firft of all duties.

This Turkifh nobleman poffeffed feveral other country-houfes. That to which we were invited he only occupies in the fpring, for he paffes the violent heat of the fummer in a charming retreat, fituated among the mountains. There, while the fun fcorches up the plain, and the whole atmofphere feems on fire, he enjoys a delicious temperature; and beholds the country round him clad in verdure, and covered with flowers and fruits.

Such, Madam, is the life led by the rich Mahometans in Candia: they pafs three-fourths of the year on their eftates, and repair in winter to the towns, to fell the fu-

(*b*) The chapter called *the Introduction*, which ferves in fact as a preface to the Koran: it breathes that fublimity, that ancient fimplicity, which feems to be the proper language of man to the Almighty.

perfluity

perfluity of their produce; the oil, which they make in great quantities, the wax, the wine, and the wool of their flocks, procure them very confiderable wealth. Content with their poffeffions, they afpire after none of thofe public employments which might endanger their fafety, but fee them, without envy, in the poffeflion of ftrangers. Uncontrolled monarchs on their own eftates, they command and receive implicit obedience. Poffeffing the handfomeft women of the ifland (*i*), they bring up their numerous offspring, in the refpect and fubmiffion due to the chief of the family. Thefe Mahometans, enjoying without pain, anxiety, or ambition, all the bounties offered them by nature, pafs their days in tranquillity and happinefs, and retain, even in a

(*i*) The Turks are not fcrupulous in their means of obtaining women: when a Greek has a pretty daughter, and has the misfortune to let her go out of the houfe alone, that moment they carry her off, and marry her. They do not force her to renounce her religion, if fhe appears much attached to it; but all the children are Mahometans. I faw at Canea a handfome Greek girl, who had been carried off in this manner from her family. At her hufband's death, fhe returned to her relations; but her children were muffulmen, and fhe was obliged to feparate from them.

very

very advanced age, almoſt unimpaired good health.

I ſhall long remember, Madam, the agreeable hours I ſpent at the country ſeat of Iſmael Aga; yet I muſt confeſs to you, that, amid the pleaſures I was enjoying, I could not ſuppreſs a feeling of regret for the abſence of the fine arts. To this, however, the Mahometans are inſenſible ; but a Frenchman cannot but deplore a want ſo eſſential, in one of the fineſt countries in the world. Were this iſland the country of a poliſhed people, how would it change its appearance! How much more delightful would its gardens become! What delicious ſhades would the hand of an able artiſt there form! How would he diſplay, in brilliant caſcades, thoſe rivulets which ruſh naturally from the hill-tops! How conjoin the ſcarlet of the pomegranate-tree with the white of the orange flower! How would the myrtle and the laurel-roſe then interweave their branches, and their bloſſoms, and the charming lilac vary the beauteous mixture! How would thoſe elegant ſhrubs, diſtributed in clumps, compoſe groves unequalled for the fragrance of their flowers, the variety of their colours,

colours, and the diverfified tints of their foliage. Under thefe fmiling arbours, the poet
would feel himfelf infpired by the Mufes,
breathe rapturous ftrains dictated by the
Graces, and chaunt hymns to Love. Amid
fuch wondrous natural beauties, letters
would flourifh as in the days of Anacreon,
whofe brow was perpetually crowned with
rofes. Pardon me, Madam, if I thus yield to
the pleafing dreams of my imagination : alas!
I fear I fhall not be able to produce the like
in the foggy atmofphere of the Seine.

I have the honour to be, &c.

L E T T E R XXXVI.

To M. L. M.

QUITTING Canea, Madam, the travel-
ler fees before him the White Mountains (*k*),
at prefent called the hills of Sphachia. This
chain of eminences is in height fecond only
to Mount Ida, which is the moft extenfive
in the ifland ; they begin at Cape Drepanum,
to the eaftward of La Sude, and extend as
far as the fouthern fea, where the little town
of Sphachia is fituated, and defended by a
fmall fort, that ferves to frighten away the
Corfairs. From this elevated centre two
branches ftrike off, which take their courfe
toward the ancient Peloponnefus. Thefe terminate in a point, and form the Capes Spada
and Sufa (*l*), which are the moft weftern
points

(*k*) The ancients called this chain of mountains *Leuci*, or
White Hills. Strabo, lib. x.

(*l*) Thefe weftern branches of the mountains of
Sphachia

points of the ifland. Thefe fecondary branches
are fteep, abounding in perpendicular precipices,
and by no means fertile ; flocks, however, are fed
on them, and we here and there find fcattered, cypreffes, pines, and various evergreens.
The villages on them are little frequented, and
thinly inhabited ; and we meet with no remarkable town. At the bottom of the bay,
inclofed by thefe mountains, is the fmall town
of Cifamo, the ancient Cyfamum, with a
wretched harbour and a ruinous caftle. Near
the promontory of Sufa, is the fortrefs of
Grabufa, built on a low rock : the Venetians defended it for a long time againft the
whole force of the Ottoman empire, and
might ftill have poffeffed it, but for the treachery of one of its governors, who fold it
to the Turks for a barrel of fequins. Between the rock and the continent, veffels
of all fizes find excellent anchorage. But
let us now quit thefe wild and defolate places,
and return to the White Mountains.

Sphachia were formerly called Tityrus and Cadifcus.
The hills of Tityrus formed the promontory of Dictynna, the modern Cape Spada ; thofe of Cadifcus, the
promontory of the fame name, now called Cape Sufa.

Thefe

Thefe hills form, in the front of Canea, an immenfe rampart, the fummit of which is loft in the clouds, and feems to feparate that city from the reft of the ifland. The loweft chain is but two leagues from the town, and may be about fix hundred yards high. Between that and the fecond, opens out a vaft plain three leagues in diameter, and of confiderable length; this intermediate chain is far higher than the former. Beyond are lofty peaks, to which, without doubt, the name of the White Mountains was given from their being, during a part of the year, covered with fnow, which, collecting in heaps, in the deep valleys, on the north fide, hardens, and never melts: the inhabitants cut it in large pieces, which they bring to Canea in the night, and thus enjoy the luxury of drinking iced liquors in the hotteft days of fummer.

Thefe mountains are an appenage granted by the Grand Signior to the Sultana Walida, and are intirely independent of the government of the Pachas. The Sultana fends a perfon fhe can confide in, to govern there, and collect the tributes. The Greeks who inhabit them are called Sphachiots; they-rear

numerous

numerous flocks of goats and sheep, keep bees, make excellent cheese, which has the taste of Parmesan, and sell what they do not consume themselves, in the neighbouring towns and villages.

The Sphachiots, confined to their mountains, are more distinct from the different nations who have possessed Crete, than the inhabitants of the plains: they speak a dialect less corrupt than the rest of the Candiots, and have retained several customs of their ancestors, and certain peculiarities of their ancient character. When Belon travelled among them, they were the best archers in the island; they had very large bows, and displayed more address, strength, and courage, than the other Greeks. Even now the musquet has succeeded to the bow, they are not less skilled in the use of the latter; and in general are excellent marksmen.

Of all the Cretans, the Sphachiots alone have retained the Pyrrhic-dance; this they perform, clad in their ancient dress, that is to say, a short robe bound with a girdle, breeches and buskins; a quiver, filled with arrows, is fastened over their shoulder, a bent

bent bow hangs on their arm, and by their
fide they have a long fword. Thus accoutred,
they begin the dance, which has three mea-
fures. The firft marks the ftep, and they change
feet in dancing like the Germans ; the movements of the fecond are more lively, and
refemble the dance of the inhabitants of
Lower Brittany; during the third meafure,
.they leap backwards and forwards, firft on
one foot, and then on the other, with great
agility. The dancers, who anfwer them,
imitate the fame fteps, and fing and dance
with them to the fame time. In the courfe
of this dance, they perform various evolutions ;
fometimes forming a circle, at others, divid-
ing, and ranging themfelves in two lines,
and feeming to menace each other with their
weapons. Afterward they feparate into couples, and appear as if defying their antagonifts
to the combat; but, in all their movements,
their ear is true to the mufic, and they never
vary from the meafure.

You know, Madam, that, in the ancient
Cretan republic, the people were divided into
two claffes, that of the youth, and that of
mature manhood; this divifion is ftill preferved among the Sphachiots, but not in the

purity of the inftitution. Formerly the young men were fubject to the reproof of the aged, and obeyed them; at prefent they wifh to command. This want of fubordination has been productive of great misfortunes to the whole nation. During the laft war with the Ruffians, the Turks imagined that the inhabitants of Sphachia intended to give up the ifland to their enemies, and pretended that fome Ruffian fhips, touching at the fouthern fide of the ifland, had formed a treaty with the Sphachiots. This was enough to make the Mahometans take up arms. They marched, to the number of eight thoufand, and climbed without difficulty the firft chain of mountains; but it was not fo eafy to fcale the fecond, and a handful of men could have prevented them. The clafs of men propofed to fight, and defend their rocks; but the youth, no doubt feduced by the promifes of the Turks, advifed fubmiffion; and, while their fathers were making head againft the enemy, had the bafenefs to introduce them, by fecret paths, to the fummit of their mountains. The moment they appeared the Sphachiots took to flight, and concealed themfelves as they could in caverns of the rocks, and among the precipices.

The

The muffulmen cruelly abufing their victory, deftroyed whole villages, maffacred many of the inhabitants, and carried off a great number into flavery; without fparing either men, women, or children. They afterwards fold them in different provinces of the Ottoman empire. The youth who compofed the Agelas (*m*) of the ancient Cretans would certainly have acted in a very different manner. We fhould have feen them fly the firft to arms, and repel the enemy far from their habitations, or perifh on the field of battle; but never would they have betrayed their country. This example proves, that the beft inftitutions become pernicious when they depart from their original principles (*n*).

I have already faid, Madam, that the winter covers the mountains of Sphachia with fnow. One morning, in the beginning of February, we left Canea to take the diverfion of fhooting. The north wind had blown during the night; and, though we enjoyed a very agreeable temperature in the plain, the cold

(*m*) Companies of the youth.

(*n*) Since that unfortunate period, the Sphachiots, who were before exempt from the *Carach*, pay it like the reft of the Greeks.

was

was sharp on the mountains. After proceeding about half a league, struck with astonish-
ment and admiration, we could not but stop
to contemplate the superb picture before our
eyes. The sun was rising majestically above
the summits of the hills, and illumined with
his rays a mantle of snow of an immense
extent, which descended from their tops to
the highest part of the lower eminences.
Through the snow the black trunks of the
firs and oaks were seen making their way,
which, at the distance we were at, seemed
as if planted by a line, and assuming the appearance of a long curtain, bounded the horizon in a most picturesque manner. The
magnificent mantle, of which they broke
the uniformity, illumined with all the rays
of the sun, must have been fatiguing to the
eye, had it covered the whole ground; but,
ending precisely at the last chain of mountains, it formed different folds, following
the elevation of the country. Where it terminated, plantations of olive-trees adorned
the declivity of the hills, in the midst of
which scattered cottages agreeably varied the
landscape. Lower down, the scenery was different. Here and there on the plain we
discovered

difcovered beautiful country houfes, fome of
which were built by the Venetians. Around
them the lemon, orange, and almond trees,
laden with golden fruit, formed enchanting groves, while innumerable violets growing under their fhade, perfumed the air with
their delightful odours.

The plain we paffed through contained
large fpaces covered with corn, a foot high,
and of an admirable verdure. This beautiful
carpeting formed a wonderful fine contraft
with that which the fevere cold of the night
had ftretched over the hills. After peram-
bulating, for an hour, amid thefe pleafing landfcapes, we defcended into the vale of Lacu-
late, which is very marfhy in winter, and
intirely uncultivated. But nature has not neglected its embellifhment. For the fpace of a
league, the earth was covered with yellow and
white narciffufes, of the livelieft hues, which
diffufed around the moft fragrant odour imaginable. Wherever the ground was fomewhat
more elevated, it exhibited a profufion of other
ornaments ; white anemonies, and violets,
yellow, red, and, in fhort, of every colour,
glittered through the verdure.

This,

This, Madam, is not a picture of the imagination: from the fummits of the hills
clad in the dazzling whitenefs of their fnowy
mantle, to the plain enriched with verdure,
flowers and fruits, we had before our eyes
all the beauties I have been defcribing. We
contemplated, at one view, the feafons of
fpring and winter, feparated only by an elevation of fix hundred yards. I do affure you,
Madam, that I add nothing to the painting;
and if I have any regret, it is in not being
able to exprefs the peculiar emotions every
one muft experience at the fight of objects
fo aftonifhing, collected within the fpace of a
few leagues.

It is true, that in the month of February,
Nature, in Crete, is, as I may fay, in the
bloom of youth; the breath of her lips is
pure and odoriferous; her robe is embroidered
with the livelieft colours; the gentle dew
of the nights, the light of the god of day,
which begins to warm her bofom, all con-
tribute to her decoration: but one of her
moft beautiful ornaments is the innumerable
golden-apples, which at that feafon cover the
branches of the orange-trees. Thefe are then

I　　　　　　　　　　　　　　　　ripe,

ripe, and invite every hand to pluck them. Their fkin is extremely thin, and their juice delicious, the fragrant odour of which remains long after they have been eaten; they are greatly fuperior to thofe of Egypt, and even at Malta are preferred to the oranges of that ifland.

Having thus defcribed the enchanting fcenes that prefented themfelves to our view; we will now, with your permiffion, Madam, continue our diverfion of fhooting. When we had traverfed the plain of Narciffus, we arrived at fome marfhes, fituated at the extremity of the gulph of La Sude (o). They are nothing but reeds and water, and there is no following the game without boots; but they are inhabited by innumerable fnipes, which afford excellent fport. The environs abound in laurel-rofes and myrtles, which are in flower almoft the whole year, and among thefe the fnipes we had fprung alighted: we here alfo found water-hens, and in the higher grounds our dogs put up a number of quails.

(o) The Plain of Narciffus, which, with its environs, I have been defcribing, is ufually called *La Culate*.

Wifhing

Wishing to prolong our pleasure, we entered the deep vallies that interfect the last chain of the hills of Sphachia, from north to south. Large woodcocks rose every moment from amid the myrtles and laurel-roses, with which this part of the country so abounds. Here are numerous fountains of water, as clear as chrystal, many of which have been embellished by the Turks, and formed into handsome basons. In this delightful spot, beneath the shade of a plane-tree, surrounded with flowering shrubs, we made our halt, and breakfasted on partridges, excellent wine, some olives, and the limpid water of the spring; we did not, however, give over our sport, but climbed up the dry channel of a torrent, till we came into a plain, which extends as far as the foot of the lower chain of mountains, and in which we found great plenty of the finest partridges and hares. Such, Madam, was the country in which we took the diversion of shooting; but we did not too prodigally permit ourselves this pleasure, and, in general, only indulged in it once a week.

I have the honour to be, &c.

L E T-

L E T T E R   XXXVII.

To M. L. M.

WE have already, Madam, vifited the moft beautiful fpots to the weft and fouth of Canea.   It now remains for us to take a view of cape Melec (*p*), which ftretches to the north and eaft of that town.   Its enormous head is feven leagues in circumference, and offers to the navigator nothing but fteep rocks, and threatening fhoals; but, among its romantic hills on the land fide, the traveller finds many places well deferving his attention.

The eaftern part of this promontory forms one of the coafts of the gulph of La Sude. Half a league from its mouth, is a rock on which is built the caftle of that name, which

---

(*p*) This cape was anciently called the Promontory of Ciamum.

refifted

refifted for fo many years the Ottoman arms. It might eafily be battered from the fide of Cape Melec, which is only a quarter of a league from the fhore, and commands it by its fituation. It could not be taken, however, without a fquadron, as it has feveral batteries ranged above each other, hewn out of the folid rock, and is fo extenfive as to contain a village with about a hundred and fifty houfes. Veffels of every fize may anchor all round this fortrefs. But were its artillery well ferved, and by expert gunners, the moft formidable fleet could never force the entrance of the bay, nor efcape, if once fuffered to enter. The fort of La Sude is one of the moft important ftrong-holds of the ifland of Candia, and was accordingly that which remained longeft in the poffeffion of the republic of Venice.

That part of the bay, which extends beyond the caftle, is a league and a half in length, and one-third of a league broad. There is no anchoring-ground nearer than at the diftance of half a league from its extremity; and in any other part, no bottom is to be found at a hundred and fifty fathoms. The anchorage, however, is fufficiently extenfive

tenfive for the moft numerous fleet; and fhips lie there fheltered from all the winds, and landlocked as in a bafon.

The extremity of the gulph of La Sude, called *La ₎Culate*, is only a league and a half from the porte of Canea. They are united by a natural valley, through which it would be eafy to open a communication between the two harbours. Nothing more would be requifite than to cut a fhort canal, which feems to be fuggefted by the very nature of the ground. This would be of ineftimable advantage to commerce. For when the north winds blow, which fometimes detain fhips a week at Canea, they might come down the ftrait of La Sude, and put to fea. Nor would it be lefs favourable to them at the time of their arrival: veffels which, from contrary winds, were unable to make one of thefe harbours, might reach the other. Such a canal would alfo have many other advantages, which I fhall not here fpecify, as plans of this nature will never be executed under the government of the Turks.

Let us now proceed toward the higher part of Cape Melec. This road is very difficult, for we are obliged to climb a number of fteep hills,

hills, which lie perpetually barren. On them the fportfman finds as much game as he can wifh for; hares and partridges in abundance; but the lover of agriculture views with regret thefe naked rocks, hill-fides covered with briars, thyme, and an infinity of wild plants, of no utility to man. The foot of the rocks is lined with the cyclamen, or fow-bread, which in the fpring covers the ground with its pleafing flowers. When we have pafled thefe rugged and defolate places, we defcend into a plain, which owes its fertility and riches to a convent of monks, who have themfelves cleared out the lands. They have enriched the barren hills with vineyards, and planted woods of olive, almond, and fruit-trees, which pro-duce them a confiderable revenue. On the low grounds they till the beft land, and fow it with wheat and barley. The Turks have the juftice to refpect their property, and though their fields have now attained the higheft ftate of improvement, do not add a farthing to the old and very trifling taxes.

We arrive at the convent of the Trinity by a long alley, adorned with lofty cyprefles. On entering the court, which forms a long fquare, we fee the work-fhops and cellars of

the

the holy fathers diftributed around it. In the centre of this court is a fmall church, the portal and fides of which are ornamented with orange-trees, forming a noble circular peri-ftyle, and which, when in bloffom, fill the air with their fragrance. This monaftery is provided with all the utenfils neceffary for agriculture: they have oil and wine-preffes likewife, and every convenience adapted to a rural life. While the priefts are offering up prayers to God, and celebrating divine fer-vice, the lay-brethren employ themfelves in ruftic occupations. It is a little republic, which derives its wealth from labour, and of which the members, attached to their refpec-tive duties, lead a laborious, but peaceable and happy life. We frequently took up our quarters with thefe good monks, to be more in readinefs for fhooting, and always expe-rienced from them the refpect and attention of a hofpitality which anticipated all our wants.

Leaving the convent of the Trinity, we arrive, after an hour's walk, through very rugged paths, at the monaftery of St. John, fituated on the loftieft fummit of Cape Melec. The level ground, in front of the houfe, com-mands

mands the adjacent country. Seated under a
single olive-tree, which rifes between two
rocks, the traveller refpires a cool air in the
middle of the hotteft day of fummer, and
difcovers an immenfe extent of country. To
the fouth he fees the chain of the White
Mountains, crowned with fnows and forefts;
to the weft the Minarets of Canea, and to
the north the diftant point of Cape Spada,
and all the veffels which commerce brings into
thefe feas. His ideas expand in proportion to
the magnificence of the profpect before him.
If he contracts his horizon, he difcovers the
hill-fides ornamented with vineyards, mountains full of rocky precipices, and in the
plain, country houfes furrounded by delightful groves. His imagination ftraying beneath
their fhade, beholds the fruit fufpended from
their branches, and the flowers which decorate the myrtles. Abforbed in a pleafing re-
very, he views with rapture this enchanting
landfcape. But, ah! What horrid noife fuddenly awakens him from his dream? He
hears the hollow found of the diftant tempeft;
and the dafhing of the waves againft the rocks
fufpended over their abyfs. Their roaring is
tremendous; and they threaten to undermine
the

the foundations of thefe huge maffes of ftone,
and ingulph them in their waters. How do
they foam and lafh continually the refounding
fhore! Surely this is the anger of nature!
Adieu, ye fmiling fhades! delicious profpects,
adieu! no longer can you attract the attention of the alarmed fpectator. Cafting his
eyes around him, he difcovers nothing but
precipices, calcined rocks, and barren hills
piled one upon the other, while he fhudders
at their horrid afpect. Such, Madam, are
the different fcenes which occafionally prefent
themfelves to an obferver beneath the olive-
tree, before the monaftery of St. John.

From this hermitage a narrow path, hewn in
fome places out of the rock, leads to a grotto,
embellifhed by the wonderful powers of nature. To arrive there, we muft continue to
defcend for half an hour into a very fteep
valley; but the pleafure amply repays the labour. This vaft cavern is full of brilliant
ftalactites; fome of which are of a pyra-
midal form, while others refemble the pipes
of an organ, and, pendant from the roof, feem
to threaten the head of the curious examiner.
They line all the fides, reflect, like chryftal, the
light of the flambeaux; are as polifhed as glafs

and

and extremely brilliant ; but they are not fluted, nor do they hang in feftoons, like thofe of the grotto of Antiparos, the moft beautiful in the world. The forms of the latter are much more varied, and their effect, by confequence, far more aftonifhing.

The apple-fage (*q*), defcribed by Tourne. fort, grows in abundance along the valley leading to the grotto. The botanift has rea- fon to lament that this learned naturalift re- mained fo fhort a time in the ifland, and examined it at a feafon when the country, burnt up by the fun, could afford him nothing but parched plants. Had he feen it in the fpring, he would have enriched his catalogue with feveral fpecies, which had difappeared before his arrival. The beautiful fhrub, known by the name of the ebon-tree of Crete, is found among the rocks on the fea- fhore. It does not grow to any great height, but the lively purple flowers, which glitter among its filver foliage, render it very pleafing.

Let us now defcend from Cape Melec, and return towards Canea; in our way, we meet

(*q*) This fage is not confined to this fpot. Large tracts of ground are covered with it in Mount Ida.

with

with the convent of Acrotiri, which is a
convent of nuns. It is a frightful folitude,
in the environs of which nothing is feen but
dreary rocks, and at their feet the wild thyme,
briars, the thyme with the odoriferous flower,
the labdanum, and a few ftraw-berry bufhes.
The nuns here are not cloiftered, and make
no other vow but that of virginity. Each
choofes a companion ; and, thus coupled, they
refide in fmall houfes, built round a chapel,
to which a Greek prieft comes to fay mafs.
Thefe couples perform all the mutual offices
of friendfhip, affift each other, and poffefs, in
common, an inclofure, more or lefs confiderable, appropriated to the double cell. This
is their garden and orchard, in which we find
orange, almond, and olive-trees. They likewife keep bees, which are not fhut up in
hives, and have no covering but planks, laid
crofs-ways on two pofts, beneath which fhelter
alone thefe induftrious creatures depofit their
honey and wax. The firft combs are the
largeft, and gradually diminifh to a point.
They are all in the fhape of an inverted py-
ramid, and it is furprifing how faft they are
made by the bees. The honey of thefe infects is produced from the flowers of the different

ferent kinds of thyme, and an infinity of odoriferous plants and fhrubs, with which the country is covered; nor can any exceed it in purity or'fragrance.

But to return to our nuns. I have already told you, Madam, that, united in pairs, they inhabit a building, confifting of three or four apartments. Each of thefe little dwellings contains various conveniences within itfelf. They have here likewife a vaft ciftern, a neceffary precaution on an eminence without water, a wine-prefs, an oven, and one or two looms for making linen. They generally rear filkworms, and gather cotton, which is an annual plant in this country. One of the fifters fpins, while the other weaves, and fome of them knit ftockings. When they have provided themfelves with what is neceffary for their own ufe, they fell the remainder of the fruits of their induftry, in the town.

In their cells we fee neither fumptuoufnefs nor magnificence; we find only convenient utenfils, and fimple and abfolutely neceffary furniture, which is kept perpetually clean and neat. In a word, thefe nuns, without being rich, enjoy a comfortable fubfiftence, for which they are indebted to their induftry.

Cheerfulnefs

Cheerfulnefs is their conftant companion, and
we fee among them no melancholy faces.   In
general, a young fifter unites herfelf to one
older than herfelf, to folace and relieve her
from the burthen of the more laborious employments.   I frequently vifited a Greek lady,
who every year paffed a few weeks in this
monaftery, and always found, among thefe
voluntary nuns, a mildnefs, modefty, and
livelinefs, very remote from that four and auftere chara&ter, which is abfolutely inconfiftent
with virtue.

At the moment I am writing, Acrotiri contains within its narrow precin&ts the decrepitude of age, the vigour of riper years, and
all the charms of youth.   I have feen three
of thefe females well deferving to employ
the pencil of a fkilful painter: a nun of
a hundred and nine years old, another of
thirty-fix, and a novice of fixteen.   The firft,
bent like a bow, with difficulty hobbled along
by the aid of a fmall ftaff, and feemed every
moment ready to fink with feeblenefs.   She
had ftill preferved all her fenfes, though blunt-
ed, and in a kind of ftupor; to extra&t any
converfation from her, you muft give her a
glafs of cordial, or of excellent wine, which
gradually revived her heart.   She told us,
fhe

fhe was born in the village of La Sude; how the Turks had feveral times befieged that fortrefs, and how the bombs they threw fell upon the roofs of the houfes, and fpread terror among the inhabitants. After the taking of the fort, fhe retired to the convent of Acrotiri, where fhe has refided near four-fcore years (r).

The fecond was tall, with an animated countenance, and elegant features; her air was majeftic, her eye-brows black, and her eyes fparkling; but the rofes of her cheeks, and the lilies of her complexion, began to fade; fhe was ftill handfome, but her beauty was the beauty of maturity; the delicacy and foftnefs of blooming youth was evidently paft, and each fucceffive day robbed her of a charm.

The third—you muft have feen her, Madam, to conceive a juft idea of her beauty, which my powers of defcription are totally infufficient to convey. Unite, in imagination, all the charms which fometimes adorn

(r) The fort of La Sude was ftill in the poffeffion of the Venetians, when M Tournefort vifited this country, in 1700. They continued mafters of it feveral years after; and it was only taken from them in 1707, or 1708.

the faireſt of nature's works, in all their
delicacy and perfection, in all their aſtoniſhing harmony and grace, and you will have
a feeble image of the novice of Acrotiri. Her
features had uncommon animation, and her
eyes ſparkled with a luſtre that ſeemed more
than human, and which it was impoſſible to
ſuſtain unmoved. How indeſcribable muſt
have been her ſmile, would this beauteous
virgin have conſented to ſmile. Tranſcendent
as were her charms, her dreſs was of the moſt
ſimple kind, yet it ſeemed as if no ornament
might be added that could embelliſh her.
Every action, every attitude, made her appear
ſtill more lovely. Abſolutely unconſcious of
her beauty, ſhe with apparent pleaſure waited
on the nun, whom ſhe conſidered as her mother, and anticipated all her deſires. Her whole
air and manner were free from the ſlighteſt tinge
of affectation; ſhe appeared abſorbed in ſublime
ideas, and only aſpired to the happineſs of
being received among the nuns of Acrotiri.
I cannot deny, Madam, that I was ſenſibly
concerned at the thought of ſo many charms
being for ever buried in the depth of a ſad
ſolitude, and that ſhe, who ſeemed born to
give the higheſt felicity to ſome favoured
mortal,

mortal, fhould be feparated for ever from the
fociety of man ! I went often to the monaftery,
and never failed to vifit the good nun, who
was to her as a mother.

Let a painter try what his art can effect,
and if he would reprefent the bloom of youth,
the maturity of riper years, and old age in
its decrepitude, let him pourtray the three
females I have endeavoured feebly to defcribe. But he muft fail in the attempt. To
fucceed, he muft, like me, have feen the originals. The imagination only traces with
fidelity what the eye has obferved. Then
genius meditates and compofes, and by its
powers becomes creative : for perfectly to reprefent fuch objects, is rather to create than
to imitate. This was the perfection to which
Protogenes attained. The froth, on the mouth
of the panting dog, appeared to him imitated,
and not natural ; an ordinary artift would
have been fatisfied, but the Rhodian painter
afpired to the perfection of nature ; that is,
to be like her creative.

Let us return to Canea, from which we are
only a league diftant. As foon as we defcend
the mountain, we pafs through a country
abounding in all the treafures of agriculture,

fmiling

ſmiling paſtures, and plantations of olives and orange trees. Alas! Madam, the riches with which the earth is covered, the beauty of theſe ſhades, the flowers and fruits with which the trees are loaded, have no longer any charms for me. Let us re-enter the walls of Canea.

I have the honour to be, &c.

L E T T E R XXXVIII.

To M. L. M.

THE iſland of Crete, Madam, is at preſent governed by three Pachas, who reſide at Candia, Canea, and Retimo. The firſt, who is always a Pacha of three tails, is, as I may ſay, the viceroy of the iſland. He is inveſted with the ſupreme power, has the inſpection of the forts and arſenals, nominates to vacant military poſts, and to the governments of La Sude, Grabuſa, Spina Longua, and Gira Petra (s). The governors of theſe forts are called beys. They have under them a governor of the caſtle, and three general officers, one of whom is general of the artillery, the other of the cavalry, and the third of the janiſſaries.

(s) Gira Petra, formerly called *Hierapithna*, was a city with a harbour, ſituated on the ſouth ſide of the iſland. At preſent it is but a ſmall and wretched town, only the ſmalleſt veſſels can enter the harbour; and the fortreſs, which is incapable of defence, ſerves merely to frighten away the Corſairs.

The

The council of the Pacha confifts of a Kyaia, who has great influence in all public affairs, and the difpofal of almoft all appointments; of the Aga of the janiffaries, who is colonel-general of the troops, and principal fuperintendant of the police; of two Topigi-Bachis (*t*); of a Def- · terdar, treafurer-general of the imperial claims; of the keeper of the imperial treafury, and of the firft officers of the army. It is plain, therefore, that this government is purely military; and, which is the natural confequence, that the power of the Pacha Scrafquier is abfolute. There is no appeal from his fentence, which is inftantly carried into execution.

The great officers of the law are, the Muphti, the fupreme head of religion, and the Cady. The former expounds the laws relative to the partition of property among children, inheritances, and marriages; in a word, all thofe laid down by Mahomet in the Koran; and decides on every thing refpecting the ceremonies of the Mahometan religion. The Cadi cannot pafs fentence in difputes originating in thefe laws, until he has obtained, in writing, the opinion of the Muphti, which

(*t*) General of the artillery.

B b 2 is

is called a *faitfa*. His office, therefore, is to receive declarations, complaints, the prefents of individuals, and to decide in the common *cafes of litigation. The Pacha muft confult thefe judges before he can legally put a Turk to death; but when he has attained the dignity of three tails, he often raifes himfelf above the law, and at once dictates the fentence of death, and orders it to be carried into execution by his own authority.

Each mofque has its Imam, a fort of curate, who performs divine fervice; and fchool-mafters are diftributed in different quarters of the town. Thefe men are greatly refpected in Turkey, and bear the title of Effendi (*u*).

The following is the number of troops of which the garrifon of Candia confifts.

Five companies of Janiffaries, the number of which varies.

Twenty companies of Jerli, of one hundred and twenty men each.

Two companies of Ifdarli.

(*u*) Effendi is a title of honour, beftowed on perfons confidered as deferving refpect.

Four

Four companies of gunners.
Four companies of cavalry.
Four companies of volunteers.
One company of bombardiers.
One company of miners.

In the whole forty-fix companies, com-
poſing an army of about ten thouſand men.
All theſe troops are not in the town, but
would be collected in an inſtant. They receive their pay regularly, and punctually, every
three months, except the janiſſaries, whoſe
officers alone are paid. The different poſts
in this militia do not depend on the Pacha.
All promotions are regulated by a council of
each company, confiſting of the officers on
duty, and the veterans. Theſe offices can
only be held two years, except that of the
Sorbagi, or captain, which is purchaſed at
Conſtantinople, and held for life. The *Oufla*,
or cook, is continued likewiſe in his employment as long as the company are contented
with his ſervices. There is a chaplain, or *Imam*,
to every company.

The garriſons of Canea and Retimo, regulated on the ſame plan, are much leſs numerous

merous. The firſt conſiſts of about three thouſand men, the other of fifteen hundred. But as all the male children of the Turks become members of the corps of janiſſaries at their birth, their number would greatly augment in time of war. There is not much, indeed, to fear from them, the greateſt part having ſcarcely ever ſeen a muſket fired. They are' never exerciſed in military evolutions, and are totally ignorant of that dreadful art, which. in our days has been brought to ſuch perfection, and which, reduced to certain rules, triumphs, without difficulty, over blind force and numbers.

A Pacha of Canca, who diſtinguiſhed himſelf in the laſt war with the Ruſſians, was deſirous to try the ſkill of the gunners of that garriſon. He ordered a bark to be anchored, at the diſtance of half a mile from the walls, and a large barrel placed on the deck. The ſea was perfectly calm, and the mark exceedingly diſtinct; but, notwithſtanding a reward was offered to the perſon who ſhould knock it down, the gunners kept firing the whole day, without touching either the barrel, or the boat.

The

The Pachas of Canea and Retimo are not lefs abfolute, within the limits of their govern- ments, than the Pacha of Candia. They en- joy the fame privileges, and their council is compofed of the fame officers. Thefe go- vernors are only intent on rapidly enrich- ing themfelves, and ufe every means to ex- tort money from the Greeks, who are op- preffed in a manner not to be defcribed. But, to fay the truth, thefe unhappy people ftretch out their willing necks to the chains that weigh them down. Their envious difpofition is con- tinually arming them againft each other. If one of them has had the good fortune to ac- quire a little property, others endeavour to difcover fomething of which to accufe him before the Pacha, who avails himfelf of thefe diffenfions, to rob both parties. It feems as if the Greeks, dejected and debafed by their misfortunes, were no longer capable of a ge- nerous fentiment; nor are they in the leaft amended by the cruel examples they have every day before their eyes.

It is not, therefore, furprifing that, under this barbarous government, the number of Greeks fhould daily diminifh. At prefent Crete is

fuppofed

fuppofed to contain, at moft, only   150,000
Sixty-five thoufand of whom pay
the carach (x).

The Turks, though they have only
poffeffed the ifland one hundred and
twenty years, as they are not fubject to the fame oppreffion, have
multiplied, and flourifh on the ruins
of the vanquifhed. Their number
amounts to   -   -   -   200,000
That of the Jews only to   -   -   200
                                      _____

                                      Total   350,200

Is it not aftonifhing to find fo few inhabitants on this ifland, which is above two hundred and fifty leagues in circumference? Is not
this diminution of men a fufficient proof of a
deftructive government? I am aware that Crete
is interfected by chains of high mountains,
where we cannot expect any great population. But there are rich valleys, and immenfe plains, capable of being rendered pro-

(x) The carach, as I have faid, is the tribute paid to the
Grand Signior by all his fubjects, not Mahometans. But it
is levied only on men arrived at maturity; women and
children are exempt from it.

                                      digioufly

digioufly fruitful. Nothing is wanting to this teeming foil but labourers and fecured property, to make it furnifh fubfiftence for four times the people it now contains.

The hundred cities of Crete have been ce-lebrated by the writers of antiquity, and Geo-graphy has preferved to us their names and fituations (*y*). Several of thefe contained thirty thoufand citizens ; if, therefore, we allow fix thoufand to each, on an average, I imagine we fhall be rather under than above the true number.

This calculation will give for the hundred cities - ∙ - - - - 600,000

We may alfo eftimate the Cretans difperfed in the towns and villages, at the fame number - - 600,000

               Total   1,200,000

This cannot be efteemed an exaggerated calculation. When the Venetians were in poffeffion of the kingdom of Candia, it is faid

(*y*) The cities of Cnoffus, Gortyna, and Cydon, muft have contained, each of them, at leaft 30,000 citizens, if we may judge from their power, and the extent af-figned them by hiftorians.

to have contained nine hundred and ninety-six villages.

Thus we find that, when Crete was a free country, it maintained eight hundred and forty-nine thoufand eight hundred inhabitants more than at this day. But fince thofe happy times, this unfortunate ifland has been deprived of her laws by the Romans; groaned under the difaftrous reigns of the corrupt princes of the lower empire; been ravaged by the Arabs during a hundred and twenty years; exchanged their government for that of the Venetians, and, at length, has been finally fubjected to the defpotifm of the Turks, who, in all the countries they have conquered, have occafioned a frightful depopulation.

I might produce many examples of this deftruction. When Candia was in the poffeffion of the Venetians, the towns of Sitia, Gira Petra, Sifamo, and Sphachia, were crowded with inhabitants; at this day they are but wretched villages with ruined fortreffes, and harbours, nearly choaked up. Candia, the capital of the kingdom, was prodigioufly populous, and carried on a very extenfive commerce in wines, corn, filks, and wax. It was, indeed,

a fecond

a second Venice ; but is now almost de-
serted.

It is true, that the Turks, during a five
and twenty years war, destroyed many thousand of the Candiots ; and that the plague,
the constant attendant of their armies, followed them into this island, and was the de-
struction of a still greater number ; but if the
Ottoman government had considered men as of
any importance, it might have been able, in
the course of a whole century of peace and
tranquillity, to repair these ravages.

The Turks have left the Greeks the free
exercise of their religion, but do not allow them
to repair their churches and monasteries, without permission, which is only to be obtained
by money, and brings in confiderable sums to
the Pachas. They have, as formerly, twelve
bishops, the principal of whom assumes the
title of archbishop of Gortyna. He resides at
Candia, which is the seat of the Metropolitan
church. Nominated himself by the patriarch
of Constantinople, he fills up all the vacant
sees of the island (z). He bears the triple
crown

(z) These bishoprics are, at present, *Gortyna, Cnossou,
Miralella, Hyera, Gira Petra, Arcadia, Cheronesus,
Lambis,*

crown on his tiara, figns in red, and is re-
fponfible for all the debts of the clergy. To
fulfil thefe engagements, he levies heavy contributions on the other bifhops, and efpecially
the monafteries. He is acknowledged as chief
of the Greeks, whom he protects as far as
his feeble influence extends. To him the
government applies in matters of importance;
and he alone, of his whole nation, has the
privilege of entering a town on horfeback.

I have the honour to be, &c.

Lambis, Milopotamo, Retimo, Canea, Cifamo. They are
nearly the fame as under the Conftantinopolitan emperors.

L E T T E R   XXXIX.

To M. L. M.

T H E olive-tree, Madam, that precious tree, confecrated to Minerva, has almoft difappeared from Attica. The Albanians and Turks, who have alternately ravaged Greece, feem to have been intent on deftroying it. I have been affured, that, within twenty years, they have cut down two hundred thoufand feet of thefe trees. Is it poffible to imagine greater barbarifm ? Do we perceive any thing refembling this in ancient wars ? Thus has the Morea, fo rich and flourifhing, when poffeffed by the Venetians, become a poor and miferable country.

The ifland of Crete has not in this refpect fuffered the fame fate. The olive-trees, which delight in a fandy foil, a mild temperature, and the vicinity of the fea, grow in abundance on the hills, and in the plains. The cold is never fevere enough to injure them, and the

heat

heat is always fufficient perfectly to ripen their fruit. We meet with fome which feem coeval with the foil that bears them; they grow to a vaft fize, and attain the height of fifty feet. Their produce conftitutes the chief wealth of the inhabitants, and their principal branch of commerce. The crops, however, are not equally abundant; in two years, one is generally excellent, and the other moderate. Exclufive of the prodigious confumption of oil by the inhabitants, and efpecially the Greeks, who make ufe of it as fauce to vegetables and fifh, during the four Lents; befides what the Turks of Canea, inftructed by a native of Provence (*a*), make ufe of in their manufactories of foap, which they export throughout the Levant; befides the great quantity of preferved olives, which are ferved at every table, the Turks annually load four and twenty fhips with oil. Thefe veffels contain, on an average, one hundred and fifty

(*a*) The inhabitants of Candia had no manufacture in their ifland, and it is not long fince a native of Provence taught them to make foap, of which they have now feveral manufactories at Canea. This betrayer of his country's intereft has greatly injured the trade of Marfeilles.

tons

	l.	*s.*	*d.*
tons each, the value of which is about 90,000 livres, - - | 3,750 | 0 | 0 |

Five only of thefe fhips belong to foreign nations, and their exportation amounts to 450,000 livres, - - | 18,750 | 0 | 0 |

The other nineteen are of Marfeilles, and their lading amounts to 1,710,000 livres, - | 71,250 | 0 | 0 |

The French merchants, fettled at Canea, annually export, befides, in wax and other articles, to the amount of 80,000 livres, | 3,333 | 13 | 3 |

which makes an annual exportation, from this ifland, on account of the French, to the value of 1,790,000 livres, - | 74,582 | 10 | 0 |

They import to the amount of 450,000 livres (18,750*l.*) in the cloths of Languedoc, and to about 100,000 livres (4,166*l.*) in fugar, coffee, Englifh fhalloons, &c. which make 550,000 livres, | 22,916 | 0 | 6 |

Deducting this from the preceding amount of exports, we fhall find that the balance of commerce, between France and

the

the ifland of Crete, is in favour   *l.*   *s. d.*
of the latter 1,240,000 livres,   51,666   13   3

The Marfeilles houfes, eftablifhed at Canea, are connected   .
with thofe of Smyrna and Conftantinople, and the balance is
paid in Turkifh piafters.

Now, as almoft all the exports
from the ifland of Crete are
made at Canea, where the trading fhips of different nations arrive, by eftimating at one-third
more the articles fhipped by the
Cretans from their other ports,
we fhall rather be above than
below the truth, if we eftimate
the total at 2,986,666 livres,   124,444   8   4

This commerce is certainly very inconfiderable for an ifland of fo great an extent.
But it is in the poffeffion of the Turks,
who are ignorant alike of the arts and fciences ;
and the Greeks, who, · harraffed by every
fpecies of oppreffion, dare undertake nothing,
either· for private advantage or public utility. The ifland does not contain a fufficient
number of inhabitants for all the lands to be
cultivated.

cultivated. We pafs over, with fympathetic concern, plains of three or four leagues extent, watered by fertilizing ftreams, without meeting with the flighteft trace of cultivation. Delightful vallies, where the luxuriant earth produces an infinity of wild fhrubs and plants, lie wafte, for want of hands, encouragement, and induftry. The indolent Turk paffes his life in the midft of his poffeffions, without thinking of improvement : and fhould the Greek obtain permiffion to clear out a piece of ground ; after bedewing it with the fweat of his brow, and at the moment he is about to enjoy the fruit of his induftry, his powerful neighbour wrefts from him the fruit of his labour. Within thefe few years, however, feveral of the land proprietors in the environs of Canca, have become fenfible of what is their true intereft, and begun a few olive plantations.

When the kingdom of Candia was under the dominion of the republic of Venice, it produced great quantities of grain, amply fupplied the wants of the inhabitants, and made confiderable exportations to foreign countries. At prefent the ifland is obliged to import corn ; and I have feen feveral fhips

C c

laden

laden with it arrive at Canea. This is not to be attributed to any change in the foil, which is ftill warmed by the fame fun, and watered by the fame ftreams. The tyranny of the Turkifh government muft alone be confidered as the caufe.

Objects of the laft importance, which would infinitely extend the commerce of the Cretans, are almoft totally neglected. The mulberry-tree thrives admirably in the ifland, and nothing would be more eafy than to rear filk-worms. The little cotton which is cultivated there, is of a very fine quality ; and the wool, though not remarkable for its finenefs, is fo for its quantity ; yet is there not a fingle manufacture in the country which may employ thefe valuable materials ! Little attention, therefore, is paid to the filk-worm ; cotton and flax are cultivated in fmall quantities ; and never will it occur to the imagination of a Turk, that under a mild and favourable fky, which would allow the flocks to be folded the whole year in the open air, it might be poffible, by paying due attention to their feeding, and properly crofling the breed, to obtain wool even equal to that of Spain.

What advantages might not a polifhed nation

tion derive from an ifland, which, after fatis-
fying the moft effential wants of man, would
ftill farther fupply him with every thing
that contributes to utility, eafe, and even
luxury ! How might they extend their various branches of commerce ! What benefits
might they not derive from manufactures calculated to give them value ! The delicious
wines of the country, fo little known, would
be in requeft over the whole world. Its forefts of pines, oaks, and cedars, under proper
management, would be of ufe for fhip-building. The hufbandmen, excited by the hope
and certainty of enjoying the fruit of their
labours, would clear out vaft tracts of wafte
land, now abandoned to fterility, would fow
every fpecies of grain, increafe their plantations, and, after enriching the ftate, live in
plenty, in the bofom of their numerous families. Men would multiply without end, in the
fineft climate in the world ; villages and im-
poverifhed towns would again become populous cities ; again would the arts return
to their native country ; again would they
flourifh ; and, in a word, the fuperb ifland
of Crete revive out of her afhes. To produce this extraordinary, this happy change,

C c 2   nothing

nothing is neceffary, but the encouragement and protection of a wife government.

Thefe reflections, Madam, are not the dreams of a heated imagination, or of a traveller who has haftily paffed through the country. I continued in the ifland of Candia fifteen months; I have vifited its mountains and its plains ; I am acquainted with its productions ; I know in what they are fufceptible of improvement; and I can affure you, that in the whole world, there is no country that combines fo many real advantages. The lofty trees of the frozen regions crown the fummits of the mountains ; while lefs lofty hills are covered with the fruit-trees which are common in our climates (*b*) ; the declivities are embellifhed with vineyards, producing wines equally various as agreeable ; the vallies abound in trees bearing delicious fruits, many of which thrive under the torrid zone, while the plains are enriched with every fpecies of grain the earth produces. Ob-

(*b*) The apple, chefnut, pear, and cherry trees, thrive incomparably on the hills of Crete, and produce fruit ; which, if it be not fo good as ours, it muft not be imputed to the quality of the foil, but to the indolence of a people who know nothing of the art of grafting.

ferve,

ferve, too, that nature has placed the fineft harbours, Palio Caftro, under Cape Solomon, Spina Longa, La Sude, and Grabuge, on the eaft, weft, and north fides of the ifland, as if its commerce was deftined to extend to every quarter of the world. I fhall add only one word : Crete, placed as it is, almoft at an equal diftance from Europe, Afia, and Africa, feems the central point of thefe three quarters of the globe ; nor do I believe it pof-fible to affign a more favourable fituation.

I have the honour to be, &c.

L E T T E R XL.

₊ *The following Letters were intended to form a second volume, in which the author proposed to treat on the other iflands of the Archipelago which he had vifited. It has not been thought proper to give the public any more than thefe three letters, the author not having put the laft hand to the others before his death.*

To M. L. M.

I HAVE left, for fome time, Madam, the ifland of Candia, and made an excurfion into the Archipelago ; I fhall now give you an account of this little voyage. I embarked in one of the decked boats with which the Greeks carry on their coafting trade in fummer. The eldeft fon of M. Breft, vice-conful of France, at Argentiera, and two merchants going to Conftantinople, were of the party. Our veffel was but fifteen feet long, by five broad, without either cabin or deck ; fo that we were obliged to remain expofed to the burning rays of the fun, and fleep in the night without any other covering than our cloaks. A

fudden

fudden fquall might overfet us ; and were the
fea ever fo little agitated, we muft be deluged
by the waves. Before they leave the harbour, indeed, thefe light barks always wait
for a fair wind, and then they appear to fly
over the furface of the waves. They are
built to go both with oars and fails, which
is a double advantage.

You may poffibly begin to think, by this
time, Madam, that this mode of navigation
is not the fafeft, and you are certainly right.
But that of the Greeks, who failed to the
fiege of Troy, was ftill lefs fo ; fince, if we
may believe Thucydides, undoubtedly an authentic hiftorian (c), their veffels were without decks. They were, therefore, obliged to
coaft along the fhore, and navigate from cape
to cape ; unable to keep the fea with open
barks, which the firft wave might have fent
to the bottom, they dragged them upon land
at the leaft appearance of a ftorm, and waited,
fometimes for whole months, the return of
fine weather. With fuch veffels it was impoffible to tack, and the wind was favourable
for them only when right abaft.

(c) Thucydides, lib. i. The Grecian fleet, which failed
for Troy, confifted only of veffels that had no decks.

We

We left the port of La Sude at fun-rife : a freſh breeze filled our triangular ſails, and we continued rapidly to plough the ſurface of the deep. Our courſe lay towards Argenticra. We long kept in view behind us the majeſtic head of Cape Melec, and the lofty mountains of Sphachia, which loſt themſelves in the clouds. As we advanced, they diminiſhed in the horizon, and about noon wholly diſappeared, leaving us ſurrounded only with the vaſt expanſe of ſea.

The firſt time you venture on the ocean with theſe little boats, which, in the grand ſcene that preſents itſelf to the eye, appear like walnut-ſhells, the mind is ſtruck with aſtoniſhment. Seated on the deck, you touch with your hand the water, foaming under its ſides. On the brink of the abyſs, you ſeek in the horizon a place of refuge againſt the tempeſt ; but the eye diſcovers nothing but the immenſity of the waters and the heavens, and a ſentiment of fearful awe penetrates the ſoul. Experience, however, ſoon diſſipates theſe vain terrors, and man, to whom habit familiarizes every thing, delights to brave, with ſuch feeble means, the fury of the waves. The Greek mariners, well acquainted

quainted with all the harbours of the Archipelago, and guided by prudence, put their veffels before the wind, when the tempeft begins to threaten, and feek for fhelter in fome neighbouring ifland. Not lefs prudent than their anceftors (*d*), they lay up their boats in harbour during the winter, and wait for the return of fummer, before they truft themfelves anew to the inconftant element.

During the whole day we had a ferene fky, and a favourable wind, which enabled us to make a great way, and at nine in the evening we anchored in the port of Argentiera, after a run of thirty fea-leagues. M. Breft prefented us to his father, who received us with great politenefs, and invited us to take up our refidence in his houfe.

I have the honour to be, &c.

(*d*) The ancient Greeks and Romans, not having a navy like ours, nor fhips capable of refifting tempefts, feldom made voyages in winter, but waited till the fpring, and the return of fine weather.

L E T T E R XLI.

To M. L. M.

I LEFT Canea with an intention to go to Conſtantinople ; but on our arrival at Argentiera, learning that the plague was then ravaging the capital of the Ottoman empire, I immediately laid aſide my projeᵗ. In vain did my travelling companions, who had buſineſs in that city, ſolicit me to proceed with them. I had ſeen too much of the dreadful effeᵗs of this terrible diſtemper ! The diſmal ſcenes I had witneſſed were ſtill preſent to my memory. I already imagined I beheld the unhappy viᵗims, ſtruck as with lightning, ſuddenly dropping down dead ; others, with haggard eyes, and inflamed counte-
ᵣnances, expiring in the convulſions of a horrible delirium. I ſeemed to hear the ſhrieks of the women, and the howlings of the public mourners.

mourners. Thefe fad fpectacles, which recurred to my imagination in all their horror, rendered me immovable in my refolution. I refifted every importunity, wifhed my companions a good journey, and remained at Argentiera.

This little ifland, which was formerly called Cimolus, is only fix leagues in circumference: the foil is extremely dry, and deftitute of fprings, nor is there any water here but what is collected in cifterns, or brought from Melos, an ifland at a little diftance; the hills, vales, and the whole country ftript of trees, do not offer a fingle fhade to defend you from the heat of the fun. The Venetians, during their war with the Turks, cut down all the olive-trees, and did irreparable damage to the ifland; nor do the prefent inhabitants dare to make frefh plantations, left they fhould draw on themfelves heavier impofitions. Thus does the Ottoman government uniformly act towards its fubjects; if they manifeft any induftry, it is immediately taxed, and ftifled in its birth!

Argentiera prefents nothing but rocky hills, deftitute of verdure, and vallies producing worthlefs fhrubs, and thorny thickets.

The

The vales are generally covered with a white and flat clay, called by the ancients *Terra Cimolia*, or *Cimolia Creta* (Fuller's-earth), and which the inhabitants employ, inftead of foap, to wafh their linen. This barren foil feems but ill adapted to agriculture; yet the induftrious iflanders make it produce them a fubfiftence. They fow barley and wheat at the beginning of autumn, which is the rainy feafon, and reap in March. Their vineyards on the hill-fides furnifh them with fruit only for the table. They procure their wines from Santorini, Milo, and other iflands of the Archipelago. They rear poultry, and flocks of goats and fheep, the flefh of which is excellent. The country affords them quails, hares and partridges in abundance. The women knit cotton ftockings, and the men employ themfelves in fifhing and navigation. Excellent fifh are taken round the ifland, efpecially the *Rouget* (e), which is very delicate eating.

The little tribe which inhabits Argentiera, is compofed of about five hundred perfons.

(e) This fifh is well known, and highly efteemed on all the coafts of the Mediterranean; it is met with at Marfeilles and Toulon, and throughout Provence.

Their

Their enjoyments are not many, but, thanks to their induſtry, they want none of the neceſſaries of life. This little iſland indeed does not groan under the immediate oppreſſions of the officers of the Porte; here are no Agas, nor Cadis. The Turks would not venture to reſide here, as there is no fort to prevent the Malteſe from making them priſoners, whoſe privateers come hither, from time to time, to ſpend in feaſts, entertainments, and pleaſures of every kind, the money they have taken from the Mahometans. This is a tribute they pay to the pretty women of Argenticra. In a word, the Greeks who inhabit this rock would be happy, were the Captain Pacha but to forget them in the annual contributions he levies, frequently with barbarity, on the iſlands of the Archipelago. Beſides the poll-tax, to which all the Greeks are ſubject, he exacts preſents ſometimes amounting to the value of the tribute; and his officers know perfectly how to imitate his example. Theſe extortions are attended with the moſt fatal conſequences, and reduce the iſlanders to the moſt extreme miſery.

During my ſtay in this country, I lodged with M. Breſt, the French vice-conſul, an

intel-

intelligent man, with much firmnefs of character, and a noble and generous foul. He.
is perfectly acquainted with all the ports of
the Mediterranean, and has often ferved as
a pilot to the French fhips in thefe feas. He
has made himfelf adored by the inhabitants,
by faving them from the plunder of the Corfairs, and by interceding with the officers fent
by the Captain Pacha to lay them under con-
tribution ; he may be confidered, therefore, as
the chief of this little republic, or the king
of the ifland. This worthy man has refided
upwards of forty years at Argentiera, and
has two fons, the eldeft, whom I have already
mentioned, and a younger, now at fea ; both
are great travellers, and well educated ; they
fpeak French, Italian, Greek, and Turkifh
perfectly, and appear worthy to fucceed
their father. He has alfo a daughter, who
is young, tall, handfome, and of a moft
amiable difpofition ; fhe is the delight of the
good old gentleman ; and, by the endearing
attentions of filial tendernefs, confoles him
for the frequent abfence of his other children.

The drefs of the Greek women of Argentiera is, in fome particulars, a little whimfical.

I   In

In France, a neat leg and a fmall foot are in
high eftimation, but the belles of Argentiera
are of a different opinion; they fwell out
their legs by wearing fevcral pair of ftockings,
and appear as if they were booted, which
ftrange kind of ornament they confider as
an effential part of drefs; and left it fhould
be loft to the eye, their garments do not defcend above two inches below the knee.
Thefe too are fo contrived, as abfolutely to
fpoil their fhape, and render it impoffible to
form any idea of the beautiful proportions
with which they were formed by Nature. I
am at a lofs to conceive what can have induced them to adopt fo very extravagant a
drefs.   In other refpects they are cheerful,
lively, and handfome.   M. Breft, who is no
indifferent judge of beauty, introduced me
into fome houfes where I was aftonifhed to
find, under ruftic roofs, young women with
the moft charming faces.   If you reprefent
to them that they difguife, by fuch prepofterous
ornaments, fome of the lovelieft of their charms;
their anfwer is, " Our grandmothers were clad
" in the fame way; we do but follow the cuf-
" tom."   Shall cuftom then always tyrannize
over reafon?   But in a fmall ifland, which

the

the women never quit, and where they hardly ever fee any ftrangers, the difference of whofe drefs might make impreffion on them, fafhi- ons, however abfurd, muft be unchangeable, nor can it be expected that any individual fhould dare throw off the yoke.

Fronting Argentiera is a long barren rock, called the Burnt Ifland; in the channel be- tween, fhips find fafe anchoring; and fmall veffels may enter the harbour, where they have fufficient depth of water. This is the only land- ing-place, for in every other part of the ifland the fhore is fteep, and furrounded by inaccef- fible rocks. The village, built on the fum- mit of a pretty lofty eminence, commands the fhipping; the declivity is fo fteep, that if a battery were erected there, to afcend it would be impoffible.

I have the honour to be, &c.

LETTER XLII.

To M. L. M.

FROM Argentiera, Madam, the ifle of Melos is in full view, and is diftant only half a league. Its modern name is Milo or Mile. Anciently it had a town of the fame name, built by the Phœnicians *(f)*. That maritime people, attracted by the beauty of its port, undoubtedly made it an emporium of their commerce. This harbour, the mouth of which faces the North Weft, retreats within the land, forming various windings, and fuddenly opens out into a fpacious bafon, in which fhips of all fizes may anchor, fheltered from every wind, and even the largeft fleet ride with fafety and convenience.

This ifland was long rich and populous, and in early antiquity enjoyed perfect free-

(f) Stephan. Byzant. The city of Melos was founded by the Phœnicians.—Feftus Pompeius adds, Melo, leaving the coafts of Phœnicia, built the city to which he gave his name.

dom.

dom. The Athenians, unable to bring the people of Melos to declare in their favour, in the Peloponnefian war, made a defcent upon their coafts, and laid all wafte before them with fire and fword. Twice did they fail in their enterprize; but returning with more numerous forces, they laid fiege to Melos, and having reduced the befieged to furrender at difcretion (g), put to the fword every man capable of bearing arms. They fpared only the women and children, whom they carried off into captivity. This atrocious action makes us blufh for humanity, and difhonours the Athenian name. But war was then carried on with a barbarity of which we have now no example. Republics know not how to pardon, and always carry their vengeance to excefs. Lyfander the Lacedæmonian general, having, in his turn, fubdued the Athenians (h), obliged them to recal the colony they had fent to Melos, and reftored to the ifland the wretched remains of its inhabitants.

This ifland loft its liberty when the Romans, afpiring to the empire of the world,

(g) Strabo, lib. x.
(h) Plutarch, in Vitâ Lyfandri.

I   conquered

conquered the whole Archipelago. In the partition of that monarchy, it fell to the eaftern emperors; was afterwards governed by its own dukes, and finally was conquered by Soliman II. Since that period it has groaned beneath Ottoman defpotifm, and is completely deprived of its importance. M. Breft affured me, that, in his youth, it was extremely fertile in corn, wine, and fruits, and contained upwards of twenty thoufand inhabitants. M. Tournefort, who vifited it in 1700, gives a delightful defcription of this ifland. " The " earth, conftantly heated by fubterraneous " fires, produces, almoft without intermiffion, " wheat, barley, cotton, exquifite wines, and " delicious melons. Saint Elie, the moft " beautiful monaftery in the ifland, and fitu- " ated on the higheft ground, is furrounded " by cedars, and orange, lemon, and fig-trees. " The gardens are watered by copious ftreams. " Olive-trees, which are rare in other parts, " are very numerous round this monaftery, " and the adjoining vineyards furnifh excellent " wine. In a word, all the productions of " the ifland are of incomparable excellence. " Its partridges, quails, kids, and lambs, are " in high eftimation, yet extremely cheap."

Could

Could M. Tournefort return to Milo, he would no longer find the beauteous ifle he has defcribed. He would ftill fee the feathered alum, with filver threads, fufpended from the roofs of caverns, fragments of pure fulphur filling the crevices, of the rocks, numerous mineral fprings, hot baths, and the fame fires which, in his time, heated the bofom of the earth, and rendered it fo fertile. But inftead of the five thoufand Greeks paying the capitation (i), he would now find, on a furface of eighteen leagues in circumference, only about feven hundred inhabitants. He would figh to behold the fineft parts of the country without cultivation, and fertile vallies changed into moraffes. Milo has affumed a very different appearance within the courfe of the laft fifty years. The plague, every where propagated by the Turks, has cut off the greateft part of its inhabitants; and the deteftable government of the Porte, and the oppreffions of the Captain Pacha, have completed its deftruction. At prefent, the want

(i) I have faid that adults alone were fubject to the capitation; if, therefore, we add women and children to the above number of 5000, there muft have been, in the time of Tournefort, at leaft 20,000 fouls.

of

of labourers prevents their giving a free courfe to the water, which ftagnating in the valleys, turns fetid, and infects the air with putrid exhalations. The falt-marfhes, which have multiplied for want of care, produce the fame effect. If to thefe inconveniencies the fulphureous vapours which rife on every fide are added, you will not be furprifed to learn, Madam, that the inhabitants of Milo are tormented with violent fevers during three quarters of the year. Nay, poffibly, they will be under the necefity of totally abandoning their country. Their complexions are univerfally of a yellow, pale, and deadly hue ; nor is the look of health to be found in any one of them. The prudent traveller fhould take care to make but a fhort ftay in this unhealthy country, if he would not expofe himfelf to a fever. Only to fleep a fingle night in the ifland, nay even to pafs the day there, is fometimes fufficient to contract that difeafe.

An enlightened government might remove thefe calamities which have fo depopulated Melos. Its firft care ought to be to eftablifh a Lazaretto, and prevent the approach of infected veffels. Canals fhould then be be cut to drain the marfhes, from which arife peſtiferous exhalations. The iſland would repeople : for the fulphureous vapours are not what moſt render it defolate ; it produced them equally in the time of the ancients (*k*), yet it was extremely populous. M. Tourne-fort, who viſited it at a period much nearer the conqueſt of the Turks, and before they had time wholly to lay it waſte, ſtill reckoned twenty thoufand inhabitants. To the defpotiſm of the Turkiſh government, therefore, and its deteſtable politics, muſt we attribute the deſtruction of the iſland of Melos. Let me not be accufed of painting the Turks in colours blacker than they deferve. I have travelled through their empire, I have feen the injuries of every kind which they have done to the fciences, the arts, and the human race. I fee them carrying the plague with them, from iſland to iſland, from country to country, without fuffering their eyes to be opened by the example of every other nation ; and ſhall I not raife my voice

(*l*) Pliny (lib. xxxv. cap. 15.) ſpeaks of the great quantities of fulphur produced at Melos, and eſteems it as the beſt any where to be found.

againſt

against the abominable indifference of this
barbarous people ! Shall I not inveigh against
their deftructive fatalifm, and endeavour to
find words fufficiently forcible to paint the
crimes and horrors of their government, of
that government, the enemy of the human
fpecies, which has deftroyed more men by its
odious tyranny, than ever fell by the fword of
the moft cruel conquerors ! At the fight of
thefe melancholy fpectacles my heart groans,
and is filled with indignation ; my blood boils
in my veins, and I could wifh to excite all
Europe to combine againft thefe Turks, who,
defcending from the mountains of Armenia,
have crufhed the nations in their paffage, and
waded through rivers of blood to the throne
of Conftantinople. Nor have the beautiful
countries they inhabit been able to foften the
ferocity of their character. Power is their
law ; their juftice is the fabre.

I have the honour to be, &c.

T H E E N D.

I N D E X.

A

Acrotari, convent of, — Page 363
Air, varieties of, in different countries, — 294
Alexander Severus, pillar of — — 6
Amphitheatre, ruins of one, near Caſtel Roſſo, 27
Anaphe, iſland of, 53
Aptera, — 279
Arcadi, monaſtery of, 264. Library of, 267. Wine-cellar, — ibid.
Archbiſhop of Gortyna, power of, — 379
Archery, expertnefs of the Cretans in, — 179
Argenticra, iſland of, 393, 395. Number of inhabitants of, 396. Whimſical peculiarity in the drefs of the women of, 398
Ariadne, in love with Theſeus, aſſiſts him to kill the Minotaur, 248, 250
Arſinoe of Lycia, 30
Artemira, Mount, 97. Extenſive profpect from, ib.

Aſomatos, monaſtery of 260, 264. Entertainment of the French travellers there, — 261
Aſthmatic diſorders, not known in Egypt, 296
Atabyris, Mount, 74, 97

B

Bartavelles, a kind of partridge in Crete, 333, 337
Bedchambers of the Turks, 336
Benediction of the new wines, form of, as given by the ſuperior of the monaſtery of Arcadi, 267
Biſhop (Greek) puniſhment inflicted on the Greeks for one entering Canea on horſeback, 292
Biſhoprics of Crete, 379
Breſt, (M.) French vice-conful at Argenticra, character of, — 397
Bryaxis, Coloſſal ſtatues of his workmanſhip at Rhodes, — 64
Burnt Iſland, — 400

Cadiſcus,

INDEX.

INDEX.

F I N I S.

www.ingramcontent.com/pod-product-compliance
Lightning Source LLC
Chambersburg PA
CBHW021339110726
47900CB00005B/1531